DOING THE RIGHT THING

A VALUE BASED ECONOMY

Arjo Klamer

]u[

Ubiquity Press
London

'This is the most disturbing book I ever read.'
  - **Honors student** *at the Erasmus University*

'Klamer's "value-based approach" is, in another way of talking, a "humanomics," an economics with humans and meanings left in. It returns to the great tradition of Adam Smith, Joseph Schumpeter, and John Maynard Keynes, and meets up with the younger tradition of Vernon Smith, Elinor Ostrom, and Albert Hirschman. Klamer does not abandon standard economics. He radically and eloquently supplements it, yielding an entirely new way of doing the right thing.'
  - **Deirdre McCloskey,** *distinguished professor emerita in Economics, History, English and Communication at University of Illinois at Chicago*

'Arjo Klamer's "Doing the right thing" is a manifesto for everyone. For every cultural shareholder who knows that "in the end it is culture that matters". Is proactive, altruist, value-based approach to culture, politics and economics sustainable? Read and find out. Reading Klamer may be the right thing.'
  - **Slawek Magala,** *Erasmus University Rotterdam & Jagiellonian University Cracow*

'Arjo Klamer's "Doing the Right Thing" is at one and the same time a plea for economic thinkers to return to their roots in moral philosophy, and for social and political thinkers to reorient the practical affairs away from the 'iron cage' of economic obsession to consider values other than some technically defined notion of "efficiency". Klamer asks us to redirect political economy away from the economist's instrumentalism and instead to incorporate a broader set of values in the discussion of the "good society".'
  - **Pete Boettke,** *University Professor of Economics and Philosophy at George Mason University*

Published by
Ubiquity Press Ltd.
6 Windmill Street
London W1T 2JB
www.ubiquitypress.com

Text © Arjo Klamer 2017

Second edition 2017

Cover design by Cyprian Koscielniak
Design: Anna Klamer and Myrthe Montijn
Editing: Chloe Brown and Renée Albada Jelgersma

Printed in the UK by Lightning Source Ltd.
Print and digital versions typeset by Siliconchips Services Ltd.

978-1-909188-92-1 (paperback)
978-1-909188-93-8 (PDF)
978-1-909188-94-5 (EPUB)
978-1-909188-95-2 (Mobi)

DOI: https://doi.org/10.5334/bbb

The full text of this book has been peer-reviewed to ensure high academic
standards. For full review policies, see http://www.ubiquitypress.com/
Suggested citation:
Klamer, A. (2017). Doing the Right Thing: A Value Based Economy. 2nd ed.
London: Ubiquity Press. DOI: https://doi.org/10.5334/bbb.
License: CC-BY 4.0

To read the free, open access version of
this book online, visit
https://doi.org/10.5334/bbb or scan
this QR code with your mobile device:

Dedicated to all those seeking another economics for another economy

And to those striving for a good life and desiring to contribute to the good society

CONTENTS

Preface   IX

Part 1: Framing and raising awareness   1

    Chapter 1: Doing the right thing starts at home; in the end it is the
         culture that matters   3

    Chapter 2: Different ways of making sense of culture in relationship
         to the economy   11

    Chapter 3: Doing the right thing is a matter of realizing values   21

    Chapter 4: Phronesis is the virtue in making values real   27

Part 2: The conceptual framework   45

    Chapter 5: About values   47

    Chapter 6: To realize values we need to procure goods, the most
         important of which are shared   75

    Chapter 7: The goods to strive for are our ideals   101

    Chapter 8: The sources for doing the right thing; about richness
         and poverty   125

    Chapter 9: Realizing values in five different spheres:involving others 145

    Chapter 10A: An exploration of the five spheres: logic, rhetoric,
         values and relationships. The oikos and the social and
         the cultural spheres first   171

    Chapter 10B: The market and governmental spheres, and the
         spillovers, overlaps among the five spheres   193

    Chapter 11: So what?   217

Bibliography   231
Index   237

PREFACE

How about doing the right thing?

Doing the right thing is just that: doing the right thing. It is what I am trying to do while writing this sentence. It is what you, my reader, probably are trying to do right now: figuring out what this book might mean for you. It is what artists do when they make art, mothers and fathers when raising their children, politicians doing politics, managers managing, teachers teaching, plumbers plumbing . . . who doesn't?

Yet wanting to do the right thing is something different from knowing the right thing to do, and that in turn is something other than actually doing the right thing. Is it right to ask a great deal of money for a painting when you yourself doubt the quality? Should you charge more for seats in your theatre even when that scares away people with little money? Is charging 1000 euro for a lecture to a local group the right thing to do? How about paying your kids for household chores? How about selling the company to the highest bidder? And why do we talk and think so much about monetary issues? What is the right thing to do?

Even though I am an economist, I too wonder why people are so quick to focus on monetary issues. It is my profession to do so, you might note. But after many years of struggling with such issues I have gained the insight that the right thing to do for me as an economist is to push the questioning, to ask myself and you: why are we doing what we are doing? The purpose is to move our conversation beyond the monetary. Why am I writing, and why are you reading? Why are you engaged in the arts, or in anything for that matter? What purpose does it serve? What is so important to you? This gets us thinking and talking about our values. And that is where I want to take our conversation. To get us to think and talk about our values, about what is really important to us, about how values work and how we can work with them.

It is only midcourse in the writing of this book that I got to write this beginning. At first I was still stuck in the usual academic mode of distancing myself from the here and now, to invite you to a lofty position where we can oversee the follies and fortunes of those toiling away in the worlds of arts and culture. I shared with my wife what I was thinking and told her that I actually wanted to understand what it is to be doing the right thing. We were still in bed and she was eager to return to her morning slumber. "Why not call your book *Doing The Right Thing*," she murmured and turned around. I got up and realized I had my topic and my title.

For the sake of a good life, a good society and – what the heck – for a strong and inspiring civilization.
It is only fair to direct the same questioning to this project. What for? What is so important here?

This is what I figured out. I am doing this because I strive for a good life and as part of that I want to contribute to a good society. And if you were to really push me, I would say that I am fending for the survival and vitality of the civilization that you and I are enjoying. As for civilization, I fear that the barbarians are at the gate, in the form of movements that want to do away with Western civilization and its values; and, more importantly, I fear they are already entered in the form of forces that disparage and dismiss the importance of the manifestations of our civilization. I sense these forces within the university, for example, where economists dismiss their own history and are proudly ignorant of the philosophical underpinnings of their discipline. I sense these forces in the hardening mentality, in the waning compassion, in the loss of direction in spiritual and cultural life. I sense them also in the turning away or sneering at the sources that have formed our civilization. As I am involved primarily in the worlds of the arts, the sciences and, to a lesser extent, religion, I want to contribute especially to doing the right things in those worlds. I do so by engaging in all kinds of situations, as you will notice, because I make plentiful use of the insights that I have gained from these worlds.

My hope is that the ideas and insights in this book stimulate scholars and practitioners of economic theories to think about what it means to do the right thing, as they have done for me. The idea is to get you and me thinking about the values that we want to realize, and what goods of value we have to offer to others, so that they can realize their own values. Writing the book is clearly valuable for me—otherwise I would not bother. But will it enable you, as the reader, to realize something of value for you? To explore this question, I have first applied the book in my teaching and shared it with professionals in special seminars. It appears that the answer is yes. It pleases me when bachelor and especially master students make use of the framework presented in the book. Influencing scholarly work is another important objective of the book.

While perhaps it is wishful thinking on my part, I would be truly satisfied if the value based approach that I develop here contributes to the development of another economics, and with that to another economy.

What follows is intended to be an alternative for the instrumentalist reasoning that currently prevails.
In other courses my students mainly learn "instrumentalist reasoning." That is, they learn about the instruments that presumably are geared towards some kind of policy goals like the increase in economic growth, lower inflation, lower unemployment, lower debts, greater efficiency, minimization of costs or the maximization of profit. The focus in the teaching is on the quantification of desired outcomes. Perhaps as a consequence, too many students see their study merely as an instrument for additional income and a good career.

Instrumentalism, or the prevalence of instrumental reasoning, is one of the three malaises of modern life that the Canadian philosopher, Charles Taylor, identifies (Taylor, 1991). He associates it with an eclipse of ends, or the difficulty that professionals and politicians nowadays have in answering the question "what is what you are doing good for?" I concur. Answers like "more economic growth," "more profit," or "more personal growth" leave unanswered what more growth or more profit is good for.

The other two malaises of modern life that Taylor identifies are individualism and a loss of political freedom. All three are related. Individualism refers to the tendency to stress the autonomy of the self and to think of people as independent choice makers, as is common in standard economics. The question that the individualist perspective prioritizes is "what is a rational choice or decision?" The social and political nature of people is imagined to be secondary. According to Taylor this perspective is responsible for a loss of meaning, as meaning can only be realized in a social and political context.

As to the loss of political freedom, Taylor refers to a politics that is becoming increasingly technocratic and instrumental, forcing people to accept systems that are imposed upon them for reasons of efficiency, maximization of growth, controllability or uniformity. The prevalence of instrumental reason alienates people from political discussion and political life and renders them therefore instruments for instrumental exigencies.

When I became a part-time politician in May 2014, while continuing my professorship, the dominance of instrumental reason became even more apparent to me. Civil servants are focusing on achieving quantifiable results and procedures, their customers are welfare recipients and they are keen on organizing competitive market processes for youth care, reintegration and other such services. They seek greater efficiency and better services for the "customer." As a result, when quality is at stake, these are often monitored with quantitative indicators. But what if the pursuit of those indicators actually distracts from the qualitative objectives? What if counting the number of publications in top journals distracts from the quality of scientific research? What if the pursuit of an optimal number of job placements takes place at the expense of the quality of work generated? And what does the number of visitors to a theatre reflect about the quality of its performances?

When I tell civil servants that their actions and words betray a neo-liberal perspective, they look at me puzzled. Virtually nobody is able to explain what is meant by neo-liberalism and how it differs from the liberal perspective associated with economists such as Friedrich Hayek and Milton Friedman. This baffles me, since the term is so widely used nowadays to describe policies in the US, the UK and the European Union. Apparently it does not resonate in circles where neo-liberalism is actually practiced.

Neo-liberalism breathes instrumental reasoning, but it is different from the practice of instrumental reasoning as it shows up in most economic textbooks. There, students learn how to devise instruments to promote certain policy objectives. It is the engineering approach that was promoted by my erstwhile hero Jan Tinbergen, the Dutch econometrician, who won the first Nobel Prize in Economic Sciences. It considers the economy as a machine that politicians can tinker with using the insights of economic research. Liberal-minded economists like Friedrich Hayek and Milton Friedman are opposed to such tinkering and advocate small governments and a minimum of government intervention. Neo-liberalism, as defined by Michel Foucault in his lectures on bio-politics (Foucault, 1975-76), differs from liberalism in the sense that it refers to the practice of governors (including civil servants) who embrace the market approach as their policy. Neo-liberalism incorporates the logic of markets in the logic of governance.

In the neo-liberal perspective, politicians and especially civil servants talk about the world as if it was one big market. They view citizens as customers, seek market solutions for their problems (such as the high expenses of health-care), are result oriented, stress the importance of free choice and competition and speak in terms of products, demand, supply and efficiency. It is just as if they ingested an introductory economic textbook. But they are working for governments, not market-oriented organizations. It is the powerful result of what is called New Public Management and portrays mistrust towards governmental practices. The reasoning is even more instrumental than it was in social democratic regimes; the goals are mainly instrumental, such as greater efficiency, lower costs and more economic growth. (Justice would be a substantive goal.) The practitioners are apparently not aware of this.

My aim is to confront the people around me with this frame of thinking, and to suggest that there is an alternative, as I articulate here.

Another economy. . . ?

The alternative to instrumental reasoning is substantive reasoning. Such reasoning focuses on what is important, on values and also on what is worth striving for. Substantive reasoning aims to articulate the substance of what we

-and others- are doing, what *qualities* individuals, organizations and groups of people are pursuing.

All around I observe explicit striving for quality. When it is not in the arts and the sciences, I see it in movements that stress the quality of the environment, health care, public life, democracies or social life. So many are seeking alternatives to the instrumentalized and financialized worldview that appears to be prevalent now. They want another economy, an alternative to the policies that assess everything in financial – and therefore quantifiable – terms, to focus instead on the important qualities. But how to articulate such policies? How to determine that what we do actually contributes to a better quality of whatever kind?

Proposals and initiatives for another economy abound. They aim at a sharing economy, a circular or a creative economy. While digital technology and robotization create new possibilities in this respect, craftsmanship is back in vogue. Work is being re-conceptualized and experiments with new forms of organization are underway. McCloskey and others plea for humanomics: an economics that does justice to the fundamental values of faith, hope and love. Buddhist economics appeals to the imagination as an answer to the largeness of scale of contemporary society. And, of course, the commitment to a sustainable economy is strong.

Having witnessed the sterility and ineffectiveness of standard economics when it comes to substantive and therefore qualitative issues, and to an undergirding of innovative ideas, I now want to contribute to an alternative way of reasoning, another approach. I call it the value based approach to the economy.

. . . calls for another economics!

The value based approach is intended to offer a substantive, a quality-oriented approach that is so obviously needed in the realms not only of the arts, the sciences and religion, but also in politics, organizations, social life and certainly in private life. It is meant to better understand what other people do and especially of what we do ourselves, or would want to do. It should motivate coming up with and identifying the emergence of new alternatives.

It is an economics that restores an old and long tradition in economic discourse, including thinkers like Aristotle, Thomas Aquinas, Adam Smith, John Maynard Keynes, Carl Menger, Thorstein Veblen, Max Weber, Joseph Schumpeter, Ludwig von Mises, Friedrich Hayek, Frank Knight, E.F. Schumacher, Kenneth Boulding, Don Lavoie, Elinor Ostrom, and contemporaries such as Deirdre McCloskey, Luigino Bruni, and Robert Skidelsky, as well as so many others who may not all register as economists.

This tradition contrasts sharply with the prevailing so-called neoclassical approach, which I will refer to as standard economics. Standard economics is defined – just check the textbooks or ask anyone who studied economics – as the science that studies the allocation of scarce resources, or the science of rational choice. Such a definition of economics actually stems from the thirties, more precisely from an article that the British economist, Lionel Robbins, wrote in 1932 (Robbins, 1932). In this article, Robbins sidesteps the value discussion that had dictated the scientific practice of economics until then and suggested instead that economics is all about scarcity. He made it seem that economics is about survival, overcoming hardship, with more growth, more income and more profit as the obvious conditions for surviving and sustaining. That position may have made sense at the time of the Great Depression. After all, what other goals would get the economy out of hardship? Yet, that way of thinking, such a mindset, makes less and less sense today. Sure, we still make choices. We choose to go on vacation, to merge companies, to increase prices for a performance, to provide debt relief to a country and welfare to people with no income. And so on. Does scarcity figure into those choices? Maybe. But we most certainly also make such choices because we consider certain things more important than others. In other words, we value certain things and seek not just to survive, but also to realize a good life and a good society. The clincher was the inclusion of this definition in the first modern textbook for economics, written by the brilliant economist Paul Samuelson who would later win the Nobel Prize in Economic Sciences. I began my study of economics with the ninth edition of that book.

In another definition, standard economics concerns the system of production, distribution, and consumption of goods. When standard economists think of "goods," they think of "commodities"; when they discuss "distribution," they zero in on the exchange of goods in markets. What would happen if we expand the notion of goods to include not only (intangible) services, as is common standard practice, but also goods like "knowledge," "friendship" and "freedom"? After all, such goods are certainly as valuable as "refrigerators" or "consulting reports."

My aim is to restore the discussion of values in economics or at least to contribute to such a restoration. That makes for a different definition of economics: I propose to define **economics as the discipline that studies the realization of values by people, organizations and nations.**

Standard economics specializes in the financial aspects, in the kind of activities that lend themselves to measurement in monetary terms. That is why I will generally speak of "financial" phenomena instead of "economic" phenomena. Economics, as I define it here, covers a much larger field than standard economics does.

The value based approach developed and revealed in this book has at least seven distinctive characteristics. They are:

1. When doing the right thing, people strive to realize their values. That is, they need to be aware of what those values are and then, by interacting with others, by producing, buying, selling, socializing or conversing, they try to make those values real. This perspective contrasts with the focus on preferences and utility maximization in standard economics. (See Chapter 3 and 5.)

2. The realization of values is a cultural practice; economic behavior, there-fore, is embedded in a culture and makes sense only in its cultural context. Consequently, we want to look beyond the financial aspects of transac-tions and recognize their cultural significance, or their interaction with the relevant cultural context. The idea that culture matters contrasts sharply with the standard economic perspective in which culture is given a marginal or instrumental role. (See Chapters 1 and 2.)

3. In order to work with and on the basis of values, we need to work sensibly, using *phronesis*, as the Greeks call it. We need to weigh options, deliber-ate, experiment and evaluate, all in striving to do the right thing. This is quite different from the supposedly rational choices we make in standard economics. (See Chapter 4.)

4. In order to realize values, people have to generate and appropriate goods, both tangible and intangible. The most important goods are shared with others. Consider goods like friendship, art, religion and knowledge. Goods can also be practices, such as sport, science, crafts and art. The standard perspective does not acknowledge shared goods or the role of practices. (See Chapter 6.)

5. Some goods are more important than others. Some goods are worth striving for; they render actions meaningful and make doing the right thing satisfying. When practices are worth striving for they can be called praxes. In chapter 7, I will distinguish four domains of ultimate goods and praxes: personal, social, societal and transcendental. The standard perspective offers only the ill-defined concepts of welfare and well-being when dealing with ultimate goods. (See Chapter 7.)

6. In the determination of the sources for value generation, the value based approach compels us to go beyond financial entities (e.g. financial wealth) and consider the great variety of sources that enable us to realize our val-ues. Such sources include our upbringing, our society and our memories, and – at the root of all – our faith, hope and love. (See Chapter 8.)

7. To make our values real, we usually need to involve others. To do so we can avail of at least five different logics: the logic of the *oikos* (the home), social logic, logic of governance, market logic and transcendental or cultural logic. The standard approach pays attention only to market logic and, to some extent, governmental logic. (See chapters 9 and 10a and b.)

When applying the value based approach, you will see all kinds of things in a different light, including your own actions and choices. Rather than simply trying to define your budget constraints, you want to identify your values and then figure out by what logic you can realize them. You will note the importance not only of those goods that you own yourself (like your computer and your bicycle), but also those that you own together with others (like your friendships, your knowledge, your love of a certain kind of music and your memories). You will have to rethink what it is that makes a person rich, or another person poor—(what defines richness and poverty anyway?) – and, more generally, what it is that constitutes wealth. Who knows, it may affect what you choose to do next.

The value based approach might also profoundly affect the way of doing business or conducting policy since it takes as a starting point the ends of business and policy. Such ends cannot be profit maximization or more "economic" growth. Instead, it invites and compels a serious consideration of qualities.

To get practical, this part of the book will conclude with an exposition of the quality impact monitor. It will undoubtedly elicit the critique that the value based approach is instrumental in practice and is used to serve the governmental logic anyway. While that may be so, the governmental logic must be included as part of doing the right thing; in that context we are in need of a framework for making the discussion of qualities both concrete and effective.

This is not a "how to" book, although it certainly has elements of such a book. This book does not explain how to make or lose money or what to do to get things right. It is rather a book that gets you (and me) thinking about what it means to do the right thing. And to do that, I need to get us to ask ourselves all kinds of questions, mull over various concepts, think through consequences, understand different logics in their interaction with others, pay attention to the context and get a picture of the larger context (of the creative economy, for example). There is so much to know and even more to understand. Even so, here and there you may feel prodded to do the right thing and imagine yourself reading a "how to" book.

Disturbing?

I imagine that for quite a few readers the reasoning presented in this book is strange at first. An honors student at the Erasmus University called it "the most disturbing text he ever read." I do not know what other texts he has read, but I can take a guess. I took this as a compliment. The more you are trained in the disciplines of economics, business economics and law, the stranger and the more disturbing this reasoning is likely to be. At first you will recognize little of what you have learned. To use the expression of the British poet Samuel Coleridge, all I ask of you is "to suspend your disbelief." Who knows, you may get some new insights – as have quite a few of my students and the professionals with whom I have shared some of these ideas.

I stress the therapeutic and edifying tasks of science
I may be pushing the limits of the acceptable by implying another interpretation not only of the subject of economics, but also of the role and task of science in general. The convention prescribes that science is meant to explain and to predict. Such an interpretation gives the sciences an instrumental role: to equip makers and shakers in the world with the knowledge they need to shape the world to their liking, with new inventions and effective policies. This conventional interpretation of what the sciences should do, stimulates the distancing positioning that scientists are inclined to assume, as I was at first.

I now have rather different views on the role and significance of science. Operating in a political position has only encouraged me to further recognize the ineffectiveness and sterility of the research outcomes of standard economics when determining the right thing to do. It is rare that scientific findings have a direct impact on policy, though this is contrary to what standard economists tell their students.

Following a suggestion made by Richard Rorty in his *Philosophy and the Mirror of Nature* (Rorty, 1979), I see the two main tasks of science as being **therapeutic** and **edifying**. I would argue that these are its main roles. Scientific work is **therapeutic** when it poses new questions, uncomfortable questions maybe, and makes people aware of certain phenomena. (Why would lowering wages be the solution to unemployment? Might subsidies for the arts actually be harmful to the arts? Can the pursuit of financial wealth actually be a goal in life?) The scientific contribution is therapeutic when it gets people to reflect upon what they are doing, and makes them question the obvious, the conventional thing to do. The therapeutic effect is when people come to realize that there is a problem, that they have good reason to be more critical and that they have a question of which they were not aware before. "Oh, maybe culture does matter. How then? What difference does that make?" "Is it really so that the empirical findings of standard economics leave policy mostly unaffected? What would then be an alternative?" As we all should know, knowledge is born of confusion, and the process of knowing begins by asking the right questions.

Questions require an answer, or at least a way of thinking that points us in the direction of an answer. That is where the **edifying** aspect of scientific practices comes in. Scientific work becomes edifying when it offers concepts, ways of thinking, models, insights and findings with which people can make sense of the questions they encounter and enables them to see their world in a different light and act accordingly. Standard economics has been edifying because it provided accounting frameworks that produced numbers about profit, total production, consumption, investment, foreign trade, government deficits and debt, and so forth. It edifies with notions of the market, of rational choice, of externalities, of public goods, of asymmetric information, risk, games and so many more concepts that have proved to be helpful in thinking about all kinds of questions. Now people and organizations are getting questions about qualities, about values and about goals and meanings, for which the standard approach appears to fail in providing answers. Therefore another edifying framework is called for.

Part of the edifying task of scientific work is the **characterization**, or **interpretation**, of what is. When people become overwhelmed by the world around them, they need to establish what they are looking for and identify the relevant features. Scientists, including economists, play an important role here as they provide glasses with which to look at the world. Economists, for example, make people distinguish market processes and individuals who are consuming, producing and laboring, and do that for certain prices. They present a particular worldview. The value based approach aims to change that worldview and, with that, the characterization of the world as we look at it. Once you adopt the value based approach, you will distinguish shared goods, observe social behavior, co-production and co-creation and will have a new perspective on what constitutes richness and poverty.

So, although I have no reason to deny the explanatory and predicting task for the sciences, it is their therapeutic and edifying role that renders the sciences particularly relevant for daily, organizational and political life.

Getting inside the elephant

At a conference I suggested that the value based approach is but one of many perspectives on the beast that we call economics. I used the anecdote of the blind men as an example. This anecdote that originated in ancient India tells of four blind men who are asked to describe an object that is in front of them. The first observes a string, the second a tree trunk, the third a tube and the fourth a sharp object. They all have a specialist perspective. Only when they share their perspectives will they realize that they are in fact observing an elephant.

In economics there are all kinds of perspectives, including the standard one based on rational choice, a game theoretic perspective, an institutional perspective, a behavioral perspective, an Austrian perspective, and so on. So why not add a value based perspective to get a more complete picture of the beast that we call economics?

Then I realized that I was trying to do something different. All perspectives that I listed have in common that they are the perspectives of spectators. They all require that you step away from the beast and observe it from a distance. The value based approach suggests instead to get inside the elephant, inside the beast, to figure out what the beast needs to do in order to do the right thing. The beast can be a person, an organization, a city government or any other moral entity.

By getting into the beast we are made to wonder what it takes to do the right thing and why it is often so difficult doing the right thing.

A standard critique is that the focus on doing the right thing is hopelessly naïve. Those uttering the critique see ugliness all around, including selfish behavior, power mongering, abuse, corruption and exploitation. As if I do not see all of that. I admit that the following exploration is not for those who seek action that is self-serving or corrupt. I prefer to engage in conversation with those who seek to do the right thing. After all, that is ultimately the only way to realize the values and thus to true happiness.

Accordingly, let us try to get inside the elephant!

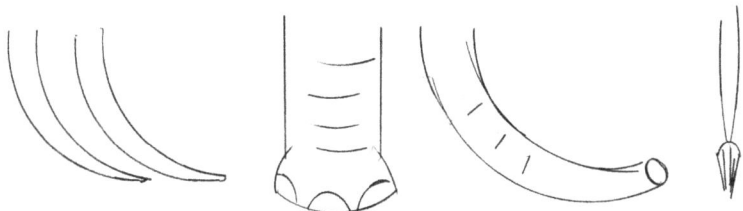

Figure 0-1 Looking at the elephant

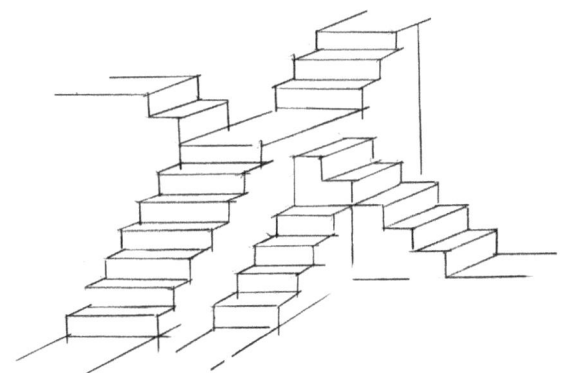

Figure 0-2 Getting inside the elephant

Is the value based approach to economics normative?

The question inevitable pops up in the company of economists. They have grown up with the idea that economics as a science should be "positive," that is, focus on the world as it is. Economists should abstain from imposing their own values, or norms, on their analysis, that is, they should not be normative.

Let me state clearly that the value based approach is not normative by studying the realization of values. It becomes normative just as standard economics does a) by the stance it advocates for the economist and b) by the appeal it makes for a conscious realization of the good life and a good society. Where it differs from standard economics is that it calls for involvement in real life—and not the detachment that standard economics propagates—and encourages people not just to consider economic processes from a distance but to become aware of one's own participation in them.

The credit should go to . . .

In order to do the right thing, all kinds of knowledge and understanding are necessary. We do not operate in a void. Fortunately not. We are part of a civilization and that means that we can benefit from the knowledge and insights that people have generated up till now. Much of the knowledge that I needed for writing this book and that we need to do the right thing is within reach; it is stored in numerous texts that scientists, humanists, philosophers, theologians and sages have left to us, forming the core of civilization. We only have to do some work to retrieve that knowledge and to interpret it so that it is of use for doing the right thing.

A lot of the material in this book is a product of my teaching in all kinds of courses and programs. Quite a few of the ideas that I include here I developed in seminars, in conversations with students and professionals. I benefit from my involvement in the program of cultural economics and cultural entrepreneurship at the Erasmus University, and programs of Creare in Amsterdam, Uganda, India, Brazil and Japan. The theme of doing the right thing for leading the good life and creating the good society, I developed in the context of Academia Vitae, a university for and about life. That university came to pass, unfortunately, due to the economic circumstances at the time. Presently I am involved with its successor, the Academy for Liberal Arts. The students of the Academy for Liberal Arts are professionals eager to reflect on their life, their work and the world around them. The questions that they contemplate are almost all concerning the meaning of their life and their work. The teaching is on the basis of mainly classical texts. So when I start with Aristotle, you can imagine where I learned this (and that is certainly not in the conversation of economists!). So this book is a product of teaching and hopefully will in turn serve as a text for teaching. I hope that both students and professionals will learn from it. Then again, aren't we all students when it comes to living the good life?

In the last stage of writing this book, I became more or less accidentally a politician, part time that is. It was a sobering experience at first. I felt like the blind man having to figure out what this large beast is about. It changed my perspective. Before I merely had purported that the standard scientific approach is not very effective in business and politics; now I experience the sterility of scientific work daily. As a governor responsible for welfare, poverty and employment, including the employment of people with a disability, I am in need of all kinds of knowledge but could not figure out where to get that knowledge. What will motivate employers to hire people and what will motivate people to actively look for work? And what can I do? At that point I realized that I benefited most from the ideas that I develop here in this book. Just how I benefited, should become clear in the second part.

As to the practice of citing, I follow the advice that the philosopher Alasdair MacIntyre once gave me. Say what you have to say, work with what others have said, but limit the references to a minimum. They only distract. Yet, I defy the advice somewhat by elaboration of the more technical and academic issues in the footnotes and a few boxes. I do so in anticipation of the standard critique of academic colleagues concerning aspects that I have not considered or elements I have left out and so on. Nevertheless, as I am the one pleading to engage in conversation, I should make an effort to show that I take my partners in conversation seriously. And I do; without McCloskey, Seiz, Fisher, de Beus, Verbruggen, Prins, Van Heusden, Frey, Throsby, Hutter, Taylor, Amariglio, Velthuis, Dekker, Goto, Magala, Zuidhof, and so many others who have put their ideas on paper, I would not have been able to write this. Everything that this book contains, every idea, every insight, is borrowed from others. Only the ordering is original.

Even so, I immediately admit that the discussion that follows does not do justice to what others have written and rarely engages with other approaches and arguments. I could offer a few lame excuses, such as a lack of time to do so, and the number of pages that would need to be added if I had done all that. However, the honest argument is that I prefer doing it this way, even at the risk of being criticized or worse, ignored.

Finally, I would like to thank Mark D. White and Carlos Hoevel for peer reviewing the manuscript for Ubiquity Press.

Let us begin the conversation

The book starts with the kernel of the approach, which is what it means to be doing the right thing. And that is the realization of values, including the way of making those values real. You will learn about *phronesis* and how that differs from the notion of rationality that is usually taught.

Those who are interested, or required, to study the text rather than just read it, will find questions on www.klamer.nl and www.doingtherightthing.nl. After all, studying the text is a matter of approaching it with questions. All knowledge begins with questions.

A personal note

I am frequently asked the question why I wrote this book, why I felt compelled to argue the importance of culture and values, and why I am so arrogant to argue another definition of economics.

I am not entirely sure of my answer. I could say that I had to write this book, yet I can list so many reasons for not writing a book like this. The risk of being ignored is significant. Derision in certain circles is likely. Why bother? There must be some reasons.

When I reflect on my intellectual career, I recognize that I have always moved towards the margins of the conversation that I was a part of. I felt most comfortable with the critics, especially when they followed social and humanistic values. Cold, cynical reasoning—that I too often encounter in the conversation of economists—deters me. This may have something to do with my upbringing as the son of a protestant minister. Till I was about 14 years old, I was deeply religious and committed to the life of a minister. The minister in me is still alive, as you may conclude here and there from what follows, but my spiritual life is troubled. I am searching to recover some of what I feel I have lost, the inner dialogue with the deity. That is perhaps the reason that I stress the goods to strive for and to include the category of transcendental goods. That may also be the reason for the development of the notion of shared goods.

With this book I want to express my hope for a world that would make more sense (at least to me), for a valuable economy, for an economy based on values, for a humanistic economy. It may all be wishful thinking, yet it is the responsibility of the scholar not only to see the world as it is, but also to imagine the world as it might be.

With age comes the desire to be inclusive in the argumentation. I do not seek opponents to attack them with arguments and to destroy theirs in passing. Enough has been done to take down the bastion of standard economics. I satisfy myself with presenting the concepts and arguments that make sense to me and render my life meaningful. It will please me if it does so for others as well. If that is not the case, then I will happily take this book with me to my grave.

PART 1

FRAMING AND RAISING AWARENESS

The exploration of a value based approach requires a frame, a set up that can get us going. Values evoke the notion of culture because culture is about values. How then can we give culture a meaningful role in a conversation about the economy? What can we make of the relationship between culture and economy? What is culture anyway? The concept is used in so many different ways, so we need to be clear on that.

In the next chapters I will propose that a value based economy is about the realization of values. Realization of values in turn signifies the awareness of and the valorization of values. In this part we focus on the awareness aspect. Part II will deal with the valorization issue.

If you embrace the idea that what we do, or what organizations or governments do, is ultimately the realization of values, you will have to recognize with me that the standard economic models of rational behavior do not suffice. The realization of values calls for something like phronesis, or practical wisdom.

CHAPTER 1

DOING THE RIGHT THING STARTS AT HOME;

IN THE END IT IS THE CULTURE THAT MATTERS

The streets were dusty, the sun stood high and the atmosphere was different. There I was, in the streets of Kampala, the capital of Uganda. The next day a program would start with people of Uganda's cultural sector. This was my first time in Central Africa.

I walked by the wares spread out on the sidewalk by a street vendor. Determined to ignore the stuff, my eyes caught a glimpse of the banner shown here. Wasn't this banner stating exactly what my approach is about? Here is the message, so plain, so obvious. Can it be true if displayed on a dusty sidewalk in the heart of Africa? I paid the vendor what he asked for—the equivalent of 1 euro—and continued on my way.

The banner is a reminder for you and me that the important things in life are not for sale. We can buy all kinds of things but owning those things does not guarantee that we have what we really want. We can buy a house, but that does not necessarily get us a home. Even if the house is wonderful, it does not necessarily stand for a wonderful home.

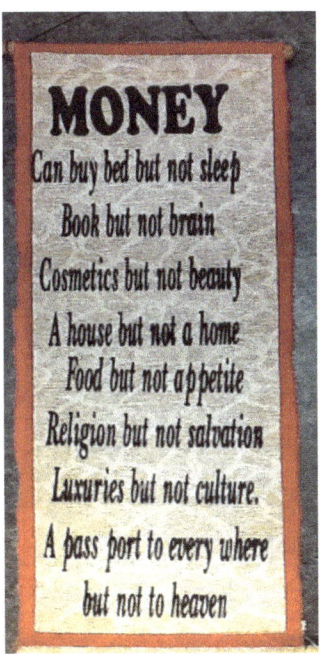

Figure 1-1: Banner

House or home

It is so tempting to steer the conversation to the house. We can know so much about it. The house is tangible. We can easily spot deficiencies and we usually know what to do about them. A cracked window can be replaced, a leaky roof can be fixed, and the attic may have space for an additional room. The house has a price.

The price renders the value of the house concrete. We can attach a number to it. In that way the collection of bricks, the wood, the concrete, or whatever the house is made of, and its shape and its design become a quantity. I can say that my house is so much. When I subtract the amount of my mortgage I am left with a number representing what I am worth, more or less, or at least what my house is worth to me.

That number is pretty high. At least that is what I think. Maybe you had expected more. I might point out that during the recent financial crunch I lost a lot of money and that my mortgage payments eat up a large chunk of my salary each month. But then, who cares? I do not, really. The loss was virtual and even after the payment of the mortgage interest, I am left with sufficient money to sustain my family and hobbies.

Here is my point. I do not care so much myself because I do not own the house for the sake of those numbers. And I am not watching each day what is happening to those numbers. The reason for this is that I am preoccupied with something else, something far more important: my home. I share the house with my wife and kids because we want to have a home. It is the home that really matters to me. Even if the house were to fall down, the home will remain standing, at least so I presume. The real loss occurs when we lose our home—as I once did because of a divorce. Then the house represents mere financial value that has to be split somehow.

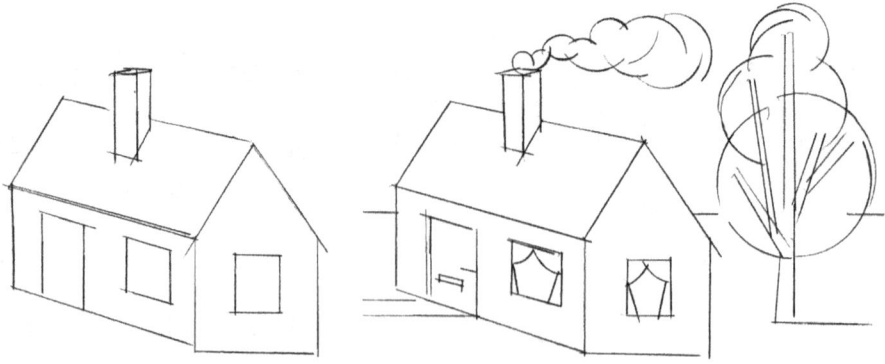

Figure 1-2: My house   **Figure 1-3:** My home

My home stands for all that I share with my wife and kids. It evokes the atmosphere in our house with its furniture, decorations and special places. Also with the memories that we generated there and now cherish together, the shared stories, the dogs and the cats buried in the back yard, the party that we gave last year, the Christmas celebrations, the dramatic scenes, the door post where we measure the height of the kids throughout the years (gosh, how they've grown!). Not to forget the gatherings with friends and families, and so much more.

My home is my *oikos*. I prefer the latter term as it evokes the original meaning of economics—*oikos*, the Greek word for home, and *nomos*, the Greek word for law. The great Greek philosophers Plato and Aristotle began the discussion about economics by pondering the laws of the household. They wondered about the right thing to do for someone running a household. One issue they encountered was whether or not to trade. (The best thing to do, Aristotle argued, was to be autarchic and only to trade in case of necessity. We would beg to differ now, but the issue remains pertinent as observed in the question of whether or not a home cooked meal is better than going out, and under what conditions.)

The economic discussion nowadays tends to focus on the numbers, on the things that can be bought and that therefore are measured in monetary terms. The numbers convey a sense of concreteness and practicality. A house is good for numbers. A house is concrete. So it is tempting to talk about the house, about its physical state and about its price. The house gets us to think of markets, of demand and supply ("As there are currently so many houses on the market, the price of ours will inevitably be going down."). A house is a product that can be sold and bought. The *oikos* is another matter altogether. It makes for an entirely different discussion, a discussion without many numbers and without the appearance of concreteness and practicality of a house. It is the quality of the *oikos* that I really care about. That is the substantive issue to me when buying a house. The price of the house is subsidiary to that.

When I brought up the *oikos* with my Ugandan students, they asked for my definition. For me my *oikos* is the circle of people with whom I have essential connections. In the *oikos*, people are connected by fate. So I said: my *oikos* makes me think of my immediate family, and possibly my parents, grandparents and siblings, their partners and kids and my parents in law. They laughed. They would consider their extended family as part of their *oikos* and some would include the local community in which they grew up as well. It was immediately clear that their *oikos* was not only larger than mine but also meant more to them, or, to put it better, it meant something different. This showed in their sense of loyalty that far exceeds the one we have in western culture. The idea that we put our parents in an elderly home, and to have others take care of them, seemed outrageous to them. If someone has wiped your bottom, it is a sign of civilization that you wipe theirs when needed, one man noted. I could only nod knowing that at that very moment a nurse might be cleaning my mother in law.

Even so, my *oikos* – small as it may be – plays also a pivotal role in my life. While writing this I am at my home. In a moment my wife will expect us to have coffee together, and that means I need to have something to say. Who knows, I might have to say something about what I feel. There may be an issue about the birthday party of our adult son tonight, or about the hockey team of my daughter that will come for a get together tomorrow night. There is shopping to do tomorrow. I have to work in the yard in the weekend. She will have to see her mother. My mother will come over for dinner. Ah well, you get the picture. The point that I want to make is that my family requires a lot of work and that I did not get any schooling for that type of work. It is the household work, but also the ever so demanding relational work. It is all about qualities. When I have my head in the newspaper at breakfast, I am not doing it right, as the other family members expect my input in the conversation. When I am not eager to go to the birthday of my son tonight, I fall short of expectations. (My wife is calling me for the coffee, so please wait.)

(When I came down, I hinted at what I was just writing. So I got a scathing remark about my confusing work and home, and one thing led to another. There was disagreement about my use of the term therapeutic—it popped up in the introduction. I could not quite explain why I was writing all this—isn't this too personal? What does it have to do with economics?—and before I knew it, we got into an old, rather painful issue. I told you that relational work is demanding. I had to hang in there to maintain at least the minimal standard of the quality that is expected from having coffee together. Fortunately, I am getting better at it, so I more or less succeeded this time.)

Work on the *oikos* is a matter of realizing qualities of moments together, of dinners and breakfasts, of relationships, of evenings spent together, of vacations and so on. It is a practice, something we do. Working on the *oikos* implies that I attend to the needs of kids and partner, visit my ageing mother weekly and try to be a responsible father and husband. In other words, I am trying to do the right thing to maintain the qualities that make up my *oikos*.

Sure enough, I also enter the market place for the sake of my *oikos*. Every Saturday I go to the local farmers market, to buy supplies for the meals of that weekend—supplies such as fish, vegetables, fruit, bread, and milk. And I finance expenses such as my daughter's membership for the sport club, her clothes, her allowance. I pay the interest on the mortgage, the repairs of the house, the vacations and, every now and then, I buy something for myself, like books, underwear and shirts. Though most things I buy with my money are intended for my *oikos*.

These personal references may strike you as strange, or awkwardly private. The reason for sharing them is to point out that the *oikos* is not only the basis for my life; it is for all people in all societies. Everyone needs to have an *oikos* of some kind or another. You may not need a family as I do in order to have an *oikos*. A group of intimate friends may constitute an *oikos*, or people may have chosen to live by themselves and create their *oikos* in a most personal way. However the *oikos* is shaped, it is where we start our lives and it is most likely also where we end our lives. When people are lonely, it is often because they lack an *oikos* in their life (although you can be lonely in an *oikos* too). Students every now and then question the importance of the *oikos*, but they are usually in transition from one to another of their own making. We grow up in an *oikos*; the *oikos* shapes us and makes us what we are.

The anthropologist Stephen Gudeman speaks of the base instead of *oikos* (Gudeman, 2008). The phrasing is appropriate as it rightly suggests that the *oikos* is the base. It is in the *oikos* where most people grow up. It is an *oikos* that many will try to reproduce, and it is the *oikos* that has a profound influence on most of our lives, as any psychologist will tell you. In the Latin American communities that Gudeman studies, the base is more extended, as it is in Uganda. However, the core idea is no different. In the US and Europe the *oikos* is to be conceived as the base, as the place where our lives definitely begin and usually end.

Home also stands for culture and content

The home is a good metaphor for what an organization, a society is about. When a theatre group owns a theatre, a building that is, it may be fortunate for having the building, yet having the building is not the point or the purpose of their activity. The group wants a home and the home is constituted by the content, the plays, the people who come to watch the plays, the atmosphere in the building, the energy, the excitement, the shared values and the shared memories. A building is just a building.

This is no different for a company. Also a company is about something, things of value, meaningful things, meaningful practices. Take an engineering firm. The boss of an engineering firm had asked me to speak with his management team during a daylong session. I came in the beginning of the afternoon. The entire morning had been spent discussing the financial numbers, the balance sheet, the turnover, the profits and the like. Using the metaphors of the house and the home, I suggested that all that they had discussed was the value of their house and the value of the things flowing in and out. But those were not the most important things for them. Much more important were the qualities they had realized like the qualities of their craftsmanship, the motivation of the people they work with, the ideas that were generated, new contacts, new clients, opportunities, their shared values and their shared aspirations. After all, I suggested, that is what their business is about. They agreed enthusiastically. So why not start the discussion next time with what is really important, with their home that is, and leave the discussion of the financial matters for a later moment? When the qualities are clear, the finances would be most probably clear as well. They looked at me with the expression of "Yeah, you're right," but I saw them wonder how they could ever do the right thing at this time in this age.

The proposal is similar in discussions with people of theatres, museums and other such organizations: focus your attention on the home, on the qualities of what you are doing. With these people the suggestion usually resonates with what they already believe and do. In their case, the doubt sets in when they face a financial shortage, as they unfortunately often do. Yet, the money issue is only instrumental and subsidiary in the end, as they readily acknowledge. Money is not what defines their success, even if it may be an indication thereof.

Economists may identify in this proposal a reference to their notions of happiness, welfare or well-being. By suggesting that we should focus on the content, I seem to suggest that we are seeking happiness and welfare, or well-being. I will address this argument later, but let me note here that when you and I seek happiness, or well-being, we still need to know what it is that makes us feel happy and well. We need to know what constitutes the kind of home that works for us, that makes us happy; we need to know the qualities that really matter. The conventional economic discussion assumes that the things we buy contribute to our happiness and sense of well-being somehow. It bypasses the critical issue and that is how the things we buy, like a house or a car, contribute to the quality of our home, that is, the thing that we are ultimately interested in. Something crucial happens between the purchase and our sense of happiness, and that is the realization of the *oikos*, or something similar. The purchase of something is not doing the right thing in and of itself. It never is. It is in realizing our *oikos*, or whatever else we value, that we are doing the right thing.

If you go along with this, you might associate anyone who pours over financial data, or insists on quantification of whatever, with the drunkard in the following drunkard joke. The drunkard is standing under a lamppost and looking at the ground. When asked what he is doing there, he says that he is looking for his keys. "So why are you looking here?" "Well, don't you see? Here at least there is light." Even if we can measure things in terms of money that does not mean that those things are what life is all about. If we really want to look for our keys we will most likely have to grope in the dark. That's life.

In the end culture is what matters. Culture is tough; money is soft. *Oikos* is all that gives meaning to intimate life. It constitutes my personal culture. Culture is all that gives meaning to shared lives. With our actions in the company of others, like family members, colleagues, fellow citizens or fellow professionals, we generate and sustain cultures. Those cultures define who we are; they provide us with a context of meanings, with a sense of belonging, with inspiration hopefully. When we are groping in the dark, we will inevitably end up needing the notion of culture.

Culture, as I use the concept here, has three distinct meanings.

Culture in the anthropological sense (C1) connotes the stories, history, expectations, artefacts, symbols, identities and values that a group of people shares and with which they distinguish themselves from other people. In this sense a family, company, city, region, ethnic group, nation, and continent can be said to have a distinct culture. Having a culture implies having the possibility to share the meanings of life with others. Having a strong culture can be a great good for the insiders; it also excludes outsiders.

When the Germans write "Kultur," they indicate the second meaning of culture: here culture connotes civilization, usually expressed in the accumulated achievements of people in a certain region over a long period of time in the arts, sciences, technology, politics and social customs (C2), or in the words of Matthew Arnold: "a knowledge of the best that has been thought and done in the world and a desire to make the best ideas prevail." (Arnold, 1869, p. 8) This notion of culture refers not only to what people share, but also to what they have accomplished in various domains.

Common parlor culture refers often to just the arts, sometimes including design, architecture and certain crafts (C3). This notion of culture is intended when people speak of the "cultural" sector or "cultural" policy. It is a subset of the broader grouping C2. I will use this category also for other practices with a distinct content, such as architecture, design, technique and religion.

In the conversations of scholars in the humanities, anthropologists, sociologists, historians and philosophers, all of these interpretations are contested and problematized (Elias, 2000; Lasch, 2013). Their usage, therefore, calls for caution. The notion of civilization in particular is under suspicion because of its pejorative usage. People speak of civilization to imply superiority. Kultur was an argument of German national-socialists to subject other, inferior, "cultures," and exterminate so-called "degenerate" people like the Jews, gypsies and homosexuals.

Likewise, while stressing one's own culture may generate warm feelings among those included, it excludes everyone else. Because of such pejorative usage scholars have made serious work of deconstructing notions of culture, civilization and identity. Recently, we have witnessed attempts to recover the original notions from this deconstructive work as there is a clear need for them. Nevertheless, we need to continue to watch out for pejorative usage.

Culture is important. The culture of the *oikos* (C1), for example, determines its resiliency; that culture will remain standing even when the house falls down. Qualities of their culture tell us what not only an *oikos*, but also a workplace, a community or a society are all about. By way of their actions people sustain, strengthen or undermine their culture; at the same time the culture that they are part of informs and gives meaning to what they do. Although we may abstract in our thinking about human behavior from the cultural context, we may be left wondering how it is possible for us to act independently of such a context, even if we are not aware of it. As is often noted, culture is for people what water is for fish: once outside of it, we become very aware of its importance in our daily lives. In the presence of another culture we distinguish our own.

A strong culture (C1) renders communities tough in dire circumstances. When a museum experiences declining monetary numbers because of lower subsidies or lower ticket sales, the questions arise how tough is its culture (C1), how committed its people, and how strong the support. A strong museum has a strong culture.

We have furthermore good reasons to suspect that large communities (in the form of cities, regions, nations and even continents) derive strength from a lively artistic climate and active scientific communities (C2 and C3). Economic circumstances may constitute the necessary conditions, but in the end what counts are the qualities of the culture (C1, C2 and C3): they tell us how rich in content, how varied and inspiring life in that community is, and how strong and effective the shared values are.

Accordingly, culture (C1, C2 and C3) matters. In the end, it is all that matters. All the rest is subordinate, or instrumental for the realization of culture. The *oikos* is culture in the sense of the values, stories, memories and aspirations that its members share. Monetary quantities, or those values that we measure in monetary units, are instrumental at best; all too often they distract from what really matters in the end, i.e. our culture, or cultures. Culture matters for any *oikos* and workplace, but it also matters for a city. Sure, cities are important for jobs and economic activities, but it is the realization of all kinds of qualities that make a city what it is. Paris has its atmosphere, New York its energy, Vienna has its coffee houses, and London its traditions. As Jane Jacobs so famously pointed out, cities need to be livable (Jacobs, 1993). The qualities of a city determine how well it enables its people to realize a good life, how it inspires its visitors and provides a good working environment for its workers.

Culture matters for a nation, too. The qualities that make up the culture of a nation determine what kinds of lives its citizens are able to realize. Here we have a major theme that is: **culture matters**.

CHAPTER 2

DIFFERENT WAYS OF MAKING SENSE OF CULTURE IN RELATIONSHIP TO THE ECONOMY

When you and I are trying to do the right thing, we will not immediately consider the cultural context in which we are operating. Inside the elephant, culture is like water for a fish: as long as you swim in it, you are not aware of its existence. Only in contrast with another world with another culture, does your own culture become noticeable. I myself realized my Dutchness only when I began studying in the US, in North Carolina. And I am aware of the significance of culture each time I switch between the academia to political life. Gosh, how different those two worlds are.

This chapter aims to demonstrate the consequences of the "culture matters" position, how different that point of departure is from so many other approaches, including that of standard economics, but also that of cultural economics – the field in which I have done a great deal of my research. Accordingly, this chapter addresses scholarly discussions and illustrates the particular position that this book represents. The purpose is orientation for you, the reader, and to provide context for the exploration that follows.

Scholarly positions on the role of culture

Scholars like me want tools in order to explore the role of culture, how to talk about it. I am concerned with the practice and thus also with the meaning of the expression "culture matters" in practice. Furthermore, I am interested in the type of conversations that render it meaningful.

There are, for example, scholars who focus on cultural processes and discuss nothing else. We could name them culturalists. They are anthropologists, sociologists, historians, archaeologists and others who are studying culture in general (C1 and C2) or, like art historians, the arts (C3) in particular. As an economist, I cannot help but notice that their work offers little to no insight into the financial aspects of their fields. They suggest that culture stands alone. In their case culture is all that matters!

When I turn to standard economists, the discussion is biased toward the opposite side of the spectrum. Economic discussions zero in on the financial aspects of life, on the instrumental part. Culture does not figure into those discussions. So, that does not help when we are interested in the way culture (C1, C2 or C3) works in the economy and how economic processes affect culture (again in all three kinds).

Recently, scholars in a wide variety of disciplines have broken with the one-sidedness of culturalist and economic discussions and have begun to explore the relationship between economy and culture. Historians are studying cultural factors in the development of, for example, the financial sector; sociologists and anthropologists are exploring interactions between economic and cultural phenomena; business economists have turned to cultural processes in organizations; social geographers point to the importance of geographical factors for the arts and the creative industries; and cultural economists study the economics of the arts. The sociologists Ray and Sayer coined the notion of the "cultural turn" to characterize the surge of interest in the interactions between culture and economy (Ray & Sayer, 1999).

As scholars, we seek the right conversation to be in. There are all kinds of conversations for us to join. So which is the right one when we want to understand the right thing to do, when we want to understand the intricacies of economic life while pursuing what is important to us?

If you are accustomed to the standard conversation of economics, you must already have noticed that I am nudging you towards a different conversation, a conversation that does justice to the *oikos*, to culture, while taking financial phenomena seriously. I am trying to change the conversation by recovering long neglected concepts, such as values and goods. I do so by connecting other ongoing conversations.

I first need to define this notion of "conversation" that I am using.

"Conversation" is a metaphor

I will use the metaphor of the conversation quite a bit in this book, in addition to terms like "practice," "praxis" and "a commons". Earlier I dedicated an entire book to the exploration of the metaphor (Klamer, 2007), so I will be brief here. Conversation, as I use the metaphor, denotes the more or less organized exchange of ideas of a group of people on a particular subject in a particular way. A conversation can take place at a particular moment in time, or in a particular situation but usually I will refer to a conversation that takes place over a period of time in all kinds of settings with a range of participants. "Science" is such a conversation, as are "art," "politics," "business" and "sport." Each of these conversations consists of many distinctive conversations. "Science" consists of conversations like "physics," which in turn consists of conversations on "thermodynamics," "elementary particles" and so on. "Economics" is a conversation, too, made up of the conversations on "game theory," "microeconomics," "cultural economics" and many other subjects (as you can see when you consult the index of the *Journal of Economic Literature*).

When I speak and write of a conversation, I do not only intend to get you thinking about people talking. They may just as well be writing, reading, gesturing, listening, attending a conference, checking out a journal and chatting in the corridor. Economists generally prefer to refer to fields, evoking the image of people trotting around in Wellingtons. The German philosopher Jürgen Habermas speaks of communicative action (Habermas, 1984). That gets closer to what I would like to draw your attention to. I follow the British philosopher Michael Oakeshott (1901-1990), the German philosopher Hans Georg Gadamer (1900-2002), the American pragmatist Richard Rorty (1931-2007) and the sociologist Randall Collins (1941-), among others, and opt for the term "conversation." The idea is that you think about practices, about people trying to make sense in a particular context with certain topics and in a certain mode of reasoning, with certain habits, customs and rules of conduct.

A conversation, as I use the term here, is a commons, that is, a shared practice. Chapter 6 is dedicated to developing the notion of the commons and of shared goods and practices.

The question, then, is in what conversation are you or in what conversation do you want to be. Or, if you are a practitioner, what conversation do you want to consult in order to make sense of your world, and in order to figure out what is the right thing to do in your life and your line of business.

Six conversations on the relationship between culture, economy, economics, and the arts

When I survey the field, I distinguish six ongoing conversations on the relationship between the economy (**E**) and culture or, more restrictive, on economics as a science (**e**) and culture (C1, C2 or C3).

1. The "culture does not matter for economics and the economy" conversation.

This is the conversation that I learned when I studied economics. It is still the dominant conversation, also in the world of politics, business and journalism. In this conversation the notion of culture does not show up at all. It is not taught and it is not used. The presumption here is that economists do not have to bother with culture (C1, C2 and C3) as it has no significant influence on economic processes and is therefore not something economists have to account for. Quite a few economists, if pressed with the issue, will remark that they would not know how to bring cultural factors into their model. They would not see why they should bother explaining cultural phenomena, such as the existence of national cultures or the rise or decline of the arts. They will insist that culture does not matter much in economic processes and therefore does not have to figure into their economics.

According to this conversation, culture (C1, C2 or C3) is separate from economy (E).

$$E \quad \longleftrightarrow\!\!\!\times\!\!\!\longrightarrow \quad C1,\ C2\ or\ C3$$

This is clearly not the conversation I am seeking out here, although I will use some of the insights it provides.

2. The "economy does not matter to culture" conversation

Open a book on art history, read a novel or talk with scholars in history, sociology, anthropology, archeology or philosophy, and you will wonder whether something like an economy even exists. Quite a few discussions about arts and culture focus on cultural matters only and bypass financial processes altogether. You will not find references to prices, incomes, financial conditions, market transactions or any other financial factors.

$$C1,\ C2 \quad \longleftrightarrow\!\!\!\times\!\!\!\longrightarrow \quad E$$

In an even more ambitious version of this conversation, culture stands for what could be called 'the transcendental part of a civilization'. This kind of culture involves the arts, the sciences and religion, as well as other domains (like those of nature lovers, and sports fans). In general, these kinds of cultural practices reach for something that is beyond earthly matters (our daily food, social status and pecuniary income): they may express a quest for beauty, the truth, the good, the spiritual, the sacred.

If interpreted this way, these conversations comprise literary conversations in which economic processes are somehow incorporated, as in the novels of Charles Dickens, John Steinbeck and Thomas Wolfe. When I hear colleagues in the faculties of the natural sciences and the humanities speak, I suspect that they operate in this conversation. In their world, knowledge and the pursuit thereof, the esthetical, the truth, and human sensibilities and all such cultural phenomena crowd out economic (mostly financial) factors and processes. This is also the conversation of quite a few artists and people working in the artistic field: they tend to write everything artistic in capital letters and keep all things of the economy small.

More importantly, these are the conversations that engage people who are immersed in a religious or spiritual world. Not only the Pope will be in this conversation when he addresses economic questions, but so will Muslims when they plead the Sharia or ban usury. The Dalai Lama will always put economic factors in the larger context of transcendental meanings. He will characterize the pursuit of money and other such aspects of the ordinary business of mankind as a distraction from the search for enlightenment. "Let go of the ego," he will tell economists and anyone else willing to listen, "for the ego holds you back."

Although I can easily get caught up in culturalist discussions, I am too much of an economist to be able to forget about financial aspects.

3. The "economics matters to culture" conversation.

Cultural economists apply the tools of economic analysis to the world of the arts. You could call their conversation an instance of economic imperialism: the tendency for economists to consider any phenomenon, from love to suicide and so also art, religion and science, suitable subjects for their approach. Marriage, Gary Becker famously argued, is a rational choice, the outcome of a rational calculation of costs and benefits (Becker, 1976). So is the choice to have children or to abort them, whether or not to believe in God, to do art, or to do science.

In the "economics matters" conversations the standard concepts and tools of standard economic analysis are pivotal. So this conversation is about markets, rational choice, elasticities, contingent valuation, consumer surplus, externalities, public choice and more of such concepts.

As can be expected, economists dominate the "economics matters" conversation. They have applied their analysis to the phenomenon of religion and to science (for instance Oslington (2003) and Mirowski and Sent (2008)). Economists who study the world of the arts label themselves cultural economists. The well-known economist William Baumol (1922-) was a pioneer. Prominent members of this research community are David Throsby, Bruno Frey, Ruth Towse, and Françoise Benhamou.

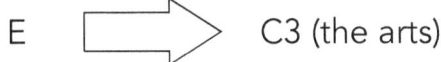

E ⟹ C3 (the arts)

When you are in love with the peculiar reasoning that economists apply (in terms of rational choice, opportunity costs, marginal costs and marginal benefits, asymmetric information, game theory and so on), you will love these conversations. If you do not, you may wonder why people get paid for developing this kind of discourse. Cultural economists will appeal to the relevance of their conversation for policy makers and to its legitimacy in academia.

4. The "arts matters to the economy" conversation

Some cultural economists, but especially people from the cultural field and policy makers, like to point at the relevance of the arts and artists for the economy. This discussion gravitates around the issue of the economic impact of culture, and of the arts in particular. The objective is to demonstrate that some economies grow better and faster than others due to the presence of artists and a creative climate, that badly functioning cities flourish because of the arts, that creative industries come to thrive in certain cities and not in others, and that culture (C3) attracts tourists (and their money).

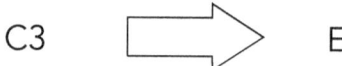

For the economic impact of the arts, the Guggenheim Museum in Bilbao is exemplary. Although the jury is actually still out, it is generally assumed to have transformed and boosted the economy of that once desolate Spanish city, by bringing in crowds of tourists, and in their slipstream, new businesses. The argument is that arts and their cultural organization can be good for the economy. Richard Florida famously argued the importance of the creative class for local economies, spurring the increasingly important creative industries and politicians will point to the economic effects of proposed investments in the arts, such as new museums, theatres, festivals and the like (Florida, 2002). The literature on "creative cities" makes more or less the same point. The conversation includes studies that show how artists can contribute to urban generation (as happened in the Soho neighborhood in New York), and how prices of real estate go up when cultural organizations move in.

Note that this conversation renders the arts instrumental for economic processes. Economic growth is apparently the goal and the arts are its maiden.

5. The "culture matters to the economy" conversation

The "culture matters to the economy" conversation focuses on culture in its anthropological meaning (C1) and as civilization (C3) as well as the economic impact that those cultures can have. Most famously, Max Weber (1864-1920) argued that protestant culture was responsible for the rise of capitalism and the concurrent economic growth in northern European countries (Weber, 2001). Economic anthropologists have pursued this line of research while standard economists have ignored it. You will look in vain for the notion of culture in economic textbooks.

Recently, economists like Deirdre McCloskey, Virgil Storr, and Robert Lane (although he is actually a political scientist) have picked up the line of argument where Weber left it (McCloskey, 2007; Lane, 1991). McCloskey, for example, argues that values and virtues affect economic processes and should account for the Dutch Golden Age in the early 17th century and the takeoff of economic growth in the late 18th and 19th centuries. In 2000, Lawrence Harrison and Samuel Huntington (1927-2008) published their book entitled: *Culture Matters: How Values Shape Human Progress* (Huntington, 1997). The title says it all. I should also mention here the French sociologist Pierre Bourdieu (1930-2002), who not only argued that economic factors influence culture, but also that knowledge of the arts and other knowledge stands for cultural capital that is needed for the accumulation of economic capital. So again, culture impacts economy (Grube & Storr, 2015).

Quite recently literary scholars, historians and social geographers have developed their own separate conversations on the "culture matter" thesis. Inger Leemans, for example, sorts out the importance of peculiar Dutch cultural traits for the Golden Age that Dutch society enjoyed in the first half of the 17th century (Leemans & Johannes, 2013; Goede de, 2005).

Also important in the "culture matters" conversation is the discussion of culture in business literature. In the seventies, the Japanese miracle got business economists interested in the value of culture in successful business strategies (Cameron & Quinn, 1999; Waterman & Peters, 1982). The Dutch scholar Hofstede made a big impression with his identification of cultural differences among IBM organizations across the world (Hofstede, 2003). This research evolved into an extensive research conducted under the name of cultural economics and dealt with questions on the role of culture in organizations, on the impact of cultural context on organization performance, and the management of culture in organizations (Beugelsdijk & Maseland, 2014). All this contributes to an increasing awareness in the business world that culture matters not only in the environments in which businesses operate, but also within businesses themselves.

Another discussion centers on creative processes in businesses and how artists can contribute to such processes.

The "culture matters" conversations appeal to politicians and business leaders to pay attention to culture in the anthropological sense and to the arts in particular. Politicians should care about art and culture--so this conversation seems to imply--because culture boosts the economy. Business leaders should understand that the culture of their organization is critical for its

performance. A strong culture makes for a strong and sustainable organization, at least that is the suggestion.

6. The "economy is embedded in culture" conversation

I now come to the conversation that is most relevant for my inquiry. This is the
conversation that views economic phenomena as manifestations of culture.
In the "economy is embedded in culture" conversation, culture is what life is
about and the ordinary business of mankind--including the trading, consuming and working that people do--are part of cultural phenomenon.

Suppose you finished a painting. What you do with the painting is a matter of what you are used to doing. It is a matter of your values and, with that,
it is a matter of the culture that you are part of. In the culture of cavemen,
painting is a strange kind of activity. When you've finished your cave painting, you must be pleased if you get your share of the food that others hunted
down or gathered. In order to get the time to paint, you most likely have a
special status in the group, such as a medicine man, or as a spiritual man. In
the culture of 17th century Netherlands, you have to realize your value as a
craftsman. In order to get anywhere with your work, you need to be part of
the guild and partake in its customs and rituals. Selling your painting is part
of the ordinary business of the guild. In the contemporary culture of high art
you will seek the approval of fellow artists, and socialize with the right people
in the hope of getting your painting into the collection of a contemporary art
museum or an important art collector. Maybe a critic will write about it! In all
three cases you operate in a different culture.

In the "economy is embedded in culture" conversation, the variations of
the conversation are what evoke interest. What do the actions say about the
culture in which the actor, you, is operating? Clearly, speaking of guilds in the
contemporary setting would be meaningless. Then again, some artists may
wish they had the status that the painters of cave paintings had.

The "economy is embedded in culture" conversations stress the meaningfulness and value-laden character of human actions, and will tend to put
them in the (cultural) context. Whether you and I go shopping, do our job,
or engage in entrepreneurial activities, we attribute meanings to things and
activities, we value them and, along the way, we generate meanings and values
for ourselves and for others. We humans are signifying people: we attribute
meanings to what we do and need a cultural context in order to make sense
of what we and what others do. See for example Van Heusden in (Klamer,
1996).

In these conversations the main purpose of studying the behavior of
people is to sort out, interpret and characterize the meanings and values
that people attribute to things and activities, and the meanings and values
that they realize with their actions. Exemplary is the work of the well-known
American anthropologist Clifford Geertz (1926-2006) who shows in his

lengthy descriptions of how culture becomes manifest in daily practices, such as cockfights in Bali. His article *Deep Play: Notes on the Balinese Cockfight* is a classic as it demonstrates how to "read" culture (Geertz, 2005).

In recent reinterpretations, Adam Smith is considered a participant in this conversation. When we read *The Wealth of Nations* in the light of his earlier *Theory of Moral Sentiments* we understand that people, in their striving to do right, answer to their moral sentiments (Smith, 1776). In *Theory of Moral Sentiments* Smith depicts people in their moral life, acting out of sympathy for others, and seeking to be virtuous. In *The Wealth of Nations*, he confronts the problem that sympathy and virtue appear to lose their relevance in market situations. The market poses a special situation since you and I cannot ask for favors and will not expect pity from others for the simple reason that we usually do not know our trading partners very well. That is why we appeal to their self-love, as Adam Smith famously argued. By acknowledging as much, Smith hastens to add that the market is but one element in society. There is sufficient space in which people can be virtuous and be benevolent towards fellow people. At least, that is the point of The Theory of Moral Sentiments, the book that he most cared about.

The "economy is embedded" vision is also present in the writings of Karl Polanyi (1886-1964). This economic historian shows how all kinds of economic institutions, foremost among them the market, are historical and therefore not universal. Markets function in some settings and not in others. Children are bought and sold in some historical and cultural settings, whereas such a practice is a taboo in the contemporary Western world. High bonuses are in some situations a sign of success, whereas in others they are considered immoral. It is all a matter of culture, this conversation will suggest.

A similar inquiry into the embeddedness of economic processes and phenomena you find in the conversations of economic sociologists such as Mark Granovetter and Viviana Zelizer, and of economic anthropologists such as Stephen Gudeman (Granovetter, 1985; Zelizer, 2005; Gudeman, 2008).

I would like to make sense of C, of what makes life meaningful, of the content of our lives, be it our *oikos*, friendships, society, art, religion or science. For that purpose I am in need of a conversation, a conversation that, for example, can make sense of the banner that I picked up in the dusty streets of Kampala. So let us see what happens when we think in terms of culture, when we focus on the things that are really important to us.

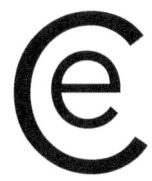

The first thing that happens, at least in this book, is that we start paying attention to values and, more particularly, to the realization of values.

CHAPTER 3

DOING THE RIGHT THING IS A MATTER OF REALIZING VALUES

Acting in a culture, or contributing to a culture – be it that of your *oikos*, the organization in which you work, your profession, your city, your society or whatever entity – implies the realization of values or whatever is important. Whether I plan the family Christmas dinner, go to a theatre, shop in a market place, consider merging my organization with another, plan an exhibition, make art, deliver a speech, vote on a new law or run with a friend, I am realizing values. At least that is what I will postulate.

When I consider how to spend an evening, I need to take into account what is important to me. I could waste my time watching mindless television, but I also could consider spending time with my children or attending a theatre performance. When a theatre group decides to do something entirely different next year, it seeks to realize something important to them. They may want to surprise other theatre makers, to test their own capacities, or to attract new groups of people to their theatre.

Is it possible that in everything we do, consciously and with the intent to feel good about it, we are seeking to realize something that is important to us? In all examples values are at stake, people are becoming or made aware of them, and then make them real by acting upon them. They may even reflect at a later stage to find out to what extent they succeeded. (When I lie down that evening I may conclude that, indeed, I wasted my evening with mindless television or that I had a great time with my children or that I still feel stimulated by the play that I attended, or not.)

My suggestion is to interpret all such considerations and deliberations **as realizing values in the sense of being aware of them, and the actions that follow as the realization of those values in the sense of valorizing them or making them real**.

Realizing values has two meanings:

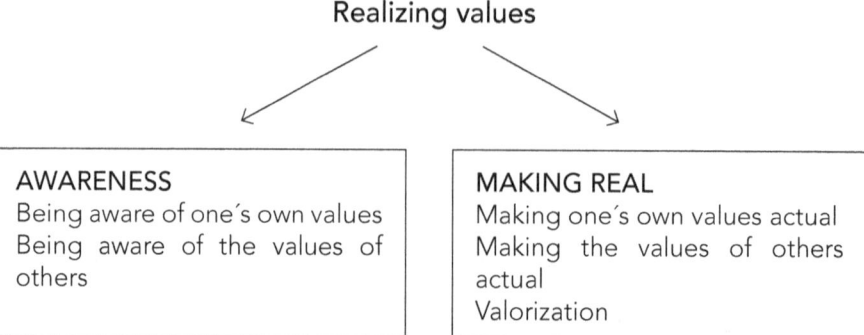

Diagram 3-1: Meanings realizing values

Focusing on the realization of values is what cultural institutions (such as museums, theatres, and orchestras), religious communities, and academic institutions do, at least in principle, and what they need to assume their stakeholders are capable of doing. Good museum directors strive to make great exhibitions to make real what is important to them and presume that museum visitors are looking for great art because that is important to them. All kinds of other organizations do the same. Charities do, but also accounting firms and law firms are doing so in the sense that good lawyers want to be just that, good lawyers, and good accountants want to be good accountants.

When I use the term *valorization*, I refer to the making real of the relevant values. It is often interpreted as implying only the realization of financial or exchange value (i.e. by selling something for a price), but I explicitly include the important values, such as artistic and social values. When someone made a painting it is one thing to sell it and quite another thing to get it recognized as a serious work of art. Valorization is the realization of relevant values, financial or not.

I focus in this book on the cultural, academic and, less explicitly, religious institutions because it is their goal to do good, that is, to do the right thing. What interests me is what it takes to do the right thing and what it is that prevents people in those institutions from doing the right thing.

Take the university. Focusing on the realization of values is what I do with my colleagues at the university when we practice science and when we teach. Sure, we scientists can be jealous, passive aggressive[1] (I plead guilty!), eager

---

1   Passive aggressive is when you agree to some action and then don't do it as a way of protesting or obstructing. It is what I do when the administration of my university issues new rules without consulting me. I do not protest but try to ignore them.

for attention and money, and rude to colleagues who think differently and to students who do not do the work, but if we sit down in a sensible mood, we will affirm our commitment to the pursuit of truth, the need for collegiality as an important value, and to honesty. See Merton, *The Matthew Effect in Science*, he describes the contrast between the scientific values of scientists and their actual behavior (Merton, 1968). By doing all that, we valorize scientific and social values.

At times my colleagues and I may confess our weaknesses. Psychologists will tell us that they are part of our shadow side. I have found the notion useful. No need to pretend that I am perfect. Yet, when I test my craving for attention, and my need of external rewards with my impartial spectator, I do not feel proud. Shame is the more appropriate feeling. I feel so much better in the pursuit of truthfulness, good conversation and good teaching.

Focusing on the realization of values is what the cultural sector is all about, at least what the "serious" leaders of cultural organizations and "serious" artists are aspiring to do. An art museum is dedicated to the arts, a theatre group to theatre. The artistic director of the Rotterdam Philharmonic Orchestra wants to have the best musicians and the best conductor to perform Mahler's Fifth as it never has been performed before. Or he wants to perform experimental music of a new composer because he truly beliefs in its power. His goal is to make great music at its best.

In the pursuit of his goals this director of the orchestra has to battle a lack of interest among regular visitors. He may have to deal with a skeptical business manager, and reluctant musicians. And he has to face the overwhelming preference for the usual, for recognizable music that makes listening easy. That is, he is up against the desire for amusement and entertainment. And because entertainment sells tickets, he has to be creative in realizing his music while avoiding bankruptcy.

The Dutch poet Lucebert once noted: "everything of value is vulnerable." People in the Dutch cultural sector have embraced this saying to characterize their recurrent dilemma. In trying to do good, to realize that what is important to them, like great art, great music, great theatre, they risk losing everything. The question is then whether they have to compromise on their values in order to be able to continue their activities. Some will tell them to pay more attention to what the public wants. Others will admonish them to be forceful in expressing their values, to stand for the art they want to make, and to persuade or seduce others to pursue great art.

Nothing new.
With this approach to the subject of economics I follow a rich tradition to which a great range of authors and endless practices have contributed. I

name the works of Thomas Aquinas and Adam Smith, any religious work, quite a bit of work in psychology (Maslow, for example) and more recently the works of Alasdair MacIntyre, Martha Nussbaum, Charles Taylor and Deirdre McCloskey. Other economists are picking up the theme like Robert Skidelsky. (These authors all operate in the "economy is embedded in culture" conversation.) A favorite source of mine is Aristotle, and then in particular his Nicomachean Ethics (Aristotle & Ross, 1959).

Acting upon values implies the striving for the good.
Aristotle (384-322BC) is the pragmatic Greek philosopher who had a profound influence on civilization. That influence began in the 12th and 13th century when scholars translated his work in Latin. Aristotle's works became a major source for philosophers through the 19th century. Thomas Aquinas (1225-1274) used the bible and Aristotle, to whom he referred as the Philosopher, as his main references when he addressed moral issues in economic situations. Aristotle was more or less ignored during the major part of the 20th century but is now back in vogue. Alasdair MacIntyre and Martha Nussbaum are two prominent contemporary philosophers who have brought his work back to life (MacIntyre, 1981; Nussbaum, 1986). In particular his Nicomachean Ethics receives a great deal of attention nowadays (McCloskey 2007, 2011, 2016; van Staveren 2001). There are even business handbooks that instruct managers how to apply Aristotle in their work.

It may be interesting to realize that Aristotle probably wrote the text to instruct his son Nicomachus. He began the instruction as follows:

"Every art and every inquiry, and similarly every action and pursuit, is thought to aim at some good; and for this reason the good has rightly been declared to be that at which all things aim." (Aristotle & Ross, 1959, p. 1094a)

A contemporary reader may have some difficulties here. At least that is my experience when I read this sentence with students and professionals. Especially the notion of the good triggers questions and doubts – as if there would be a good out there for you and me to be realized. I do not want to pursue the philosophical discussion at this point and suggest staying pragmatic by interpreting the good as the purpose that a person, a community or an organization is seeking.

In an organization the purpose is expressed in the mission that some organizations have articulated and most have not. (The mission cannot be the maximization of profit, as we will see in a moment.)

Aristotle continues by suggesting that the good varies:

> "But a certain difference is found among ends; some are activities, others are products apart from the activities that produce them. Where there are ends apart from the actions, it is the nature of the products to be better than the activities." (Aristotle & Ross, 1959, p. 1094a)

An actor wants to be a good actor. His good is in the acting, in the performing on stage: by acting he can realize his good. A craftswoman whose craft is making hats seeks to produce great hats.

Aristotle affirms such a reading when he continues:

> "Now, as there are many actions, arts, and sciences, their ends also are many; the end of the medical art is health, that of shipbuilding a vessel, that of strategy victory, that of economics wealth. But where such arts fall under a single capacity – as bridle-making and the other arts concerned with the equipment of horses fall under the art of riding, and this and every military action under strategy, in the same way other arts fall under yet others – in all of these the ends of the master arts are to be preferred to all the subordinate ends; for it is for the sake of the former that the latter are pursued. It makes no difference whether the activities themselves are the ends of the actions, or something else apart from the activities, as in the case of the sciences just mentioned." (Aristotle & Ross, 1959, p. 1095a)

Aristotle admonishes his son to distinguish means from ends. It is a lesson that seems pertinent in a wide variety of situations today. It is a lesson for business managers who mistake the instrument of profit as an end in and of itself, or youngsters who seek money (lots of it!) as their goal.

Asking about ends or goals can, therefore, be a therapeutic intervention. (As I noted in the preface, my intentions are therapeutic and edifying and not, let that be clear, normative or moralizing.) It is what coaches do when they help professionals, and it is what therapists, priests and ministers do in their therapies and ministries. When I consult artistic organizations we invariably begin with figuring out what its mission is, what it is after. The answer usually requires a bit of probing.

Swapping instruments for goals is all too common. A director of an American art museum declared in a seminar for art managers that he has three goals and they are 1) fundraising, 2) fundraising, and 3) fundraising.

(I was told this anecdote by a Dutch banker who had picked it up in an arts management course at New York University. He cited it in approval. So now you can imagine how I responded.) That sounds tough and he probably tried to unnerve his audience. Even so, he might be asked in the spirit of Aristotle what purpose the fundraising serves. It would be strange to set up a museum in order to raise funds. Such a goal also seems to make a bad proposition to those providing the funds. This director was swapping means for ends.

Money is never an end. The pursuit of money is always a means to some end or another, even if it is sometimes difficult to articulate that end. (If you disagree, tell me a case in which the pursuit of money is an end in itself.)

Asking others and yourself about what is worth striving for is probing for the good(s) that you and others are pursuing. It is the Aristotelian question.

CHAPTER 4

PHRONESIS IS THE VIRTUE IN MAKING VALUES REAL

In striving for the good we will need to consider all that is important to us. That means that we need to consider our values. We also need to know the values of others and a great deal more to assess the situation at hand and to know what works. Acting upon my values in pursuit of some good or another, and applying all available knowledge in doing so, is called *phronesis*, to use a term of Aristotle. *Phronesis* is practical wisdom. Gonzalo Bustamente wrote a thesis on *Phronesis* in which he explains that it calls for thoughtfulness, awareness of the goods to strive for and the relevant values, and a clear understanding of what other people want and need, proven practices and strategies (Bustamente Kuschel, 2012).

Aristotle considers *phronesis* a cardinal virtue, that is, a virtue that is crucial for all valuations, for all actions. *A virtue is a value that we attribute to actions.* A virtuous person is someone who has internalized the important virtues. As long as you and I consciously strive for practical wisdom, we probably have not internalized that virtue. We are not practically wise, but we would like to be. The person that others see as being practically wise, will not comprehend when told so: for isn't what he does self-evident?

Phronesis is what sensible people practice when they go the theatre "to see a serious play" instead of "slouching in front of the television," or "mindlessly playing silly games." *Phronesis* is what the director of a play does when she seeks a conflict with her actors in order to break through an impasse; it is what a student does who cancels a date in order to study for an exam. It is by *phronesis* that we figure out what is the right thing to do. It is what makes us realize whether or not an action was right.

Mind you, people are not always sensible. My choice to waste a precious evening watching mind-numbing television programs is not sensible.

Attracting a sponsor with a dubious reputation is not the sensible thing to do for a serious art museum. Being greedy is not sensible and neither is being obsessed with getting attention and appreciation for one's work. So often I have acted in ways that I regret afterwards. I have eaten ice cream when I should not have, responded inadequately to a critical remark, or accepted a speaking engagement when I should have used the time to write or be with my family or friends. Often I need others to point this out to me. Adam Smith uses in his *The Theory of Moral Sentiments*, which could be read as a treatise on *phronesis*, the impartial spectator as a device to check your actions (Smith, 1759). The impartial spectator is the voice you and I carry in us, that tells us whether or not our actions are right. It is our conscience speaking.

Phronesis kicks in when a banker realizes that his fixation on gaining high bonuses has not made him a better banker and that he needs to figure out what he actually wants to accomplish and what his values are. *Phronesis* operates when people begin considering the quality of food they consume, or when a CEO of a company decides to invest in the culture of his organization.

Phronesis is one of the four cardinal virtues that the ancient Greeks, Aristotle among them, articulated. The other three cardinal virtues are temperance (striking a balance between overdoing things or not doing enough), courage (overcoming fears in doing the right thing), and justice (taking into account interests and sensitivities of others). Thomas Aquinas and other Christian thinkers later added the three theological virtues—faith, hope, and love—to complement what later became known as the seven classical virtues. Faith stands for confidence, hope is keeping a future perspective and love is about the ability to feel a deep connectedness, the kind that my wife and I aspire to realize when dealing with situations in our *oikos*.

Well in to the 19th century these virtues were common knowledge; children learned them at school. During the 20th century, these were mostly forgotten. These virtues were slowly but surely replaced by a focus on instrumental knowledge and thus on things that can be quantified (like profits, economic growth, numbers of visitors and numbers of publications or citations). Recently they are coming back in vogue, thanks to philosophers such as Alasdair MacIntyre, Martha Nussbaum and Philippa Foot (1920-2010). I learned of them from Deirdre McCloskey who wrote a trilogy on the bourgeois virtues (McCloskey, 2007, 2011, 2016). As I will try to clarify in the next chapter, being aware of the seven virtues and knowing how to realize them in dealing with our values, is most helpful for doing the right thing. In this chapter the focus is on *phronesis*.

How *phronesis* differs from the ideas of rational behavior and rational choice

The idea of phronesis is quite different from the idea of rational behavior or rational choice that you learn about in standard economics. The idea of rationality presumes that we can *calculate* the best choice; it involves the idea that we derive the best choice by maximizing some objective function (utility, profit) under certain constraints (income, prices and the like). Economists embrace the idea because it enables them the modeling of decision making in the form of mathematical equations. The modeling gives an idea the aura of "science." The idea of *phronesis* makes us realize that too much is involved in doing the right thing, that calculation is therefore nigh impossible, and modeling quite hopeless. The process of *phronesis* is difficult to trace, and hard to catch in the form of rules and (predictable) patterns. Rationality suggests a neatly ordered process; *phronesis* evokes the image of a mess.

The idea of rationality makes perfect sense in an instrumentalist interpretation of science. When economists embraced the goal of policy relevance, as they did in the thirties of the 20th century, it made sense to assume that consumers, workers and businesses were rational. That assumption facilitates modeling of economic processes and the models that produce the results that presumably enable policy makers to conduct rational policies. At least, this was how the idea of rationality was presumed to work.

The idea of rationality furthermore alludes to a prevalent notion of knowledge as clear propositions about the world out there. This notion engenders the following misguided image: first scientists get to work by developing a model and conducting a few calculations, then there are outcomes or results in the form of propositions that dictate, for example, the best policy to be conducted under specific conditions ("When the economy has such and such characteristics, an increase in government spending of 2.8% will bring unemployment down by 0.5%"). That proposition is allegedly the knowledge that economists produce. This is also how people tend to think about the knowledge that the natural sciences generate: they think that the results come in the form of propositions that can be patented and used by engineers to design new technology.

In reality that kind of packaged knowledge plays only a subordinate role. Policy makers do not consider the outcomes of economic modeling as knowledge to be applied directly. There remain too many ifs and buts, and therefore they end up practicing what could be called *phronesis*: they try to make sense of complicated processes, taking into account different interests – and every now and then the opinions of scholars – in what may appear as a messy process. The following anecdote underscores this observation.

The year was 2000. The setting was the beautiful citizen's ballroom in the city hall of Rotterdam, one of the few buildings that survived the bombardment of May 14, 1940. Cultural economists from all over the world had gathered for their biennial conference. They were eager to hear Rick van der Ploeg, a well-known Dutch-British economist, who was then Secretary of Education, Science and Culture in the Dutch cabinet. Rick is a tall and eccentric fellow. In informal settings he likes to poke fun and make provocative remarks. In a formal setting he is dead serious, and this was a formal setting.

Rick told about the challenges he faced as a Secretary of Education, Science and Culture in the Netherlands, and explained the way the Dutch conduct their cultural policy. He talked at length about the process by which the government allocates grants to cultural organizations and about the increasing awareness of the economic importance of culture and the arts.

As the moderator of the session, I asked him how he, in his capacity as secretary, had benefited from the work of cultural economists. Did he ever make use of contingent valuation studies, for example? (Those were quite popular at the time.) His answer was brief. "Not at all," he said. I repeated the question and he repeated the answer: "I must confess that I have had no use for the results of research in cultural economics."

I am not sure whether those listening at the time realized the importance of his answer. I had expected it to hit those present with a shock. After all, most of them had dedicated their lives to do the work that should help politicians to improve their cultural policy. If even an economically astute politician has no use for their work, then what had they been working for? What if all the research in cultural economics had been to no avail?

Maybe Van der Ploeg had been too blunt. After all, politicians at the time had a keen interest in the economic impact of the arts and the creative industries and that is what economists can measure. Then again, as an economist he knew all too well the serious limitations of such measurements so maybe that had been a reason for him to eschew such studies as a politician. Or maybe he had encountered at the political table's strong resistance to the arguments favored by economists. He would not be the first economist to discover the bad rap that the thinking of economists has in the world of politics. I report several confessions of economists in chapter 1 and 7 of my book: (Klamer, 2007).

I conclude from experiences like these that policy making is not the rational process that especially economists would like to think it is, and that the knowledge of current scientific practices is not all that useful, to put it mildly. If you accept this, then you may go along with my interest in the messy practice that is *phronesis*.

The idea of rationality makes even less sense in daily life. Let us do an exercise to demonstrate why. Think of an important decision you have recently made. What was it? Was it the choice to study at a particular university? Perhaps it was the decision to study instead of setting up a business? To get married, or to have children? Was it to hire people, or to fire them? Ok, do you have a decision in mind?

Now reflect on what led you to make that decision? What were the important factors? What influenced you? Take your time.

Based on various exercises like this one done in classes and workshops, I sus-pect that you will come up with a selection of the following factors:

Intuition, gut feeling, the social environment including friends and family, values, expe-riences of others, information of various kinds, weighing pluses and minuses, the calculation of budget, the report of a consultancy group.

A report from a consultancy group comes closest to what could be con-sidered the input of science. And yet it is rarely mentioned during this exer-cise, even when the group consists of managers. In most cases, science has no influence on decisions made, at least not consciously. People who do this exercise recognize the characterization of the process as complex and messy. Most often people will describe emotions, intuition and gut feelings. A woman once shared that when she had decided to pursue a master in business, she found herself crying afterward. That made her realize that she had chosen wrongly. In many cases, people refer to their social entourage. Students often speak of the influence of parents.

It is not very often that people speak of their values. It takes a little prob-ing to get to them. This suggests that people are often not consciously work-ing with their values, but that subconsciously these values play a role anyway. When we discuss particular instances, people readily identify values that are involved. As the sociologist Max Weber would say, if we are rational we follow a substantive rationality in the sense that we try to realize important values in the decisions we take (Weber, 1968). Procedural rationality in the sense of following a strict and explicit procedure of calculation does not apply. Substantive rationality appears to be more important in real life than proce-dural rationality. Substantive rationality relies on *phronesis*, as it requires the realization of values while weighing a complexity of factors.

The question of why economists continue to be fixated on procedural rationality and why academics continue to crank out research papers that have so little relevance to daily life, I will leave for later. Though I will make one comment here: in academia the norm is to distance oneself from daily life and from actual practices and to assume the position of the "objective" spectator, or *Anschauer* in German. We teach students to disengage and adopt a distancing language or abstruse words, such as is observed in mathematics. I am determined to violate this norm and seek instead a type of knowledge that bridges the realm of inquiry and daily life. It is a science that is both therapeu-tic and edifying that I seek with the intent to affect our actions.

Creating order in the process of *phronesis*

Being about thoughtfulness, the virtue of phronesis stimulates us to be aware of what we need to know in order to do the right thing. Which knowledge is relevant? It does not take much to realize that all kinds of knowledge are called for; and most of the knowledge needed is not what you learn at school and at university.

Consider the woman who is heading a theatre group as the business director. Someone else is the artistic leader. The director comes for advice. She thinks that the artistic leader is undermining her authority, that he is taking too much risk with the new show and is not willing to listen to her objections. She fears for the company if the artistic leader gets his way. What to do? What does she need to be aware of?

To evoke the idea of rationality here is pointless. It will not help her. What algorithm would she use? What does she know?

Business economics would provide better tools for her to cope with the situation. In business books she would learn that she is in need of a vision (How does the group look at the outside world and at the future?), a mission (What is it about? What is the contribution the group wants to make and for whom?) and a strategy (How to go about it?).

To avoid the direct association with business economics and to allow for a deepening of these concepts, I propose another order and different concepts, even if they overlap with the usual ones. To illustrate, as the business director of the theatre group I would suggest the artistic leader to, first, be aware of the ideals to strive for – hers and those of the organization – and her worldview, then, to design her actions, execute those and, finally, reflect on the question to what extent her actions have contributed to the realization of her ideals.

Here are the concepts in order:

IDEALS: These are the goods that people, groups of people or organizations strive for, including the values and virtues that they want to realize. (This is also called the mission.)

WORLDVIEW: This represents all the knowledge that gives people, groups of people and organizations context when striving for the realization of their ideals. Their worldview is their perspective on the world that is relevant for them, their framing of that world, and it includes their vision in the sense of how they view the future. A worldview may be informed by scientific knowledge, but in general will mainly consist of anecdotes, fragments of knowledge, selected information and experiences or stories. (This is also called the vision.)

DESIGN: With their ideals in mind and with all the knowledge at their disposal, people, groups of people or organizations plan their actions. The plans constitute the design; it is the conscious part of doing the right thing. When people decide to go on vacation, they will have to figure out how to do so. What they figure out is their design. (This is also called the strategy.)

PRACTICE: Whatever the ideals are, whatever people know, and no matter how thoughtful a design is, often what happens in practice is something quite different. Distractions, unexpected turns of events, emotions, uncertainties and stupidities are all things that make real life surprising, interesting, frustrating and disappointing.

EVALUATION or REFLECTION: People learn from real life by comparing their ideals, worldview and design with the actual practice. Such comparison is the evaluation or reflection. The question to answer here is how effective the design has been for the realization of the ideals. Without reflection people cannot know what ideals they have realized.

People and organizations will usually not follow these steps in this order, but all steps will be part of striving for the right thing, some more expressly than others. The work of coaches, therapists and consultants is to get people and organizations to think each step through. People who are conscious of these steps and reflect on them are what Donald Schön called "reflective practitioners" (Schön, 1984).

Let us look at each step more closely.

IDEALS: How to recognize them?

Ideals are the goods and values that people and organizations want to realize, even if they know that they will never succeed in doing so perfectly. A scientist has *Truth* as ideal, an artist *Beauty*, and a monk the *Absolute Good* or *Salvation*. Ideals express longings of people or groups of people (the promised land, the shining city on the hill, paradise), and the ambitions of organizations (to create the ultimate product, the perfect technology, the ideal workplace). Our ideals are the goods we strive for. Some will speak of purposes. Others will think of something that is very important to them, of something that is a good in and of itself. An ideal is something we long for even if we know that we can never realize it. An ideal can be a practice like researching, living a monastic life, making art, and exercising one's craftsmanship.

The business director, whom we encountered earlier, may have as an ideal to be a great business director. When faced with the challenge of a recalcitrant artistic leader, a great business director knows what to do. By doing so he realizes himself as the true professional he wants to be. In case he also identifies with the ideals of the theatre group, he has to figure out how to facilitate the artistic leader without compromising the ideals of the group.

Ideals comprise the values and virtues that people or organizations want to realize. Many companies are making their values explicit nowadays.

The Boston Consulting Group has as its values "Integrity, Respect for the Individual, Diversity, Clients Come First and The Strategic Perspective." A partner of that group once told me that they really abide to those values and appeal to them daily. A theatre group that I worked with figured out that its shared values were: "Surprise, Inventiveness, Craftsmanship and Adventure." In case of disagreements or doubts, they will appeal to those values. Whatever they do, it must be surprising ("so we are not going to repeat ourselves"), inventive ("no, that is not new, not have seen that before"), adventurous ("shouldn't we change our venue?") and demonstrate craftsmanship ("sorry, that actor does not meet our standard of acting"). Whether or not they were consciously working with this set of values was not clear. Some members seemed to be more aware of them than the others.

Instruments do not constitute ideals. The hammer of the carpenter is an instrument that he uses to realize his ideal (great craftsmanship maybe). Likewise, reputation is an instrument for scientists and artists to realize their ideals. A great reputation cannot be an ideal; you and I can long for it, but the question to ask ourselves is: "What is the reputation good for?" A dictator may long for absolute power but he must still answer the same question: "What is all that power good for?" When a firm proclaims profit maximization as its goal, the question remains: "What is that profit good for?"

Ideals, therefore, are the answer to the repeated question: "What is this or that good for?" In chapter 7 I will try to be more explicit as to the ideals we may have.

WORLDVIEW: What is the required knowledge?

Our entire life we are in need of knowledge in order to do the right thing. We do so as children ("How do I know that I will make a good friend?" "Which school is best?"), as founders of a household ("Where to live?" "What job to seek?" "How to repair the faucet?"), as professionals ("What to know so I can be a teacher of economics?"), as managers ("What strategies will work?"), as politicians ("In what way is the world changing and what can I do about that?), and so on.

We need to "know that" and we need to "know how." "Knowing that" is knowing that the world or elements of the world work in a particular way: that a good conversation requires good listening, that a dropped plate probably breaks, that a higher price decreases demand, that a game theoretic situation has many different solutions, that wealthy Chinese are interested in objects of old Chinese craftsmanship, and that greater inequality makes people more unhappy. "Knowing how" is knowing how to do things, how to install a DVD recorder, how to make shoes, how to act and how to teach.

When a conflict threatens, you need to assess others involved, their interests, their possible reactions, their emotional involvement; you need to know your own motives and emotions, you need to know legal ramifications, and you need to be able to assess your chances of succeeding.

When you have a great idea for a new product, a museum, or a piece of music, you need to know all kinds of things in order to realize the idea. You may need to know technical things, organizational things, legal things or economic things. You need to know all kinds of numbers about costs and revenues, about potential buyers or visitors, about the interest rate and so on. (Are the services of an accountant and marketing specialists required?)

When we work with other people, it may help to know what motivates them, what is important to them, and we need to know about the shared culture, the common interests. When we have children, we need to know all kinds of things about pedagogy, and about ourselves (as I found out). And don't even get me started about the knowledge that we need to sustain relationships and marriages.

When you run a company, a ministry or a country, you need to know all that and then some. Bring in the reports, tally the figures, show the scenarios, calculate the risks, get the experts in and then you may decide to go with your gut feeling anyway. There is probably no singular piece of knowledge, like a scientific result or a fact, which will make you take the decision. It's all too complex for that.

Your worldview comprises all your beliefs about the world and your opinions. It is undoubtedly influenced by your upbringing and education. The economics that economic students have learned frames the way they look at the world. People who studied psychology will frame the world differently (as I experience on a daily basis being married to a psychologist). Technically oriented people will be inclined to perceive technical details around them, and artists will tend to perceive things differently from everybody else.

What I do not know—and what no one really knows—is the role that scientific knowledge has. The findings of science and the scientific perspective on things must inform our worldview. But is it the most important element of the worldview of politicians and managers? What do people do with what they learned at university? Do they apply what they learned later on? Lawyers and medical doctors undoubtedly do, even if they have to learn a great deal on the job. But how about economists and historians? What can they put to use?

Important is also the vision that leaders need in order to lead. An artistic leader of a theatre group must have an idea of where the field is at and where it is heading. If politically engaged, he better have a vision of the political horizon. In a course that I give, I work with students on their vision. Each time I observe how difficult that is for them. A vision calls for imagination and for creativity. Extrapolating current trends is relatively easy, but to imagine a surprising future is an entirely different matter. What if we were to step away from digital technology? What if old traditions were to make a comeback? What if "everything solid melts in the air," as Karl Marx predicted in *The Communist Manifesto* (Marx, Engels, Moore, & McLellan, 1998).

The point of lingering on the worldview is to be aware of all the different kinds of knowledge that are called for when we try to do the right thing. There is so much to know! How are we ever able to do the right thing?

DESIGN: A matter of planning

Once we know our ideals and know all kinds of things that we need to know, we must then determine what we are going to do in order to realize our ideals. This is a matter of design, of a conscious and deliberate planning.

So the business director will sit down, possibly with an advisor, to determine her strategy, a plan of action. Will she first set up a meeting with the artistic leader, and how will she approach the meeting? Will she come with the numbers, with some graphs even, will she be rational or will she use an emotional plea? She may also decide to consult with the board of trustees to secure backing in case of serious troubles.

When people decide to start a business, they will be asked, for example by the bank, for their business plan. So they will have to figure out how they are going to do it, what kind of organization they need, how the budget looks, how many and what kind of employees they need, how to do the marketing, what collaborations to seek and so on. All this planning constitutes the design.

Designing is also what young people do when they choose a university, a major, or a master, or when they choose to apply for a commercial job or a job in the cultural sector. All such decisions make up a design for the future in the hope that it will facilitate the realization of the ideals.

PRACTICE: To show what we are worth and to discover that things are different in reality from how we think they will be.

When someone wants to be an actor, she has to act. A musician makes music, a leader leads, a manager manages, a surgeon performs surgeries and a mother mothers. We are what we do. When people want to change the world, they have to become active somehow. People do things, groups of people do things and organizations do things. The doing of things constitutes the practice.

By doing things, we realize our ideals. In the doing of things we apply the knowledge we have and we implement the designs we have construed. In practice we prove what our plans, our values and our knowledge amount to, that is, what they are worth. We need practice, actually doing things, to valorize the relevant values.

In practice things are usually different from what we planned and in the midst of activities it is easy to lose sight of the ideals and the design. Things turn out to be more complicated than we thought, and we find out that we are ignorant or lack the appropriate knowledge.

Even if we know what the right thing to do is, we still may not do it. My doctor tells me how to handle my backache, but he himself does not follow his own advice. Quite a few economists are disastrous when it comes to dealing with money and, even though I know that I should plan my financial future, I do not do so. People put things in their mouth that they know are bad for them, and they hold on to a relationship that clearly does not work. We do stupid things all the time and choose to be ignorant even if we could know better.

Yet, it is in the doing of things that people show who they are and what they stand for. Organizations prove their merit and demonstrate their values in their dealings with their stakeholders. It is by doing things that we realize values in the sense of valorizing them.

EVALUATION or REFLECTION: How are we doing?
Because of all the stupidities, the ignorance, the bad and unfortunate practices, reflection is an essential part of doing the right thing. By evaluating our actions we have a better chance of becoming conscious of what is really important to us, of whether or not our worldview suffices for the task at hand and of how effective the design has been.

For companies and other organizations the evaluation is a monthly or annual ritual that involves accountants and sometimes researchers. Stakeholders expect information on how well organizations are doing. Shareholders want to know the amount of profit made, employees may need feedback on their contribution, financers want to know whether or not the plans worked out and delivered the desired outcomes.

Evaluation, therefore, serves different objectives. Stakeholders use the evaluation as a way of checking or controlling the organization. The leaders of an organization need evaluations in order to know whether they did the right thing. That is also the function of evaluation that *individuals* use. For them the most important question to answer is whether or not they did the right thing.

Governments need to evaluate, too. Politicians want to demonstrate to their electorates that their policies are working and therefore are in need of evaluations. For that purpose government agencies generate data of all sorts to enable evaluations. Most famous is the number for economic growth that all governments generate. The number is used to determine how well the economy is doing and, with that, how well the government is doing. (Although, whether that measure is doing justice to the qualities of an economy is questionable. Its usage has becomes a habit from which it turns out to be difficult to part.)

When it comes to organizations with ideals, such as cultural, scientific, social and religious *organizations*, the usual methods of evaluation are inadequate. Counting quantities like money generated, numbers of visitors or numbers of publications, does little for the determination of the qualities realized. The numbers do not tell of the greatness of the music that an orchestra has made or of the importance of the insights that the scholars of a particular university have generated. And how to identify the social and societal impact of organizations? When a company is intent to make significant contributions to a good society, we do not have adequate tools for determining whether or not they actually did so.

In chapter 11 I will present a quality impact monitor that enables organizations to evaluate the realization of desired social, cultural and other qualities. It is one of the concrete outcomes of the conceptual framework that I develop here.

How *phronesis* works in daily life.

You can only truly understand how *phronesis* works when you experience it in your daily life. Here is my example. It is taken from personal life, as that is the life that makes most sense for me. Please fill in examples of your own life.

Christmas was always a rough time for me and my wife. She expected a great deal from Christmas, whereas I was seeking relaxation. As it happened we had become quite ambitious in filling the Christmas days (the Dutch have two Christmas days.) On Christmas Eve we eat with a friend and attend a Christmas meeting with carols and the like. On Christmas Day we have a dinner for our family (with four children) and a few friends. On the second day of Christmas we go to my mother's for a dinner with my family, and on the day after we get everybody over again for the birthday of my eldest daughter. The events usually turned into quite an ordeal for me. They meant hard work and a dire lack of the type of conversations that energize me. Not much intellectual content here. I frequently did not make it to the last event, having declared myself sick by that time. (A couple of times I actually did have a fever.) My wife and I ended up quarreling quite a bit with her expressing her doubts about my efforts and commitment, and my complaining of too much social stuff. Rough times indeed.

So one day, a few weeks before another Christmas, we decided to be sensible. As I had learned from Aristotle we first needed to know the good we were seeking to realize. So we sat down to figure out as much. (We really did!) We concluded that we are seeking a good family and that means for us a warm, open and supportive family. I could imagine a more spiritual goal but this goal would do. We called it our ideal. With that good in mind we wanted to create good experiences for our children and friends.

We then determined our values. She submitted the value of "together," suggesting that it is important to her that we do things together, as a couple. "Together" is maybe not a real value and it could imply other values such as a common responsibility, but "together" it was. My impartial spectator told me it was right for me (while my devil's advocate warned me that this might not be in my own selfish interest.)

We subsequently settled on the value of being at the service of others (there is no satisfactory English word for the Dutch word "dienstbaar"), as we figured that we do all this for our children, our family and our friends, rather than for our own pleasure. I agreed that being at the service of others was the adult thing to do, even if I felt somewhat uncomfortable with committing myself. (How about my need for intellectual conversation and free time?)

We finally agreed that we wanted to be grateful for our ability to receive and feed people and for them to be willing to join us. Gratitude is a value that comes with the Christian tradition in which I grew up, so that came easy.

Christmas arrived and we began with our usual program. Christmas Eve went well. On Christmas Day I decided to read, while my wife began the preparations in the kitchen. After a while she appeared in the door opening and all she said was: "together?" The question mark in her comment was distinct. I rescued myself at that point with the excuse that I was preparing myself for the speech that I usually give at our dinner. But I knew that this excuse wouldn't last the day, so after half an hour I joined her in the kitchen. We worked hard, and I did my best to make sure that everyone was engaged and got what they needed. When someone appeared bored, I got him or her back into a conversation. I ran around with the bottle of wine, slipped in complimentary remarks here and there, and took care of the coffee. The conversations during the dinners were meandering as always (according to me, that is), yet I found that the experience was entirely different.

When my wife and I reflected on these Christmas proceedings after the guests had left, we concluded that our kids, the family and our friends all seemed to be content, that the dinner had been once again delicious, that I had done my best to be attentive to the needs of family and friends, and that we were so grateful that we could do all this.

I actually felt good about it all. I felt good about having done this together with my wife and about having attended to the needs of my children, my mother and friends. Frankly, I was surprised to note how well Aristotle had helped us. A good source it is, at least for me.

In the terms I am proposing here, I experienced how it works first to be aware of one's values and then to valorize them. Practicing *phronesis* made me feel content, much more so than when I was pursuing my selfish wants (as I did in the days after).

Appendix 1. The value based approach in contrast with standard economics

There is no way that a few words will do justice to the complex practice that I call here standard economics. Even so, because I use this standard economics in contrast to the novelties of the value based approach, I feel compelled to undertake the hazardous enterprise of characterizing standard economics. Hazardous, because being intimately familiar with standard economics and its practitioners, I know that they will take issue with everything I will jot down here.

The characterization of standard economics comes first. A comparison with the valued based approach follows.

A picture says a great deal. If you know right away what this picture says, you have encountered standard economics at school. If you do not, you are a novice.

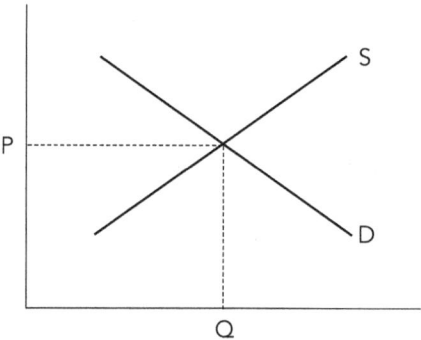

Standard economics pictures the world from a distance. This picture represents the market, and makes clear that the market is the main focus, the main theme in standard economics. The world is divided in two: the demand side and the supply side, represented by the D curve and the S curve respectively.

The picture requires quantities (Q) of products to be traded (on the horizontal axis). It attributes a central role to the price (P) (on the vertical axis).

The picture suggests that the price is responsible for establishing equilibrium between demand and supply.

Behind the demand and supply curves standard economics pictures rational individuals and firms maximizing utility or profit.

Standard economics is based on a system of accounting. Rational decision makers presumably divide the world in two, just as is done in accounting: costs and benefits, receipts and expenditures, and assets and liabilities.

Other important characteristics are: "markets are interdependent," "the price mechanism is crucial" and "rational individuals respond to changes in prices" (a matter of incentives).

The focus is on markets. Where markets fail, government actions are warranted, as in the provision of public goods, controls, regulations, taxes and expenditures, including welfare payments, establishment and protection of property rights.

Over the last few decades, standard economics has evolved to express the complexity of markets and decision making by depicting interactions as games, and recognizing risks, information problems and even cognitive problems that rational decision makers have to deal with.

The value based approach is different in all kinds of ways. What follows is a preliminary list. In the final chapter we can make sense of a more complete list, as a reward of the work still to be done.

Standard economics	Value based approach
Central problem: allocation of scarce resources	The realization of values
The economy as a system of markets	Standpoint of people realizing values
Value based/substantive reason	Instrumental reasoning: focus on meansing
Analytical and policy oriented	Interpretive, edifying and therapeutic
Quantitative	Qualitative
Basic assumptions/heuristics	**Basic assumptions/heuristics**
Rational decision makers	People coping while doing the right thing, practicing phronesis
A clear distinction between production, distribution and consumption	Consumption is also production, co-creation
Consumers maximize utility	People realize various values by way of a range of goods
Recognize only private and collective goods	Most important goods are shared
Goals are maximization of utility, profit, growth and welfare	People identify specific goods to strive for
The economy is autonomous	The economy is embedded in a culture

Appendix 2. How about the alleged selfishness of people?
When listening to standard economists, and to so many others, you begin to believe that people are primarily greedy, self-interested and money-driven. Apparently, when they try to imagine the inside of the beast that they study, they observe greed and self-interest as what motivates people to do what they do. It is not what I observe. Does this make my perspective hopelessly naïve and unrealistic?

Let me clarify how I get to a different perspective:

1. I first ask whether this observation also applies to those who make the assumption of selfishness: are they themselves greedy, self-interested or money driven? They usually respond that they are trying to do the right thing but that others are greedy and such. In that case we basically agree. The question remains why the others appear to act differently.

2. When people admit to be greedy themselves, I ask them "what is the greed good for?" When I keep repeating that question in response to the answers they give, there always turns out to be some right thing in the end. Often people express regret for their short-sightedness, ignorance and stupidities that have led them to behavior that seemed greedy and egoistic. I then point out the inconsistency: while others are greedy and the like, we are not, or wish we were not. So what if others are like us?

3. Why then do others seem greedy? This is what I think. When doing the right thing, we do need to take into account the behavior of others. Other people have different interests, and may have conflicting ideas of what the right thing is. I want to get the best seats for my family and so do you. I happen to believe that being aware of one's values is critical whereas others believe that we should take things as they come. So we are different. And then there is a great deal of ignorance, unawareness and outright stupidity. You will detect it in me, as I believe to see it in the behavior of you and everyone else. I am trying hard to improve myself but it is not right, I think, to make you and other people see things as I do. So you and I will have to take into account that other people are doing things differently, and that stupidity and ignorance are, and will always be, factors in our interactions with the world around. However, that is not a reason to assume that everyone is greedy or self-interested.

4. I will actually show in chapter 6 that the most important goods that we strive for, we share with others. That makes cooperative or social behavior the norm, and selfish behavior the aberration.

5. When the striving for ideals is at stake, as it is for many organizations and certainly for cultural, academic and religious institutions, we do better by departing from the assumption that all involved are seeking profit, power or status. Even where pecuniary profit, status, attention, ego and power are in play, we may safely assume that those are distractions. When confronted, they usually are exposed as such and the right thing comes into view.

I conclude that the presumption that people are greedy and self-interested is not helpful when we try to get inside the elephant. Greed and self-interest are false guides for doing the right thing. Even so, when we are doing the right thing ourselves, we need to take into account that others may seem greedy and self-interested.

PART 2

THE CONCEPTUAL FRAMEWORK

Part I is mainly therapeutic. The edifying part is now ahead. In order to make sense of a value based economy we are in need of concepts and directives for thinking about the economy. The concept of values has to come first. It will become clear that the value based approach answers to the question "what is important?" Price, then, is not a value. For economists this insight may be difficult to digest, so I fear.

The next step turns out to be treacherous as it takes us from the awareness of values to their valorization. We do so by the realization of goods, and most importantly, shared goods. The latter notion is new in the economics literature as far as I know. It calls for the willingness to contribute. That, too, is a new notion.

Some goods are more important than others. Some goods are worth striving for, as you will learn in chapter 7. I suggest four dimensions for the determination of values, goods and goods to strive for.

In this book sources are forms of capital. Chapter 8 spells them out and introduces a new classification of inequalities and redefines the notions of richness and poverty in passing.

The argumentation finds its closure in the model with five spheres. Each sphere stands for a distinctive logic by which people and organizations realize their goods. It is a significant extension of the two sphere model that is standard in economics.

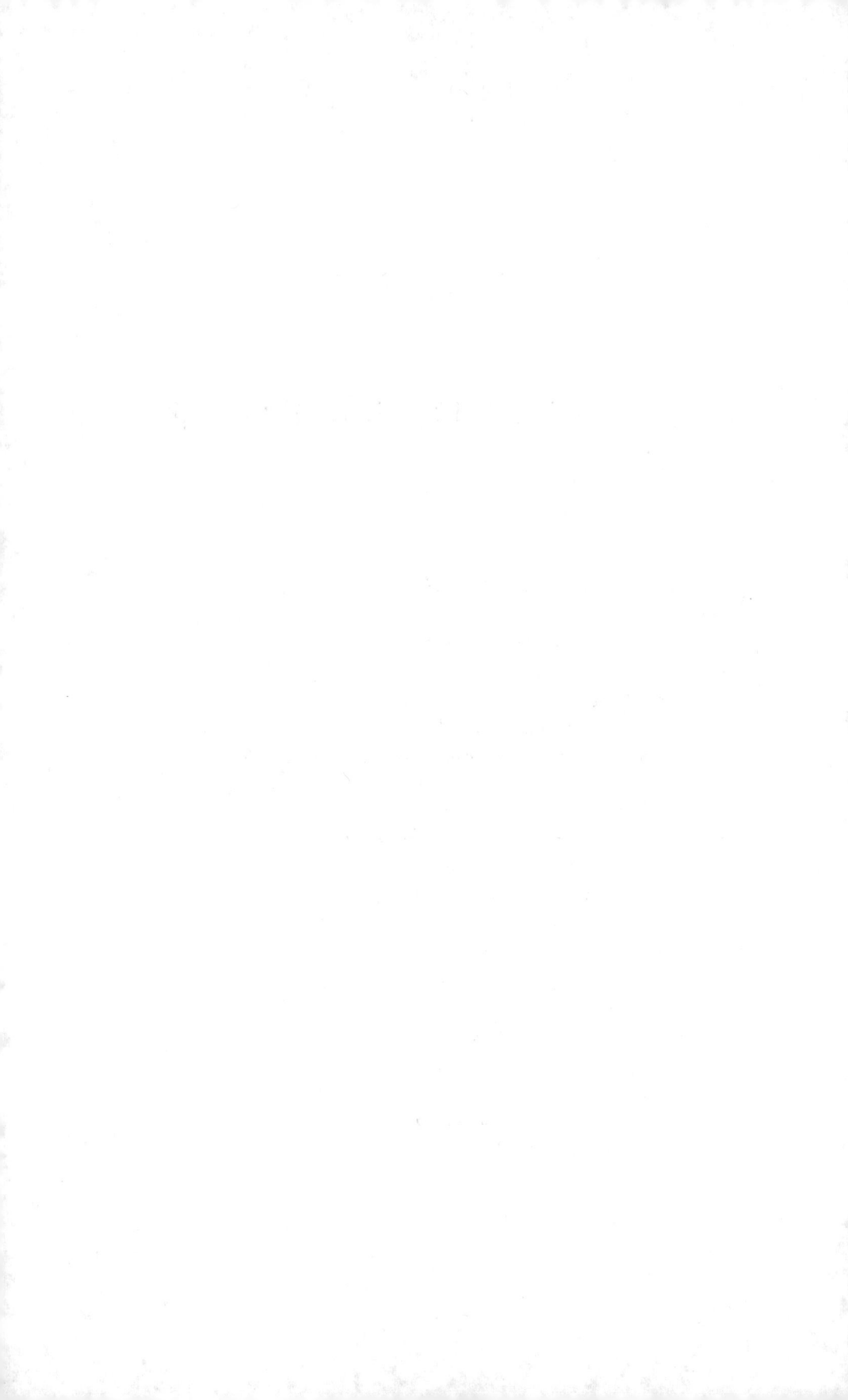

CHAPTER 5

ABOUT VALUES

We value all the time. We appreciate —"Van Gogh is a great painter" —, we use —"With this hammer I hit the nail on its head" —, we respect—"I do not like him as a person but he makes a good teacher"—,we are in awe— "This music blew me away!"; "This Rothko painting made me cry, so deep it went." —, and we are considerate—"That poor artist: let's help her out." We also humiliate, mock, despise, ignore and desecrate. Moving through life, we simply cannot avoid valuing people, things, situations and practices. Acting requires valuing.

The value based approach is about the realization of values. It encourages awareness of the values that we ourselves and others act upon. Also it will make us think about the ways in which people and organizations make their values real. Awareness comes first. In order to do the right thing we must first better understand what values are all about and what we are talking about when we use the term.

The challenge: how to supersede merely economic or financial, culturalist and moral discussions of value

The value based approach attempts to supersede and encompass the three distinctive and currently prevalent ways of dealing with values. These are 1) standard economics, 2) culturalist accounts (as in *art criticism*), and 3) moral philosophy.

Ad 1). Standard economics equates value with price. Accordingly, when the notion of value comes up, standard economists make you think of the worth of things, or their price. Price is exchange value, i.e. the value that a good realizes in a market exchange. Exchange value is price. It is the answer to the question "how much?" What matters in this discussion, then, is the pricing of things, and the willingness of people to pay that price in order to acquire those things.

Economists are sophisticated when it comes to determining the price of things, even if those things are not for sale. They can even assign a price to human life (and show that some humans have a higher price than others, an outcome that has consequences in the court of law, for example). The impression is created that everything can be priced and that price is the only value that counts.

In addition to exchange value, classical economics explains also that goods have use value. Accordingly, goods have exchange value because they have use value for the buyer. Use value alludes to the usefulness of a good. Standard economics abandons that notion of value and prefers to speak in terms of preferences and utility. The idea is that people prefer some things over others. Preference answers the question of what people like or don't like, more or less. With the motto *De gustibus non est disputandum* (taste is not a subject for discussion), standard economists usually presume preferences to be a given and do not elaborate on or explore them. The focus on price and, with that, on (monetary or financial) quantities is adequate for the instrumentalist approach that standard economics represents.

Ad 2). In a culturalist discussion, "values" usually refer to qualities of works of art, scientific contributions, organizations, cities, countries and cultures. Culturalists, as I indicated previously in Chapter 1, include art historians, anthropologists, literary scholars, historians, philosophers, archeologists and cultural sociologists. They tend to be preoccupied with qualities, with the relevance of things and of human actions and relationships. In the spectrum of values/qualities-prices/quantities, they operate at the opposite end from standard economists: the notion of "price" is practically non-existent in their discourse. (Art history books rarely mention the prices of artworks, and scientists never bring up the costs of producing a scientific article.) In light of the illustration in Chapter 1, we might say that culturalists focus on the home, and economists on the house.

> In the famous characterization of Oscar Wilde: the economist resembles the cynic who knows the price of everything and the value of nothing, and the culturalist the romantic who knows the value of everything and the price of nothing (Wilde, 1893).

Ad 3). In moral philosophy, values have a moral connotation as in "respect," "benevolence," "solidarity" or "honesty." In virtue ethics, values come in the form of virtues and concern our behavior such as "being courageous," "prudent," "just," "temperate," "faithful," "hopeful" and "loving." In classical economics, virtues played an important role. Adam Smith dedicated an entire book to the discussion of Moral Sentiments (Smith, 1759). Yet, standard economics has silenced such a discussion for being normative and therefore not scientific.

A value based approach integrates all three discussions of values. It generates a culturalist as well as a moral exploration of values while recognizing the instrumental role of prices. When doing the right thing we have to consider a wide range of values, and need to develop a sensitivity to the elusive character of values and the treacherous effects of pricing things.

A homely example makes the point
A typical episode:

"I want Uggs!"

"I really need them."

"I want Uggs."

I must have made a facial expression that inspired my then 15-year-old daughter to stress the urgency of her wish: "I really want them."

"180 euro? For those shoes? Just because you want them? There are all kinds of things I may want but that does not mean that I am going to buy them. No way. Those shoes are ugly anyway." The last remark was unfortunate. I apparently had no idea. I admitted that point but did not budge. How in the hell did she get the idea that when she wants something, she will get it? The chant "I want it all, I want it now!" ran through my head. She stormed off, frustrated and agitated.

Then my wife entered the discussion. It was not simply because our daughter wants those shoes, so she explained to me; she needs them—for her social standing, for her self-confidence. I gulped but noticed that her remarks changed my perspective somewhat. My perspective shifted even more when she continued with an appeal to our responsibility for her well-being, and my role as her father.

(As it so happened, I was scheduled to leave the Netherlands—where I live and work—for Chicago where the Uggs would be cheaper. I went to quite a bit of trouble to track down Uggs in a large department store. Upon my return my daughter overwhelmed me with her thanks but, as I found out later, I had bought the wrong ones—these were the shorties. So I ended up paying the full price anyway for the right ones).

You might read this as a story of a spoiled daughter and permissive father, which is fine with me. However, I beg to differ. I tell the story to illustrate the way a range of values affect and emerge in an everyday situation. And to show that price is not necessarily the most important value in play.

The values that operate in an everyday situation

If we were to follow standard economics, we would focus on the price of Uggs and my willingness to pay. There is not much more to say about this, other than that it is quite a high price to pay. We might wonder what other things I would have been willing to give up in order to be able to buy the Uggs. (I actually have no idea how to determine that.) A standard economist may additionally point out that my preference for the Uggs is derived from my daughter's preference. That may be so, but how will that insight affect my action?

How about the use value of the Uggs? This is clearly more than their value as comfortable shoes, although comfort is surely one of its values. Qualities besides "comfort" would include the "warmth" they provide, their "design" (which I was inclined to value negatively), and the quality of the "material" of which the shoe is made (sheep wool and sheep leather).

My decision to buy the shoes, however, entailed more than just the values of price and comfort. If we want to hold on to the notion of use value, this case suggests that there are other values operating here as well. The shoes are, or so it appeared, contributing to the realization of social values, status in particular, and personal values, such as the self-confidence of my daughter.

The high price is a signal of social values. To her friends, it signals that her father was willing to pay that much for her sake. (The high price is part of the marketing strategy of the producer of the Uggs. After purchasing the company from the Australian inventor, the American owner convinced movie stars to wear his shoes in order to generate status value for the shoes. Girls like my daughter picked up on that value and began working on their parents to get them to pay the price.)

We might conclude that the purchase of the shoes served the realization of particular social and personal values, but that is not all. I evaluated the episode quite differently. In my evaluation the purchase of the Uggs and the concomitant realization of particular social and personal values is subordinate to the realization of other, for me more important, values. To me, this episode is more about realizing my responsibility as a parent, and the affirmation and realization of my fatherhood. In this episode I was reminded of such values (by my wife), and acted upon that awareness. The price of the Uggs actually distracted me from the real issue, which was my responsibility as a father.

The story does not end here. We may need the cultural context to make sense of the way in which I interpreted my responsibility as a father. A father in China, Uganda or Spain may have interpreted those values differently. The interpretation of fatherly responsibility might be cultural, and thus subject to other values like honor, fairness, authority and autonomy. Furthermore, other fathers in the Netherlands may simply have said no to such a request; they may have argued that it is the father's responsibility to convey to his kids that there are constraints, that we need to make choices and that choosing Uggs for that price is not an option. They may think that I missed the opportunity to teach my kid about prudence.

Nevertheless, multiple values operate in the episode. Did I do the right thing? I am not sure. As the principle of *phronesis* indicates, I weighed various values, deliberated with the various interested parties and decided to buy the shoes. I did not evaluate the episode with those involved, so I only can guess as to whether or not I did the right thing. A value based approach is not paving the road to secure and predictable outcomes. *Phronesis* has uncertainty written all over it.

Is this just a homely example of trivial moments in life? I don't think so. Similar moments occur all the time in all kinds of situations. They occur in personal situations. (What to do tonight: Read? Send emails? Watch a movie? Go out for dinner with my wife? Or all of the above?) They occur in organizational settings. (What should a museum director do after learning that a major sponsor plans to withdraw: Go ahead with a blockbuster program in spite of the artistic and financial risks? Approach a bank with a dubious reputation in the hope that the bank has interest in using the reputation of the museum? Or should he prepare cuts in the staff?) And they occur at the political level (when politicians decide to raise taxes, cut unemployment benefits or lower the subsidies for the arts).

Price or value?

The challenge that I face is to articulate a conceptual framework that guarantees that the issues that really matter for doing the right thing become part of the conversation and, consequently, that relegates the otherwise dominant discussion of the transactions, the prices and anything else quantifiable to its appropriate, subsidiary position.

The framework to overcome is that of standard economics since it dominates the instrumentalist phase that (Western?) societies are going through. Standard economics makes us think of what we do in terms of choices made on the basis of our preferences. The value that matters here is the price that we have to pay, or that we receive. That value functions as a constraint; it limits what we would like to realize.

When I consider the homely situation in this frame, I am to focus on the choice I have—buying the Uggs or not—based on the preferences that influence my choice—a derived preference in this case as I have to prefer the preference of my daughter—and the constraint of the price of the Uggs. Since I ended up buying the Uggs, I have expressed my willingness to pay the 180 euros. The choice is rational because it realized the best of all possible outcomes.

The notion of *phronesis*, or practical wisdom, expresses a different frame. It suggests that we have limited knowledge (usually not a big issue in the standard economics frame), that we grope our way around, and that we weigh various options and do so in response to all kinds of values that matter to us. The price to pay, or to receive, is only one of the factors in the deliberation that is *phronesis*.

When acknowledging the notion of *phronesis*, my situation makes more sense. It does more justice to the confusion that I experienced, the groping that I did, the deliberations with my daughter, my wife and myself, and the figuring out of what really mattered to me. Realizing that I was willing to pay the 180 euros had more to do with the values of fatherhood and responsibility than with my valuing those Uggs. Even for my daughter, I felt that other values were in play, in particular the values of social status, belonging and self-confidence.

Economists who practice standard economics consider all those values to be part of what they call the *external economy*. When I point out that my value of fatherhood played a role, as well as the harmony in the family, they will say that those are external to the issue at hand: the purchase of the Uggs. Their notion of externalities works well to silence my concerns in their conversation. Yet, at the same time, it renders that conversation meaningless and quite irrelevant to my situation, since the values that they call externalities are what the interaction is all about. The value based approach that I am developing here includes that which is excluded by the standard economic conversation.

About the concept of value

The concept of value is treacherous. If you decide to embrace the concept, you have been forewarned. Values are not precise and you cannot hold onto them. People do not walk around with their values written on their forehead. (But let's face it: the utility functions that economists prefer are just as abstract as values, and just as imprecise. Unlike utility value, invites more precise characterization, as we will see shortly.) Even when you and I sense a value, we may have a hard time articulating it. When someone else articulates a value, like when a young fellow shouts at us something about respect, you and I may wonder what he means by it. (I have an idea, but does he?)

Let us try to be more specific in an attempt to further the discussion.

Values are relational concepts in the sense that they are at work in the interactions among people and in the interactions between people and things or states of affairs. We value things in comparison with other things, or the characteristics of things. At this moment I value the taste of coffee and, because I am writing, the quietness of my surroundings. Tonight I may very well value a noisy party that I will attend.

When we value something, someone, an action, a relationship or a state of affair, that someone, action, relationship or state of affair is important to us somehow. What makes something or someone important, are qualities of goodness that we identify with that something or someone.

When I want to know your values, I will first ask you *what is important to you*. Our valuation of things, relationships, actions and states of affair is based on our values, on what we consider to be important.

Asking the question "what is important to you" is different from asking the question "what do you need." My daughter's answer to the latter question would surely be "I need Uggs." Or should she rather say "I want Uggs"? We want all kinds of things, but do we need them? I want an ice cream right now. You may want a drink. But do we need them? We need things because they satisfy our needs for nourishment, security, shelter, a sense of belonging and, ultimately, self-actualization, in accordance with the pyramid of Maslow (Maslow, 1943). In that sense when asking "what do you need," you are made to think of elements in that pyramid of needs.

Asking "what is important to you" directs the attention to the list of needs but compels us to be more precise. It is asking for particular values. They most likely will still fall into the category of need—after all, we need to realize our values—but are likely to be more precise, more concrete. In the case of the Uggs I would have answered "being a good father," "a happy family," "the well-being of my daughter" or "Dutch culture." I would not have realized such answers if I had been asked "what do you need?" (I probably would then have answered something childish like "Quietness! Just leave me alone! I need to write!")

Accordingly, preferences are not necessarily values. You may be craving a drink right now, and thus have a strong preference for that good, but if I were to probe you on what is really important to you right now, you would probably acknowledge that it is not the drink itself—you may even realize that the drink is bad for you—and that you should prefer instead more study time, more brain power or something like that. Quite a few students do not care for reading serious books—it is not part of their utility function—but the hope is that this changes, that they develop such a preference and that this preference becomes a value.

In the realm of the arts and sciences, the difference between preferences and values is critical. When you first attend a modern dance performance you might dislike it, but when you go more often, you may start liking modern dance and begin to value the practice. You may even want to start dancing yourself. Changing preferences and turning certain preferences into values: that is what education is about.

Asking for the values of yourself, someone else, an organization or a society, is to ask: "What is important for you, for the organization or for this society?" This goes beyond asking: "What do you, the organization or society need?" Asking "what do you, the organization or society need" goes beyond asking "what do you want" or, as an economist might phrase the question "what are your preferences." The instrumental question is "how much." The expected answer would come in the form of a number, usually a price. The importance of things is (always?) a matter of qualities or values.

What is important for you?

I was invited to a workshop in which homeless people in my town repair bicycles for ten euros a day. It was coffee time so we sat around in a circle with plastic coffee cups. There were around twelve of them. I began asking them to tell their story. The guy sitting next to me was mainly depressed and had not much of a story to tell. Another guy had beaten up his estranged wife and had violated a restraining order. As a consequence he had lost everything. A young woman had lost a relationship and was subsequently refused by her mother. Another guy was in hiding to avoid his creditors. I was sad to learn how people have to suffer such bad fate, bad luck and outright stupidity.

I then asked them the question: "What is important to you?" If I had asked them "what do you want?" they might have asked me for more money, for a beer or for drugs. Now they answered differently. The depressed guy did not respond but the next one said without hesitation: "To belong somehow, somewhere." They all answered something similar. I pressed some of them a little and then they invariably mentioned the importance of being significant to others, to contribute soguring out what they can do to realize their values. That is why they are without home, without oikos. Giving them money or drugs surely does not address their problems. First we need to figure out what they can do themselves before we can determine the appropriate support.

We value not only things, but also states of affairs, situations, practices and behavior. When I value behavior, a practice or an action, I consider these in light of values like honesty, loyalty, sincerity, prudence, temperance, courage, justice, faithfulness, hope or love. When I perceive in your action the realization of one of those values, i.e. characteristics that are important to me, I will approve of and praise your action. In case you violate one of those values, I will disapprove and may admonish you. I will do the same when I observe the practices of a family, a group of students or an entire people. I appreciate the Arabs for their hospitality, Americans for their enthusiasm and the Dutch for their pragmatism. And I disapprove of all kinds of other practices that each of these people exhibit. Values that connect with behavior, practices or actions are also known as *virtues*.

When I value an object, a relationship, a community, an organization or whatever other thing or situation, I asses its characteristics in light of values such as beauty, usefulness, friendliness, warmth, diversity. Its value depends on the values I hold dear. When the object enables me to realize some of those values, I will like it, cherish it and maybe even adore it. When it does not, I will not buy it, discard it or forget about it. I will call such values either *content values* or *goal values*. *Content values* characterize the inner qualities of a thing, a situation or an entity. *Goal values* characterize the intent of a thing, a situation or an entity; in other words, the goal or desired result at which a thing, situation or entity is directed.

Values and culture

I hold values personally. That means that I consider new insights, veracity, loyalty, compassion, a good painting, tasty ice cream and nice shoes important for myself. In the realization of these values I may need to involve others, but I experience these values individually.

At the same time, I share my values with various groups of people. My academic values I share with some people—and certainly not all—in the academic community. My artistic values I share with all kinds of people, and my Dutch values with the Dutch. It is in the sharing of values that we experience being part of a culture.

You and I are part of, participate in and are subject to cultures. Being cultured means that you and I hold values that reflect the culture of which we are a part. As a Dutchman I value speed skating (especially the 10 kilometer), the Dutch soccer team, Dutch history, coziness ("gezelligheid"), whereas as an American (my second citizenship) I value college basketball, entrepreneurial spirit, an attractive college campus, driving through the countryside, the farmer's market and Dairy Queen. I could think of my love of speed skating as an individual value, but it clearly is not. There is no chance I would have loved it had I been born and raised in Uganda or India.

The values of a culture are shared values; the sharing of distinct and distinguishing values constitutes a culture.

Distinguishing values

There is a temptation to discuss values in abstract terms. However, once we have agreed that values are in play in what we do, the challenge is then to

Values purged from the conversation of economists.

Classical economists introduced the subject of value into the conversation of economists. Actually, it was Aristotle who distinguished around 350 BC between exchange value and use value. Classical economists picked up the distinction and used it to motivate all their intellectual attention for exchange value. The determination of use value was basically left out of the discussion.

Karl Marx

20th century economists have done everything in their might to purge the concept of value from their conversation. They judged that the effort of Karl Marx to derive an objective measure of (exchange) value of a good from the amount of labor spent making it had failed. They had furthermore realized that the subjective valuation that the marginalists had advanced as an alternative was also insufficient in accounting for exchange value.

So when John Hicks wrote his book entitled *Value and Capital* (Hicks, 1939) and Gerard Debreu a book with the title *The Theory of Value* (Debreu, 1959), they did so to eliminate the concept of value and to show how a price gets established in a (mechanical) interplay of the forces of demand and supply. Debreu even succeeded to avoid using the term *value* in his book altogether. So much for a theory of value!

Textbooks of economics, beginning with the famous textbook of Paul Samuelson (the one that I had to study), avoid the concept of value and speak of prices and utilities instead (Samuelson, 1947).

Only a few economists, such as the Austrians, held on to the notion of value.

20th century philosophers, too, began to suppress and ignore the notion of value in their conversations. In their analytical approach there was no way to articulate the conditions for such a vague concept; so it was left out. Postmodern philosophers do not like the concept because it suggests something real out there that is not. Values need language in order to be articulated and thus to become real, and that makes them suspect. At least in their conversation they do.

I am grateful for the critical contributions of economists and philosophers. At the same time, I have become convinced that they have gone overboard with their dismissal of the notion of value. See this as an attempt to rescue value and bring it back on board.

articulate which values are in play and the strength of their influence. In order to understand what drives our behavior, we must be aware of the important values. When something is not right, we want to know which values have been undervalued or ignored entirely. The point of the value based approach is to get specific about the values involved.

One difficulty is in accurately naming values. When I resist the request to foot the bill for expensive shoes, the relevant question to ask is which values are in play. What is so important for me to disappoint my daughter? If I am afraid that she is getting spoiled, then I am appreciating a sense of responsibility. That would be a virtue. Or I may question the esthetic quality of Uggs. That would suggest that I care about esthetics, a content value.

The other difficulty is that we usually do not know right away what values are in play. In the case of the shoe incident, I myself tend to resist the comfort-seeking aspect that seems inherent to so much consumerist behavior and appreciate the stimulation that people can derive from reading a good book or attending a serious play. This distinction I owe to Tibor Scitovsky as he describes in *The Joyless Economy* (Scitovsky, 1976). Had my daughter wanted to buy a book or attend a play with friends, I would have drawn my wallet immediately. This I realize only after some probing. We usually need to probe our motives, our emotions, too, in order to figure out which values are in play.

To facilitate the probing, and to remain alert to how values discipline the behavior of others, it helps to distinguish among types of values. The first distinction is one that I already made earlier: the distinction between values pertaining to behavior or practices and values pertaining to situations and things.

Virtues are values that pertain to behavior
Ask people about their values and they will name values like "honesty," "curiosity," "modesty," "courage" and "prudence." People who work in organizations will name values like "loyalty," "customer orientation," "passion," "integrity" and "authenticity." All those values are qualities that pertain to what they do, to their actions, to practices they are involved in. Apparently, they appreciate actions that are honest, courageous, modest and prudent, and that express curiosity. Those values, or qualities, are called virtues.

Virtues were a common topic of conversation for the ancient Greeks and Romans. Children learned about them at school until the end of the 19th century. They transpired in novels such as Jane Austin´s *Pride and Prejudice* and in American television series such as *The Andy Griffith Show* and *House on the Prairie*. Then they were forgotten—or suppressed?—and now they are back in the attention of philosophers and even some economists. Deirdre McCloskey in particular dedicates her magnum opus to a study of what she calls the *bourgeois virtues* (McCloskey, 2007).

In the anecdote of the Uggs I had to be virtuous in my role as father, to figure out how to be prudent, loving and wise.

As Aristotle and other Greek philosophers teach us, virtues are internalized behavioral values. An honest man is honest simply because he is, and not because he fears punishment, or expects compliments. A good friend is loyal because she just is, and not because she wants to be a good friend.

Being able to do the right thing is reserved for virtuous people. You need to be aware of your values; you need to assess the situation. But when it comes to being honest and loyal, you just do it. If you have to tell yourself "let me be honest and loyal this time," you can't do it quite right.

It takes training and endless practice to get it right, to be virtuous in one's actions, at least so the ancient Greeks and Roman philosophers remind us. They could very well be right. Most of the training we get takes place at home, on the street, in the schoolyard and later at work. Others (hopefully) correct us when we do not get it right ("that was not honest of you" or "you betrayed me, you little shit"). The culture we are part of may help shape our virtues. In a culture that celebrates friendship we may learn the meaning of loyalty more quickly than in a culture that is more individualistic.

Aristotle teaches us in his Nicomachean Ethics that there are four cardinal virtues. They are cardinal because they inform all actions directed at the realization of values. They are the following:

- *Prudence*: acting thoughtfully, cautiously, with foresight and taking into account the relevant circumstances;
- *Temperance*: doing not too much and not too little, knowing the right middle ground between the extremes;
- *Courage*: overcoming fear in order to do the right thing;
- *Justice*: doing so with regard to the feelings and interests of others.

Later Christian theologians like Thomas Aquinas added the three theological virtues to complete the seven cardinal virtues:

- *Faith*: trusting yourself, your intuition, your background, your karma, the supernatural, God;
- *Hope*: trusting that some good will come of your action;
- *Love*: feeling deeply connected with the other, others and accepting the other as he or she is.

I immediately acknowledge the gross simplification of what the virtues stand for. There is an extensive literature that elaborates and problematizes each and all of these virtues, including McCloskey's bourgeois virtues (McCloskey, 2007). But I have to discipline myself and limit this discussion to the distinguishing of the virtues. For the sake of elucidation, the following box shows how the cardinal virtues inform doing the right thing.

Acting virtuously in accordance with the seven classical virtues.

Take the value or virtue Honesty. Quite a few Dutch people, and not only they, will elect honesty as their most important virtue. Apparently Dutch culture highlights honesty as a virtue to strive for. How then to be honest? When are you truly honest or, as Aristotle would put it, excellent in honesty?

You are excellent in your honesty when a) you have internalized the seven cardinal virtues and b) you enact each one of them in your being honest. A truly honest person is in no need of being reminded of the cardinal virtues; he or she enacts them without thinking about them. Most mortals need to be reminded of the cardinal virtues from time to time. Claiming honesty as a virtue is easy, being truly honest proves to be quite a challenge as the following considerations make clear:

- *Honesty and prudence:* in order to be honest in a certain situation you need to know what the situation is, what the relevant factors are, and what brings about the situation. You may think you are honest when accusing your teacher of doing a lousy job or when accusing a student of cheating, but is that the prudent thing to do? Are you well-informed? Are you aware of the relevant factors? Have you taken into account the possible consequences? Being prudently honest implies being thoughtful and aware.

- *Honesty and temperance:* You can be dishonest by not telling the truth. You can also be too honest; in that case you are rude, obnoxious or naïve. Temperance is about knowing the right middle ground between being too honest or not honest enough. When I tell my children to be honest and they in turn tell a visitor that she has an ugly nose, I have to correct them by explaining that honesty does not mean that you say whatever is on your mind. Finding the right middle ground is, as Aristotle already taught, the crux of being virtuous.

- *Honesty and courage:* At times you need to overcome fears in order to speak the truth. When you have cheated at your work or cheated on your partner and you decide on the basis of prudence and temperance that you have to confess your misdeed, you may refrain from doing so out of fear for the consequences. You may get fired, after all, or your partner may break off the relationship. That is when the virtue of courage is required. Being honest needs being courageous.

- *Honesty and justice:* When being honest, you want to consider not only the feelings of the other to whom you are honest, but also take into account the interests and feelings of others who may be affected. Justice is the virtue of knowing the right proportion in dealing with others. When I am honest in my criticisms of a student's performance, I have to consider whether I am just towards the other students. Maybe I should be equally honest to the others. Or am I justified in taking an exception with respect to this student? As Aristotle already points out, justice is a complicated virtue.
- *Honesty and faith:* When being honest, it is important to have confidence, to trust one's own judgment. Some may speak in the name of Allah, others may pray to God, or meditate to find support for their being honest. Faith provides a backing for whatever we do.
- *Honesty and hope:* Being honest in the right way should imply the prospect for improvement, for positive change, for flourishing, or self-actualization. Being honest just out of revenge or in order to destroy is not virtuous.
- *Honesty and love:* Most important of all virtues, love stands for compassion for the other, for feeling deeply connected, for empathy. Honesty out of love is being honest with the intention to add to the flourishing of those involved or affected. It is said that if love is the virtue in charge, all other virtues are implied.

Being honest, therefore, is easier said than done. It requires the interiorization of all seven virtues in such a way that their enactment is automatic and does not require conscious deliberation. The virtuous person is prudent, temperate, courageous, just, faithful, hopeful and loving. Failing on one of the virtues can lead to criminal behavior. A criminal can be prudent, temperate and courageous but fails to be just. In that case, he most likely also fails on the virtue of love.

Overseeing this, it becomes understandable why we humans are so often clumsy, inadequate and even stupid in what we do. I beg for your compassion for the way in which I handled the case of the Uggs. How to be prudent, loving and wise in a situation like that?

(An interesting issue that arises in this context is whether we can learn to be virtuous, whether we get better as we grow older and more experienced? Adams (2006) show that virtue ethicists diverge on this issue.)

Values pertaining to situations, things, practices and people
The case of the Uggs accentuates other values aside from the virtues involved. There is a value concerning the situation as such—how to value a request of a daughter and the subsequent discussion? The Uggs represent certain values of esthetics but also social values (as in the status of owning them). The case brought out for me the values of fatherhood and family.

As noted above, values are the answer to the question "what is important." Value surveys, like the *world value survey*, gather the responses of people from all over the world in all kinds of issues, such as family, religion, gender, diversity, authority, democracy, environment, nature, individuality, freedom, discipline and justice. Inglehart and Welzel have constructed interesting value maps of the world that bring out the clustering of values (Inglehart & Welzel, 2005). This tells us, for example, that Chinese adhere to Confucian values such as harmony, and that Americans rate individuality highly. For the Dutch, the differences between their values and the values dear to their southern neighbors, the Belgians, may account for the difficulties experienced in Dutch-Belgian collaborations.

David Throsby, a fellow cultural economist, is pursuing a value based approach as well. In a discussion of cultural goods, like paintings and theatre performances, he lists an often-cited set of six values that pertain to such goods: aesthetic value, spiritual value, symbolic value, social value, symbolic value and authenticity. Each of these values point at a particular quality of the artwork (Throsby, 2001). This list demonstrates the multi-faceted character of an artwork. But when we are interested in the "realization of values" we are in need of more.

In the case of the Uggs I was not only realizing aesthetic and social values for my daughter, but I also realized other, contextual values such as the value of family and fatherhood. Like the buying of Uggs, the enjoyment or purchase of artistic goods can be in pursuit of all kinds of values, including companionship, good conversation, civilization and values not listed by Throsby, such as consolation, inspiration and craftsmanship.

That is why I suggest we consider a wide range of possible values, clustered across four dimensions. I have experimented with clustering in all kinds of settings, for example in the context of professional organizations and cultural organizations, and am satisfied so far with its applicability. The main intention of this clustering is to make some rough distinctions that will facilitate our thinking about and working with values.

I distinguish the domains of a) personal values, b) social values, c) societal values and d) transcendental or cultural values—transcendental as these values transcend the personal and the social, and cultural insofar as they evoke C2, C3 (i.e. the domains of the arts, religion and civilization). (C1—culture as perceived by anthropologists—stands for social, societal and transcendental values.)

a) The domain of personal values.

All values are personal in the sense that individuals hold them. Yet, there are certain values that pertain to the relationship with oneself. Shakespeare has personal value to me since his plays inspire me and challenge my intellectual, interpretive and emotional skills. The play King Lear has personal value because it now is a source from which I can draw to make sense of situations (of love and betrayal). I may value my skills, my health and my memories, and wished I could value my wisdom. All those are personal values. They are qualities concerning myself, my own individuality.

In the context of organizations, personal values tend to be easily overlooked. Yet organizations clearly serve the realization of personal values, such as one's skills or craftsmanship or one's ego. Thanks to the university I attended, I can realize things that are important for myself.

In the case of the Uggs, my fatherhood could be considered a personal value as it pertains to myself. Similarly, people can personally value their status, their function, the recognition or respect that they receive.

Other personal values that are often mentioned are: health, autonomy, independence, authenticity, awareness, integrity, curiosity (a good value for an academic), tenacity, perseverance, fun, joy, personal growth, flourishing and so on.

Let me point out that many of these values are ill-defined and, when considered on their own, vacuous. "Authenticity" sounds good, but the underlying question is "when are you authentic." You are actually authentic when you act in accordance with your values. So if you cannot tell me what those values are, you cannot tell when you are being authentic. Hitler was an authentic individual, as was Jesus. So what kind of authenticity do you aspire? The same could be said of "integrity": you are integer when you act your values. And what constitutes personal growth or flourishing? Hitler may have flourished and grown personally, too. When people appeal to such "values," they still need to specify the actual values that they stand for.

b) The domain of social values.

Values are social when they indicate qualities of human relationships, that is, relationships with people we know. Friendship is a good example. Of course, I hold the value myself and therefore you could consider it a personal value. But the value of friendship clearly pertains to a situation that involves at least one other person and therefore extends beyond myself. If realized the value is a shared value: friends share the value friendship. The same applies to values such as family, collegiality, community, neighborhood and coziness.

The Uggs represent a social value to my daughter, while the whole episode contributed to a social value that is (my) "family." A Shakespeare play has social values for me as it enables me to contribute to a friendship—when I attend the play with friends—to share the appreciation of theatre with others in my environment. I might also realize a social value in the form of status or prestige by being able to tell others that I saw King Lear the other night.

Friendship, status, intimacy, respect, dignity, commitment, community and family are social values. A club, a neighborhood or a team can be important for us for the relationships that they foster; they stand for a social value, too.

c) The domain of societal values.

Values are societal when they concern our relationships with a large social entity such as a society. I do not think that the Uggs episode reflects a societal value unless we consider healthy families to be important for society at large. A Shakespeare play stands a better chance of generating a societal value as it represents an important thread in the tapestry that we call (our) civilization. Performing the play contributes to the quality of life in the society of which I am a part. I may also value its educational value for young and old, for its addressing themes of hubris and loyalty that have societal importance.

Societal values include political values such as justice, solidarity, sustainability, freedom, emancipation, security, peace, patriotism and lawfulness. In political actions we realize societal values. When I plea for more attention for the arts or religion in my society, I attend to the societal values inherent to the arts and religion.

Societal values include cultural values where culture refers to C1, the shared values of a people. When we are considering a group of people in terms of what they share and in what respect they are different from other people, we will identify their shared values as cultural values. Prudence is a value of Dutch culture, while pioneering is a typical American value. Cultural values also characterize organizations as Geert Hofstede has demonstrated (Hofstede, 2003). The theatre company performing the play might have a culture of its own, and therefore operates in accordance with distinctive values.

Think of nations and you will think of cultural values like hospitality, parsimony, fun loving, serious, prudent, exuberant, authoritarian, discipline, respect for elders.

d) The domain of transcendental or cultural values.

In this domain we cherish all those values that do not pertain to ourselves, to relationships with people we know or to societies at large, but rather to something abstract, some ideal, some kind of conversation of a practice, an idea, a science or an art form. These values transcend the personal, the social and the societal, and are therefore called transcendental values.

Transcendental values include historical, artistic and scientific values. Qualities that are specific to the historical, artistic and scientific practices are historical, artistic or scientific values. Shakespeare has historical value for his having played a role in 17th century England and having contributed to a tradition through the centuries since then. His artistic values are, for example, the literary qualities of his texts, and the dramatic qualities that inspire literary critics to produce endless interpretations. Its scientific values come about in the academic discussions that his plays have generated, especially in the humanities.

Historical and scientific values include the value of truthfulness, and artistic values are the qualities of beauty, the sublime, experimental and shocking. Other cultural values are moral values. When we consider the goodness, righteousness or virtuousness of (human) actions and behavior, we take our moral values into account. King Lear is all about moral values such as the value of loyalty, of modesty (by portraying King Lear as a man who is full of himself at first), and of love (Cordelia continues to love her father even after he has denounced her). In the dramatic moment that the father compels Cordelia to profess her love, Cordelia has to weigh her options. Is she going to succumb to the deceitful behavior of her sisters or does she stick to her values? When this brings about the wrath of her father, the viewer has to wonder whether she did the right thing.

Moral values include honor, respect, loyalty and being just, compassionate, caring, faithful and courageous. And then there are the religious or spiritual values. In our relationship to the transcendental—to that what is more, to the metaphysical—we realize values such as holiness, sacredness, enlightenment. Watching King Lear may give me a spiritual experience (it did … not), a sense of being part of something magnificent, of the sublime. Young people say that they get such an experience at a dance party or when listening to music. Religious ceremonies are designed to realize transcendental values; some scientists do so in probing the mysteries of life.

Intrinsic and extrinsic values
Are transcendental values intrinsic? Are artistic values intrinsic? The question pops up in discussions about the values of the arts. There are people who adamantly defend the intrinsic values of the art and there are those who deny that there are such values. I do think that there are values intrinsic to the arts, but to make that clear I am in need of other concepts, concepts that will emerge in the next chapter. (See the section *Art is not for sale.*)

How about use values? And financial values?
Of course, we appreciate objects also for their functional value. Food has the value of nourishment and with a hammer we can hit nails on their head. Uggs are comfortable shoes that keep feet warm in cold temperatures. The performance of King Lear has the functional value of being theatre. A good

TRANSCENDENTAL/ CULTURAL

ARTISTIC, HISTORICAL, RELIGIOUS, COMPASSION, WORLD PEACE, BEAUTY, TRUTH, SCIENCE, SUBLIME, GRACE, SALVATION, ENLIGHTENMENT, KARMA, NOTHINGNESS, TAO, SACREDNESS, HOLINESS, MORALITY

SOCIETAL

JUSTICE, CIVILIZATION, EDUCATION, FAIRNESS, LIBERTY, EQUALITY, BROTHERHOOD, ENTERPRISE, SAFETY, SECURITY, PEACE, NATIONALISM, PATRIOTISM, COSMOPOLITISM, AUTONOMY, LAWFUL, INNOVATIVE, CREATIVE, EMANCIPATION, SOLIDARITY, RELIGION, KNOWLEDGE, EXPERIENCE

PERSONAL

PHRONESIS, TEMPERANCE, COURAGE, JUSTICE, FAITH, HOPE, LOVE, BEING A GOOD FATHER/MOTHER, BEING A GOOD FRIEND/COLLEAGUE, WISDOM HAVING FUN, BEING ABLE TO ENJOY MYSELF, BEING ENTREPRENEURIAL, PASSION, A U T H E N T I C I T Y , CRAFTSMANSHIP, EGO, AUTONOMY, HEALTH, INDEPENDENCE, CREATIVE, FLOURISHING, PERSONAL GROWTH

SOCIAL

SOCIAL STATUS, RESPONSIBILITY, FAMILY, FRIENDSHIP, A SENSE OF BELONGING, COMMUNITY, MEMBERSHIP, PRESTIGE, FAME, REPUTATION, POWER, COZINESS *(Dutch: gezelligheid)*, HUMILITY, LOYALTY, COMRADERY, IDENTITY, CREATIVITY, BEING AN ARTIST/LEADER/DIRECTOR/MO THER, DIGNITY, RESPECT, COMMITMENT, HEROISM

Diagram 5-1 Four domains of values

saw is good for sawing; a knife for cutting.

When classical economists spoke about use value, they usually had functional values in mind; nowadays most economists will recognize that other values are involved, but it is not common to make such values explicit as I am doing here.

Use value is practical. I value my computer for its usefulness. With my computer I can process this text. But that is of another order than the scientific or inspirational value that this text hopefully has for others. I do not write in order to use my computer; I write in order to be truthful and realize my values of good writing, scholarship and our civilization.

Use values are instrumental. You and I are dependent on all kinds of things due to their usefulness to us—hammers, computers, advice, haircuts, vegetables, cars and roads, for example. Standard economics focuses on what is useful and the pricing thereof. The value based approach takes us beyond that what is merely useful and directs the attention to what is important to us.

How about economic values? It is common to suggest that things have economic value for their ability to be exchanged for a monetary amount. The Uggs are good for 180 euro and a play of King Lear is good for subsidies, the sale of tickets and a source of income for the actors and other professionals involved in the production. Much of the economic discussion focuses on those financial values, for that is the form that economic values take in these instances: they represent a monetary amount. So should I not include them as a separate category?

In a value based approach financial values are instrumental values; they are functional. The reason is that a monetary amount has no personal, social, societal or transcendental value in and of itself. Money needs to be transferred into some kind of good in order to realize values that really matter to us. When actors use their income to buy food, pay the rent and pick up the tab at a restaurant, they realize the things that they want, need or find important. The theatre company will use the revenues of ticket sales and subsidies to realize a great performance of King Lear, to create a great artistic team of actors and a director and, who knows, to contribute to a rich tradition of theatre. Prices, or the quantities of money they stand for, are intermediaries.

A bundle of money on its own is just that: a bundle of money. It has value because it holds the promise for some goodies that can be acquired with it. Those goodies enable the realization of actual values. People are willing to pay an amount of money for a ticket because in doing so they anticipate the realization of values that are important for them. The ticket itself is just that: a ticket.

A price can have social value as in the case of the price of the Uggs. The extravagant price signals among girls the sacrifice parents are willing to make for their daughters. It transforms the good into what is called a *positional* good;

that is, a good that conveys to its owner a special social position.

Accordingly, exchange value or price is, as a rule, not a true value. It is the number that is the outcome of rather complex processes. It serves an important function as it tells the spenders what they have to give up in other goods (or values) and it tells the receivers what goods (or values) they can acquire. The price affects their actions; spenders refrain from spending when the price is too high, and the receivers will stop performing when the price is too low. That is more or less it. It does not tell much, if anything at all, about the other values at stake.

To both parties exchange value, or the price, has a merely instrumental function. It is a means to realize the relevant values. Price in itself is meaningless and worthless. It is just a number. What matters to those dealing with it, are the values that it enables to realize.

An important function of price or exchange value is that of signaling. An increasing price for an artwork signals that the seller anticipates a higher willingness to pay. When the price decreases, market participants read that as a signaling of waning interest in that work. A zero price for water, that most useful good, signals abundant supply; a high price might mean that the water is scarce, as it may be in the middle of a desert or in a hut high up the mountain. A high price for a concert tells many people that they better refrain from attending, or it must be so special that the sacrifice has to be worth it. When people are not willing to pay the price for a performance, the theatre director may infer that a) the performance is no good or b) the price is too high or c) both. Accordingly, participants in the market will act on the basis of how they interpret prices.

Thinking about exchange values stimulates the makers to think of the others, of what the others value. Exchange value signifies the encounter of different worlds, of the world of making art and all other worlds, including the worlds of someone writing books, or being accountable in a difficult marriage, or being young and eager for some meaning in life.

But that does not render prices valuable in and of themselves. Furthermore, the number that represents a price is an imperfect indicator of the values realized. It leaves out a lot; it hides the values that really matter.

What, then, is the reason that exchange value receives so much attention in everyday conversation and in political discourse?

One reason is that exchange value is a means to acquire the things that we want or need. If the theatre company is not able to realize sufficient means for exchange, then it cannot pay its actors and will have to close down.

Another reason is that, in an instrumentalist age, people are used to thinking in terms of numbers. The big advantage of exchange values is that they can be numbered.

Another reason is that exchange values refer to all kinds of values that they command without the need to specify them. Exchange value is generic. So when we hear that someone like Warren Buffet or Bill Gates owns billions, we are free to fantasize about all the goods they can acquire: about the yachts they can buy, the large houses, the luxurious vacations and the company of the rich and famous. We are not compelled to know what values they actually realize, how warm their homes are, how solid their friendships and how much they are in touch with their deeper or spiritual self.

So what to say when the manager of a theatre tells triumphantly that all performances of King Lear have been sold out? I will first compliment him and then, if I have a chance, ask him how he knows that the play has been a success. When he looks at me strangely, I will point out that in order to know about the success, he will need to know more about the values that the people involved have realized. How did the play work for those who watched it? What has it meant for the actors? Is the government or foundation that provided the subsidy satisfied that its criteria were met? If he is frank, he will grant that the numbers of visitors and the receipts say little to nothing about those values. Might a smaller number of visitors who were more involved mean more success? It is possible. So much for the numbers.

During a dinner with colleagues I could make the point as follows (after they had expressed their skepticism). I first ask what the dinner is good for. Sure, we were in need of nutrients, but that is not why we are sitting here. No, the point is that we want to have a conversation. Accordingly, the value we really care for is the value of the conversation we share, the contact we make, the hope maybe of a future collaboration. Those are the most important values that we take away from the dinner table.

Yet, what counts in the statistics is the amount we pay for the dinner and drinks. That will be counted as consumption and that is what economic models will work with. With that amount, accountants can determine the income that our dinner generated for the people of the restaurant. All that is interesting all right, but it says little to nothing about the point of the dinner and that is our conversation. Accordingly, the important values that we realized are unaccounted for and the standard economic analysis misses the point.

Values, (social) norms, and virtues.

- **Values** are qualities of actions, goods, practices, people and social entities that people find good, beneficial, important, useful, beautiful, desirable, constructive and so forth. Values are personal in the sense that individuals experience them as such and they are social in the sense that values derive their impact from being shared among groups of people. Veracity is an important value to me; it works best in conversation with people who share veracity as a value.

- **(Social) norms** are rules that guide, direct and discipline social behavior. They usually are manifestations of one value or another. When I greet you, the norm is that you return my greeting. Such a norm expresses a value like politeness, or maybe even respect. In an artistic circle the norm might be that you do not say that a work is beautiful. An "uhm" or a softly expressed "interesting" works better. I gather that the value here is that the value of art needs to be unspeakable.

- **Virtues** are (internalized) characteristics of behavior that is directed to the good. Virtuous is the person who acts upon his or her values and does so being prudent, self-disciplined, courageous and just. Prudence is a virtue, as is temperance, courage and justice. These are the so-called cardinal virtues that we find in the *Nichomachean Ethics* of Aristotle. Together with the theological virtues faith, hope and love, they constitute the seven classical virtues.

Phronesis: **working with values**.

Being aware of one's own values and of those of others is one thing; acting upon them is quite another. We will need to evaluate and appraise those values and then figure out how to make them real.

The problem with values is that we cannot grasp them. An artistic or social value is not concrete; it has no number attached. Moreover, when we act upon our values we are usually not aware of them. We act, we go to a Shakespeare play, or stay home because we feel like it. We can try to derive the values that others hold dear from what they do and don't do, and from what they say and don't say. That, too, is not an easy task, as I found out in numerous workshops.

It is in such workshops, as well as in everyday life, that I have discovered how important it is to be aware of one's values and to be more conscious of how to work with them. It is especially important when you and I try to do the right thing.

Of course, you can continue to act while remaining unconscious of what is important to you. But if you really want to know what gets others to pay attention to what you do, or have to offer, and what gets them willing to pay or to contribute, then you may be in serious trouble when you do not pay attention to their values. Seriously. That is what the practice of marketing is all about. When you allow yourself to participate in a leadership program, you will discover that it is all about awareness, mindfulness, getting in touch with your soul, knowing your passion or, in short, being aware of your values.

Working with your values is a matter of *phronesis*, or practical wisdom. It is what we learn to practice early on, for example, in figuring out whom to invite to your birthday party or how to tell the teacher that she is wrong about your fooling around. It is what we are supposed to do better when we grow older and become more experienced. It is what we do all the time (whereas the making of calculated choices we do rarely, if at all any time.)

Take the visit to the Shakespeare play. First I need to decide that the values that I will realize by going will be more valuable than the values that I will compromise (such as the value of working on this book). In my case this is an intuitive and emotional matter. When I sense a feeling of guilt at the thought of not going and feel kind of excited about going, then I am moved to go. (But because my emotions are not always that clear, and I am able to suppress some emotions, I have to be cautious in interpreting them.) I surely do not make any calculation. When I receive an email to remind me of the intention to go together, I respond promising to book the tickets. And there we go.

The real work is in the attending and during the aftermath. At least, it was in my case. There was the social setting that compelled me to meet the expectations of my company (my wife and a befriended couple). I felt responsible to contribute to the good mood in our group and that meant bringing in topics for conversation, paying attention to the others, remembering to ask how well they are doing and stuff like that. During the play I had to pay serious attention, and to battle the fatigue of a day of writing. I struggled with what the play meant, why Cordelia refuses to please her father, and why he was so unreasonable. I discovered that I got into the play and went with the flow. So it surprised me when my wife expressed some doubts during the intermission. What to say to that? I had to scramble to find the words to express my own experience and was relieved that I could draw from some reading I had done in advance—a return on investment! She was not (and never is) easily convinced so I had to work really hard at it. It is a matter of *phronesis* that I know that I need to respond well for the sake of a good evening together.

After the play we drove home with the other couple. I did my best to keep the discussion focused on the play (since other topics such as other people, politics or therapy are so much easier). Being able to talk about what we experienced together is not only a way to realize artistic values, but also social values. I tried to appeal to their experiences as therapists. Did they understand why Claudia did not respond to her father´s question? Their response surprised me. All three surmised that the explanation was in her past. They noted that the mother (and the wife of King Lear) was never mentioned but her absence was, in their interpretation, critical and could account for the actions not only of King Lear, but also especially for those of the sisters. They sensed that in the imagination of King Lear, Claudia, the youngest daughter, had taken the place of her mother. It has made her sisters jealous of her and had put her in an impossible position. That was an insight to me. I tried to bring up the loyalty of the Lord of Kent, but that did not get us very far.

Maybe it was because of the discussion afterwards that I remembered the play so well. Even now I am writing about it. The makers can be pleased. Yet my wife confessed to me recently, that she had not thought of the play any further. If we were to do a head count of the audience once again, her head should count for less than my head.

You can explore your own actions in similar situations. It helps you to become aware of the values involved, of the values realized, of the deliberations and the evaluations, and therefore of what *phronesis* is all about.

Accordingly this is what *phronesis* is about:

- ***Identifying and articulating values***. What is important to you? Which values matter to you? In the case of the Uggs, I became aware of my personal value of fatherhood and the social value of having a good and harmonious family.

- ***Being virtuous***: Aspiring to do the right thing, I want to be virtuous; that is, I want to act in accordance with the relevant virtues. Therefore I try to be prudent when necessary, temperate, courageous, just, faithful, hopeful and loving. It is a matter of being integer and authentic. (See also the box on being virtuous.)

- ***Valuing:*** you need to assess the values of the things you aspire to own, of the relationships you have, the conversations you are involved in and so on. What am I willing to sacrifice in order to hold on to my marriage? How much am I willing to spend on an evening with theatre? What am I willing to contribute to a social cause?

- ***Valorization:*** With the theatre I want to realize social and cultural values. Valorization of this book signifies the realization of its

financial, cultural and social values. Valorization is the making real
of values.

- **Evaluation:** How important is a value compared to others? (If you
cancel the appointment with a friend in order to go to the theatre
instead, what does that say about the values of your friendship and
the values of going to the theatre?)

- **Transforming or changing values:** I can change my values in the
process. Having experienced a Shakespeare play, my valuation of
Shakespeare play may increase. Some people in the audience will
discover that Shakespeare is their thing, while others may realize that
their expectations were not met, causing them to choose a leisurely
evening the next time around. Like religions and universities, cultural
organizations often have it as an explicit purpose to change the values of people.

This goes to show that the process of *phronesis* involves a great deal more
than the rational decision making that economic models imagine. The usual
construction of rational choice suggests an analytical process on the basis of
a well-articulated algorithm and explicit numbers with a clear, unambiguous
outcome. The process of *phronesis* is more interpretive than analytical. It is
much more allusive and therefore much more difficult to study. *Phronesis* is also
much more difficult to practice. Then again, I do not think you and I practice
rational choice as imagined in the economic model. But we practice *phronesis*
all the time, no matter how complicated it is. For that is life. That is what the
story of the Uggs tries to tell.

Finally: do we choose our values or do we discover them?

One reason for resistance against the value based approach is the fear of fixed
values, of practices that hold values firm and absolute and impose them on
others. It is the image of zealots who rally under the banner of family values,
who destroy in the name of Christian or Islamic values, who imprison those
who do not subscribe to communist values.

The need for the notion of *phronesis* is indicative for the feebleness of
values, for the difficulties of articulating, interpreting and acting upon them.
In reality values are the subject of continuous deliberation. Sure, people can
claim that they know their values; that their values are sacred and holy and
therefore true. I would like to ask such people how do they know; on what
grounds do they know better than others.

At the other extreme, people deny the usefulness of values because we
cannot know them, their significance is contingent upon numerous conditions

and, consequently, there is nothing sensible to say about them. If so, I wonder, how then can we act? How are we able to do the right thing, or at least able to have the idea that we do the right thing every now and then? Apparently, we are able to have a sense of what our values are. The value based approach works with that sense.

Are we then determining our values ourselves, or are we discovering them? Every now and then, students raise this question. Usually they do so because they want to believe that they are autonomous individuals and should therefore be able to determine themselves what is important to them.

In that discussion I tend to stress the other option: that we discover our values. This position is more consistent with most beliefs, like Christianity, Islam, Confucianism, Taoism, and Buddhism. But also Gestalt, Jungian and Freudian psychologists would suggest the same. Accordingly, you and I are groping our way, figuring out in all that we do, what is important to us.

In the end I take a pragmatic position, like that of Dewey (Dewey, 1915). Whether we determine or find our values, we have to cope with our values one way or another. As long as solving the dilemma is not critical for acting upon our values, I leave it—along with topics such as the free will, the proof of God or the end of humanity—to discussions during a Sunday evening meal.

Appendix 1. How to determine your own values?
When I want people to figure out their own values, I make use of the Aurelius exercise.

The Aurelius exercise. The exercise is named after a beneficent Roman emperor. In a book of reflections he lists the people that have been important to him and specifies for each one the qualities that make them important to him. He starts with his grandfather Annius Verus from who learned "to be gentle and meek, and to refrain from all anger and passion. . . [from my mother] to be religious and bountiful [. . .] and to live with a spare diet." (Aurelius & Gill, 2013) And so he continues.

Do the same. To increase the effectiveness of the exercise, narrow it down to the three or four people that are most important to you. List no more than two qualities for each that make them important to you. Only choose people with whom you have a relationship (so not the Nelson Mandelas, the Ghandis or the Dalai Lamas unless you have related to them personally).

Specify the qualities you have listed as your values. List them in order of importance.

Appendix 2. How to work with your values.
Being aware of your values is one thing, realizing or valorizing them is quite another. It is easy to forget your values after only having figured them out in the exercise that I just described. You have to work with them daily in order to make them work for you. Many organizations nowadays make an effort to specify their most important values. It happens all too often when I ask leaders of such organizations what those values are, that they have to look them up. That means that he or she is not working with them. Doing some exercises is a good start, but the real exercise is daily practice.

Exercise: Ask participants for situations that they were in and about which they have a bad feeling. It has to be a situation in which they did something. Then ask them to determine what they would have done if they had acted in accordance with their most important values (that they just determined).

CHAPTER 6

TO REALIZE VALUES WE NEED TO PROCURE GOODS, THE MOST IMPORTANT OF WHICH ARE SHARED

When doing the right thing we want to realize our values. In the previous chapter we were concerned with all the values that might come into play. That is the awareness part. Now we turn to what we do when we try to make those values real. And that requires becoming aware of the goods that we acquire and generate. So we move up the awareness part.

Suppose someone cherishes the value of friendship and finds himself lonely. So he is aware of valuing friendship. He can just live with that ideal but he can also act in order to make the value real, that is, to valorize "friendship" in his life. The question is then how he can do so. The answer seems obvious: in order to make the value "friendship" real, he needs to approach people to generate a friendship somehow. In that way he transforms the ideal "friendship" into an actual friendship. The same transformation is required for someone valuing personal love. Without a relationship this person does not stand a chance of having love. It furthermore has to be a special relationship in order to generate the kind of love that this person is seeking.

The point is this: the friendly or loving relationship is a good in the sense that it is something to gain and something to lose. This person either has such a relationship or not. It is a good as it services to realize all kinds of values, like friendship, love, or both, companionship support, attention, and the possibility of parenthood. Accordingly, in order to make the values "friendship" or "love" real, we need to acquire a good like "friendship" or "a loving relationship"; a good we cannot buy and that the government cannot procure for you.

Values need to be acted upon to become real, and an important way of realizing them is to acquire or generate goods. Goods enable us to realize values. They can be things like a cup of coffee or a computer, but they can also be intangible things, like relationships, communities, ideas and artistic expressions.

Goods are good for all kinds of things. You and I can "have" or possess goods, although often not in a legal sense. "Having" a relationship is the same as "possessing" it. People have houses and they have kids and a home. Goods are whatever we have that enable us to realize values.

Really?

This characterization of goods may seem odd at first. It certainly is when you are accustomed to thinking of goods as things you can hold onto, like a cup of coffee and a computer, or when you think of goods as things that you can buy or sell.

I now will do two things to convince you that we are in need of a broad category of goods, a much broader category of goods than what shows up in a standard economic account. Sure, in the conversation of economists you will come across intangible goods like services (think of a class or a therapy session) and the hard to grasp collective or public goods, like safety, or cultural heritage. However, we need to go even beyond these classes of goods to include goods such as friendship, home, society, faith, art and science. You better think twice before continuing from this point, since the consequences are far reaching for the way you and I conceptualize our world and understand phenomena such as the arts, poverty, richness, altruism and so much more.

The first consideration comes by way of another reading of Robinson Crusoe that shows the importance of company and conversation. Why not call them goods?

Defoe´s story about Robinson Crusoe, who got shipwrecked and found himself all alone as the sole survivor on an island, is standard fare in an introductory economics course. It perfectly illustrates, for example, the tradeoff that we need to make between consumption now and consumption later (by planting seeds from his harvest now to have a greater harvest later), investments and division of labor (between him and Friday, the fellow that he rescues from being the meal for a bunch of cannibals). In this reading, Robinson Crusoe is the archetypical homo economicus; a perfect example for anyone who wants to understand how homo economicus operates.

In another humanistic reading, the story turns out to be a human drama. This is the story about Crusoe's struggle with his father and his seeking faith. It is about the purifying experience that spending twenty eight years on an island can be. That is what makes Robinson Crusoe a *Bildung* novel.

Though it is not so strange that economists read their perspective into the novel. Already in the very beginning of the novel Crusoe does a cost-benefit analysis, weighing the advantages and disadvantages of his stranding on an island. But a careful reading shows that the accounting of Crusoe is quite different from the accounting that is customary in standard economics. For these are his lists:

Good	Evil
Still alive	Cast away
Singled out to be saved from the wreckage	Singled out to be miserable
I am not starved	Divided from mankind-solitaire
There are no wild beasts	I have no weapons
It is warm	I have no clothes

He could have added that he had been able to secure plenty of supplies from the shipwreck, including a few bibles (which served him well in his search for his faith). He also found some coins in the ship, but they are useless in his economy. (Note that economists latched onto a story that has no use for exchange! Strange, isn't it?)

His account stresses his social situation or, better said, the lack thereof. All alone he is barren from any social interaction. That is why his encounter with another human being after a long period of loneliness is so important to him. Friday is not only someone who can do his share of the chores, but he is also company for Crusoe. Crusoe teaches Friday some English so that they can *have conversations*. The conversations have a great deal of value for Crusoe, a social value as we can observe after the previous chapter. He feels better, even richer because of them. Of course he does. We humans are in need of company and conversation. They are basic needs.

Were you to wear the glasses of demand and supply, exchange and price, costs and benefits, you do not see such things. With the value tinted spectacles, the values of company and the conversations are becoming pronounced.

In a valued based approach to economics, friendship is a good. And so is a conversation. They resist having them. That means they do not come free; Crusoe has to make efforts and some sacrifices to acquire them. And they are good for all kinds of things.

The second consideration comes after answering a question.
I have made it a habit to ask classes of students and audiences at lectures to name their single-most precious possession. Sometimes I begin by asking them to name their drive. In one class, every single student mentioned money

as the main goal. One guy wanted it to be on the record that he was going for lots of money. Only one female student took exception and said that she wanted to be happy. The guy pointed out to her that she needed money for that. She had to agree to that. There we were: money is what moved them.

And then I put the big question to them: what is your most precious possession, what is the last thing you want to lose? The lots-of-money guy wanted to know whether it had to be something tangible. I told him that it was up to him. He immediately had his mind made up: his most precious possessions were his family and friends. Others followed suit. One student thought of her freedom, another mentioned her brains. And as almost always happens in such a round, a few named their health as their most precious possession. No-one spoke of money, cars or something tangible. One time someone mentioned her iPhone but—judging by the burst of laughter among the students—this was clearly not a serious option. Sometimes the answer surprises me, like when a guy from Botswana mentioned his fear as his greatest possession. I doubt whether "fear" is a good (after all, how does it resist possession?), but I understood his reason for saying so when he explained that his fears are what give him his urge to accomplish something.

So here is my question to you, my reader: what is your most precious possession?

Would you even consider something that you have bought, or something that the government has provided? Is it something you own in a legal sense?

Let me pause here, as I would do in class.

Strange, isn't it? Money may be what people want, yet money does not buy what is most important to them. You do not buy friends and family with your money. Yes, money helps to secure your health, but then again, you do not own your health legally.

Leaving out what is most important to us does not make a great deal of sense. Standard economics does not consider family, friends, freedom and such as goods. The value based approach does. Doing so will change a great deal in our worldview.

What are goods?

Aristotle defined goods as "the means of life and well-being of men" in his work *Politics* (Aristotle & Ross, 1995). So goods would be the means to realize values. And so we are back to the definition I gave at the beginning.

In the late 19th century, Carl Menger, an Austrian economist, probed the nature of a good and concluded that whatever satisfies a need, qualifies as a good. That opened the way for a wide range of goods including families and friendships. But he shrank away from that consequence and decided that economists had to restrict the definition of good to those categories of goods that lend themselves for exchange in the market place. Later, economists had to break this restriction in order to allow for collective goods (Menger, 1871).

A value based approach stresses the values that goods enable us to realize and recovers the wide range of goods that qualify, including collective goods and all the other goods that cannot be priced and cannot be bought and sold at a market.

Goods need to be acquired or generated and the acquisition requires some kind of sacrifice. To speak of "having" or "possessing" a good only makes sense if a good resists possession. When we happen to see a splendid sunset it would be strange to claim that sunset as "ours." It would be different if you have to climb a steep mountain in order to see a particularly beautiful sunset: in that case you might say that it is yours to cherish. In general, goods require an effort to acquire. We have to give something up to "have" them or to enjoy the benefits of goods. Even a sunset requires some work in order to be able to enjoy it.

Therefore, I define goods as follows:

> *Goods are tangible or intangible things that an individual, a group of people or a gathering of people possesses; they are good for all kinds of things and their possession requires some kind of effort or sacrifice.*

> *Goods are important to us, because they enable us to realize values.*

The time is ripe for a general notion of "goods." We are already accustomed to thinking of experience goods and imaginary goods. The lottery sells an illusion, that is, an imaginary good. And a fair or festival is all about experience. But is that really it? Just try to determine what you buy when you pay for a ticket for a museum. What is the good you are buying? An experience good? Continue reading and you will realize that it is not just that. You can be certain that values play a role!

Goods that are most important to me, and you.
In an earlier version of this chapter I proceeded to list the types of goods and started off with the goods that are usually recognized as such; those are private goods—or the goods we buy—and collective goods. Only later did I introduce the shared goods. Then I realized that by doing so I went along with the standard scientific approach that makes us consider things from a distance, speaking of "the system" or "the processes out there." But my approach is

to consider the world from the standpoint of the subjects themselves, of us, that is, as a people trying to make a life, realizing values. So I had to delete everything I had written and start to make sense of the life you and I live. Let me give it a try.

My day starts when I get out of bed. Please join me, and imagine yourself doing so also. The first thing on my mind is not that I have to buy or sell something, as the standard economic perspective would suggest. Come to think of it, the buying and selling of things is not much part of the day of a family man, a politician and an academic. I am rather focused on doing things with the members of my family, at the university and in the city hall. Most of the time, I am engaged in conversations of all kinds. I talk with Ph.D. students, other students, colleagues and research assistants, and I teach classes, of course. In the city hall I have endless meetings with civil servants, citizens and politicians to discuss a wide range of topics. At other times I am working on this book, reading and writing emails and, every now and then, I have to cope with faculty meetings and the like. In the evening, if I do not give a lecture somewhere, have a meeting or meet with a friend, then I look forward to having dinner with my family. At the end of the day I will not talk about the amount of money I have earned or spent. I do not even think about it. If I were to reflect on my day, I would instead care about the qualities of the time spent with my family, of the classes and lectures I've given, of the interactions and conversations I've had, and whether or not I am still politically alive and about the worth of my friendships.

If I were to follow Crusoe's example, I would try to assess what my activities have contributed to the goods I care for, such as the good "family." the good "collegiality," the good "knowledge,", the good "conversation," the good "academic community," the good "democracy", the good "fairness" or the good "friendship." All those goods are important for me. They are good for a variety of my values.

I do buy a few things, off and on. All the things I buy are instrumental and usually serve the realization of the goods that are really important to me. The gas that I buy gets me to the places I need to be. The food I buy nourishes me so that I have enough energy to get through the day or it serves to accompany a conversation with colleagues or other people. The vegetables I buy are ingredients for a family dinner. By paying the interest on the mortgage I am able to share the house with my family. Every so often I buy a book that I need for my research. There have been days that were all about a purchase, like the day I bought my house. But most of my days are about conversations, teaching and meetings. The things I buy during those days are subsidiary and instrumental.

During the day I also benefit from a variety of collective goods, such as the roads, the sanitary sewer, the water supply, police protection, relatively clean air and the university system. I am very pleased with these goods, when I think about them. Usually I am not aware of their values. They, too, are instrumental for the goods I really care about. I am not living and working for the sake of the university. I need the university in order to have a good academic community, to be able to teach and to have "good conversations."

"Yeah, but you are privileged. You do not have to worry about how to survive." This is a standard reaction. It usually comes from people who are as privileged as I am, in the sense that we do not need to worry whether or not we will have food on the table the next day and a roof over our head. Sure, I would respond, when people are in survival mode, like when they are in a war zone, going hungry, trying to immigrate, scrounging for food, searching for a shelter or seeking a residence permit, it is all that is on their mind. But they, too, are seeking to overcome the mode of surviving in order to "have" a life. Having a life implies being able to focus on conversations, companionship, a community, knowledge, a skill and all those things that render life meaningful.

Accordingly, doing the right thing is about acquiring all kinds of goods, most of those—and the most important of those—we cannot buy and do not own legally. Standard economics is all about private and collective goods, about property rights. So that domain is covered. We now need to understand the other goods as well. What are their characteristics? How do we acquire them? How do we value them? Can we order them?

The most important goods are "shared goods"

Let us have a look at the good "a good conversation." It happens to be a good that is important to me: I am always trying to make it happen, at home, with friends and at the university. It was also what Crusoe was looking for. There he was, all by himself, trying to survive, but with no one to talk to. People who have stranded at islands all by themselves, or who are locked up in isolation, are known to have a hard time being without any conversation. Alexander Selkirk, a well-known castaway at the time of Defoe was actually unable to speak and socialize after his rescue and ended up living in a cave in his back-yard. He had been on the island for only five years, versus twenty eight years in the case of Crusoe. The advantage of the latter was that he was able to have conversations with this Friday guy, a cannibal whom he had saved from a cannibal feast. Even though they did not speak the same language, they quickly developed a language that they both could understand enabling them to communicate. After some time they shared feelings, discussed what needed to be done and so on. Crusoe enjoyed the company and appreciated the ability to have a conversation with another person. This was presumably also true for the other fellow.

What does the companionship mean? Even when this person does not help Crusoe in adding to the amount of goods for his consumption—he may put in some work but has to eat and needs a place to stay, too—he may still decide that he is better off with his presence because of the possibility of having a conversation with someone. He may even come to that conclusion in the event that the amount of goods available for his consumption actually declines. He gladly gives up some bread and meat in exchange for the conversation.

The bread and meat are private goods in the sense that he raised the sheep and planted, harvested and milled the grain. Those goods are his and it is his decision to share them with Friday. If Friday were to grab them without asking, he might get angry and throw him off the island.

The conversation that they are having is another matter, for it is theirs. *They share the conversation.* It is *a joint production.* Friday makes an effort and so does Crusoe. A conversation in which he does not participate is not the same as one in which he is paying attention to what the other is saying, responds and contributes himself by telling things. The more effort they both put into their conversation, the better Crusoe will feel and the better Friday will most likely feel as well. (He finds himself whistling again while walking along the beach and catches himself looking forward to the evening's meal because of the conversation they will be having.) It matters to him that Friday enjoys the conversation as well. They do not only produce the conversation together, they also "consume" it together. The enjoyment is mutual. Their conversation is what he and Friday share. It is a shared good.

Maybe it is strange to call a conversation a good at all. From an economic point of view, however, it is not all that different from a good like bread. A conversation requires the input of time, effort and human and social capital. A conversation does not come about effortlessly. It is not free either. Even if the direct costs are zero, there will be opportunity costs (the benefits of alternative activities that are forsaken). And like bread a conversation gives satisfaction. Thus far a shared good is like a private good. The conversation, however, cannot be a private good because no one can claim sole ownership of it. Crusoe cannot claim that the conversation is his and exclude others, including Friday, from enjoying it. A conversation is not *divisible.* We cannot say: "this part is mine and that part is yours, I give you this for that." A conversation cannot be exchanged; it cannot be bought or sold. It is shared.

A conversation is not a collective good either. A pure collective good is both indivisible—when you and I are the collective, I cannot consume it without your consuming it as well—and non-rivalrous—my consumption of the good cannot be at the expense of your consumption. Although a conversation cannot be split up and although Crusoe cannot have the conversation by excluding Friday, Friday and he can easily exclude others (like the members of Friday's tribe) from their conversation. Their conversation is between them; it is theirs. Maybe one of them will give it up for another conversation when the occasion presents itself. Crusoe may exclude Friday, as he actually did after being rescued. Conversations have rivalry and exclusion written all over them. A conversation, therefore, is a good that does accord neither with the class of private goods, nor with that of collective goods. It is a shared good. Both Friday and Crusoe enjoy having or owning it.

The good "conversation" comes in different qualities, of course. A conversation with a lover will have a higher quality from one with a stranger. A conversation with a colleague can go deeper and can be more intense than one with a layperson. And the participants may not benefit equally from the conversation. It helps him in his conversation if Crusoe were interested in the phenomenon of the wild man; in that case he will get one kick after another from talking with Friday. Otherwise he may find Friday's talk mainly strange and incomprehensible. Participants may put in different efforts and therefore get something different out of their conversation. It remains a shared good, though, as no party can appropriate it entirely or exclude the other.

A shared good as defined here is different from the notion of a common good, or a commons, in the standard economic discussions. Common goods are accessible to all—they are non-exclusive—but they allow for rivalry. Economists tend to see great problems for the sustenance of common goods because of the free rider problem. Take the sea, for instance. This is a good that all people have in common. The whales swimming in the sea are a common good. Catching them is lucrative. Here the free rider problem occurs because whale hunters have an incentive to catch as many whales as they can. When they voluntarily agree to limit the number lest the whales die out, individual whale hunters have the incentive to exceed that limit to have more than the others. They are said to be free riding (like what people do when they do not buy tickets for public transport). The point is important since common goods lose their footing in the classic economic analysis because of this problem.

However, the problem does not apply to shared goods! When one party shirks, by pretending to be in the conversation while being instead with his thoughts somewhere else, the conversation will be different because of it and will have less value than a conversation to which all parties contribute. When there are more than two parties involved, one party may shirk and let the others do the work, but risk losing the conversation. When Friday and Crusoe are having a conversation, you may want to join in. Imagine they let you in and you subsequently shirk by not contributing yourself. Apart from what they will think of your passivity, you will benefit differently from the conversation than they do, if you benefit at all. You may gain some information, some insight maybe, but because you will not partake in the conversation, it will not be yours. You can only have a conversation by partaking in it. (Of course, you can exploit a conversation that others are having, drawing gainful information from it, but then you cannot go home and tell your partner about this wonderful conversation you had.)

Once you have identified shared goods as goods, you will notice them all around. Friendship is an obvious example, as is "home," "family" and "collegiality." "Trust" is a shared good, as is "knowledge," "music" and "art" (about which more later in the chapter). A "community" clearly is, and so is a "team" or "team spirit." When people list their most important possessions, they are almost always shared.

When I lecture I like to use "knowledge" as an example. "Knowledge" is presented as if it were a package of information, ideas, models and the like; as if you can take it over, buy it as it were, to make it your own. But that is not how "knowledge" works. I will point out here that I try to convey knowledge in a hopefully interesting, maybe even inspiring, exposition. Why do I do so?

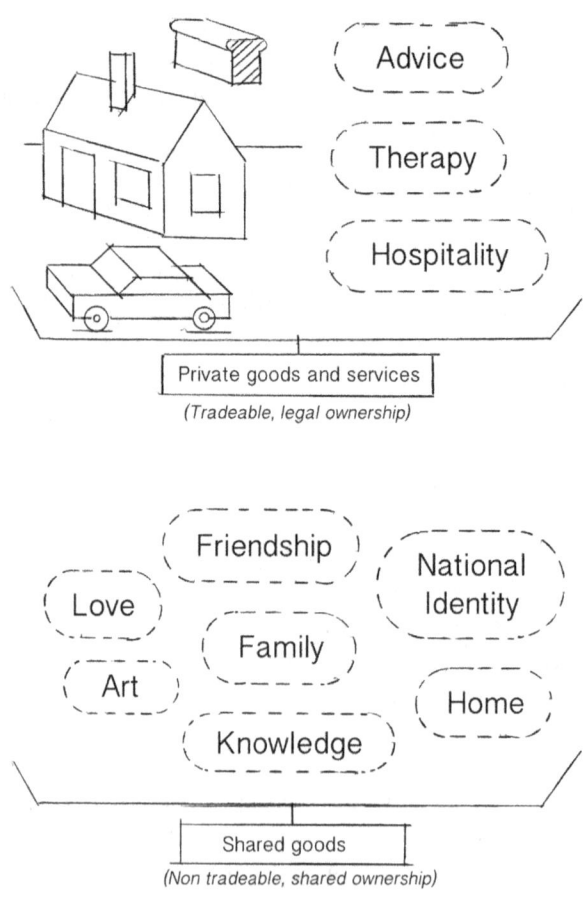

Diagram 6-1 Private goods and services, and shared goods

It is certainly not for the money, since the pay is usually limited. My reason for doing so is that I want to share my knowledge. But that is not going to happen if I am the only one doing the work. The people sitting in front of me are actually having to do the hard work because they have to make sense of the noise that I make, transform that noise into something that has meaning to them and appropriate that somehow. Of course, I have to make an effort seeking a connection with what people already know and, of course, most of what I have said will get lost anyhow. But hopefully some of us will share part of the knowledge conveyed.

It is the sharing that renders "my" knowledge relevant and valuable.

A shared good is usually a practice
It is not only that knowledge, like the knowledge contained in this book, needs to be shared in order to become knowledge; most knowledge also requires a continuing activity. When the general response to what you just read is "sure, friendship is a shared good" and that is it, then this knowledge will quickly be forgotten and get lost. Knowledge is an active good; it is a practice. In doing, the knowledge becomes valuable. So people have to think when it comes to the notion of shared goods, apply it in situations, in their research, in their conversations. Some people need to probe it further, explore the valuation of shared goods, differentiate types of shared goods and so forth.

Friendship, too, is a practice in the sense that to sustain, enjoy and further the friendship friends have to do things, all kinds of things. They may have to talk with each other, think of the other, bring the friend up in conversations, share important experiences and do things together. The phone calls and the outings serve the friendship; they are activities intended to valorize the friendship.

> **The practice of a shared good, therefore, consists of all activities and interactions that are directed at generating, sustaining and valorizing the good. Put differently, the shared good stands for the practice that constitutes it.**

Think of the concert pianist, the dancer, the craftsman: they all have to practice their skill day in and day out in order to sustain and further it. Likewise we have to practice our knowledge, friendships, family and art in order to be able to say that we "have" them.

The (creative) commons
The notion of the shared good points out that when we go through our daily life we do all kinds of things, go to meetings, have chats, read, exchange compliments for the sake of sustaining, furthering and valorizing shared goods of

all kinds. The valorizing refers to the realizing of values, all kinds of values.

When going around, seeking to realize our values, we benefit from ongoing practices out there. Other people have developed ongoing practices generating a certain genre of music, a scientific discipline, an artistic environment, a social space, websites, some of which will be of interest to us. Such a practice is called a commons. You benefit from it by participating in and contributing to it.

A commons is out there, available to anyone who is willing to make an effort. The traditional commons is the pasture that surrounds the village. It is free for all villagers to make use of. The common room is the place where people get together to share conversations. The sea with the fish in it is a commons. Wikipedia is also, as are all open sources on the Internet. The commons is optional: you have the option to make use of it, or not. Other terms are a common pool resource, or a creative commons as in the case of the arts (Ostrom, 1990).

We make use of commons all the time. A painting has value partly because it shares with other paintings the commons of the arts. The commons of the art, that is, the institutions, the conversations and the activities that constitute the worlds of the arts, is the resource that feeds and informs the value of the painting. Whether I listen to music by Pink Floyd or watch a Shakespeare play or a French movie, I benefit from others who like the very same music, theatre and movies. The entrepreneur makes use of all kinds of commons, like skilled practices, a culture of hard work and of loyalty, a vital financial system, knowledge practices and so on. It is almost impossible to get the value of art realized in an environment that lacks a commons for the arts, or to be entrepreneurial in an environment that lacks an entrepreneurial commons.

A commons is a practice. It is not a practice that is for sale, so it is not a private good. It is most likely not a collective good as it is not provided for by the government, and requires the participation of many, but not all. People can make use of the commons without anything in return. You and I can consult Wikipedia or any open source program with no strings attached. That is why Hardin in his famous article *The Tragedy of the Commons*, concluded that a common is unsustainable (Hardin, 1968). The only safeguard from overuse would be the privatization or collectivization of the good. Privatization involves the creation of private property rights (cf. the discussion on intellectual property rights); such rights turn the good into a commodity that can be bought and sold. Collectivization implies that the government takes over and makes the use of the common subject to public law. The government can allocate rights to usage and regulate and finance the production of the commons, which then has become a collective good.

But a commons can also remain a social practice, as is the case with Wikipedia, open source programming, and the creative commons in cities and other places. Even though many only make use of such a commons, some people are apparently willing and able to sustain and further the commons. The latter contribute and apparently derive some satisfaction from doing so.

Because a commons is open to outsiders, it is not a shared good as defined here. A shared good excludes people who do not participate and contribute. A commons is shared by those working on it, participating and contributing, but it does not exclude outsiders from using it.

A commons is something social. The term contains the Greek term *koinonia*, which was understood to have the following five characteristics:

"(1) participation must be free and unforced; (2) participants must share a common purpose, whether minor or major, long term or short term; (3) participants must have something in common that they share such as jointly held resources, a collection of precious objects, or a repertory of shared actions; (4) participation involves philia (a sense of mutuality, often inadequately translated as friendship); and (5) social relations must be characterized by dikaon (fairness)" (Lohman, 1992).

All these characteristics appear to apply quite well to the commons of an artistic conversation. The artists are free to participate, (1) those who participate share the objective of furthering the case for their art form (2) and share things like a (usually) informal association, coverage in certain media and a tradition as laid down in art-historical accounts; they will care for each other in some way or another (3) and within the arts the norm is to be fair in dealing with other participants (4). The same applies to scientists, and I gather that people working with open source software will recognize themselves in these five points.

Ownership of shared goods requires contributions

How to acquire a shared good? The knowledge example and the discussion of the commons already gave a clue. Let me elaborate with the shared good "friendship" as an example.

Like a good conversation, a friendship has shared ownership (of the friends involved), is costly to acquire (friends need to make sacrifices) and is good for the realization of all kinds of values. How do you acquire a friendship? It is not by way of a purchase: friendships are not for sale ("hey, I am too busy; want to take over a friend of mine?"). It is also not driven by some governmental program.

I once had an Asian student who came over to the Netherlands to do a PhD with me. Before he came he had been living with his family. At our first meeting I instructed him that he had to make friends. "How do you do that, Sir?" he wanted to know. I involved other Ph.D. students to address the question. How do they make friends? Just asking someone to be a friend is not going to work. That much we agreed upon. Paying someone is out of the question, of course.

A friendship requires the sharing of experiences, doing things together and doing things for each other. That was clear to all of us. "Friends have all things in common," the ancient Greeks would say. But that does not mean that having a friendship is a passive thing. Clearly, potential friends have to do something in order to acquire a friendship. And friends have to keep doing things to sustain or to strengthen a friendship. That is the practice a friendship stands for. Aristotle pointed out that some degree of reciprocity is required. One friend does one thing for the other, and the other does something else at another time. They need to help each other, by lending a listening ear, helping the other to move, making dinner, giving support and so on. All actions and gestures that serve the friendship somehow **contribute** to that friendship.

> **Contributions to a shared good are intended to sustain, enjoy and add value to a shared good. Contributions are a key activity in the practice that constitutes a shared good. In order to claim a shared good as yours, you need to have a willingness to contribute.**

Contributions will play a critical role in the framework that I am developing here. In an exchange situation, people pay an amount of money in exchange for a private good. Economists speak of **willingness to pay** to indicate the willingness of people to pay a certain amount of money. **Willingness to contribute** indicates the willingness to contribute to a shared good. In this case there is no immediate return of something, of equivalent values, as in an exchange. When someone makes a contribution to a friendship, say by paying a sick friend a visit, the giving friend does not get anything in return except for the affirmation of the friendship. The receiving friend is made to understand that in order to sustain the friendship he will have to make a contribution somehow sometime later as well.

> To repeat: **willingness to contribute** differs from **willingness to pay**. In the case of the latter, the expectation is a return of equivalent value. In case of willingness to contribute the expectation is that the contribution will add values to a shared good.

In the case of shared goods the notions of consumption and production—those that do so well in the case of private goods—fail to make sense. The consumption of a private good implies the destruction of value; you eat the ice cream and when you consume your computer, the price of the thing goes down. When you "consume" a friendship, its value may go up. By making use of your friendship, you are actually producing it. The more time Friday and Crusoe spend conversing, the more likely they are to enjoy their conversation. Converse frequently but lightly and you have "companionship." Converse a great deal and you have a relationship. Converse more and you have friendship. Converse even more, and you will have love. Or not.

Because the value of shared goods depends on the inputs of all owners, we can speak of the **co-creation**, or **co-production** of the good. Put differently, shared goods require some form of collaboration.

As I noted earlier, standard economists will subsume all these effects under the category of externalities. They are, in other words, external to the market exchange and the pricing that a market exchange requires. To this I would retort that the market exchange is rather an epi-phenomenon, that is, external to the social practice that constitutes a shared good, or a commons. Standard economics misses the point entirely, and therefore cannot distinguish the most important goods that we try to realize each and every day.

Valuing shared goods.
Because shared goods cannot be bought or sold and do not have a price, their values are not quantifiable. But people weigh the values and the qualities of shared goods anyhow. They will assess some friendships to be more valuable than others. They will tend to contribute most to shared goods that they value most. At least, that is, when they are doing the right thing.

Weighing the values of shared goods and acting upon that is a matter of *phronesis*. Awareness of the values involved and all kinds of knowledge are required. One challenge is the assessment of the values that shared goods realize. A good conversation, for example, is good for social values when it realizes warm feelings, a sense of companionship or even friendship. It may also realize cognitive values when it generates new insights and ideas. Knowledge is required for the right contribution to the conversation and for a proper understanding of the situation.

The value of a shared good is far from fixed. The value of a conversation will change all the time. Each contribution, or lack thereof, will change its value, even if in a minuscule way. The conversation differs from the one we were having yesterday because of what has happened in between.

I realize that these observations do not exhaust the topic of valuation. For example, when people are unaware of the values of friendship, or family, they are likely to miss doing the right thing. The hard working businessman may later regret that his hard work was done at the expense of his family life; and although he will tell everyone that he does what he does to support his family, he may risk losing his family for being away so often. Likewise, people may neglect friendships, the reading of serious books, or a spiritual life to only regret doing so later.

That is why an important component of the value based approach is awareness: we need to be aware of our values and we need to be aware of the goods that enable us to realize those values in order to do the right things.

Categories of goods

Goods come in all shapes and forms. We buy them, acquire them by contribution and then there are goods out there to enjoy without individual effort (like the clean air). It appears useful to indulge in some categorization to allow for distinctions among this great variety of goods.

A few definitions

Goods are those tangibles and intangibles that have value for people, and for the possession and enjoyment of those goods, people would be willing to sacrifice resources. Goods resist possession. Goods are good for the realization of all kinds of values.

Shared goods are shared by a few people or a group of people without a clear legal definition of ownership. As a rule, no single person or legal identity can claim ownership of a shared good. The members of the group enjoy the fruits of their shared good; they cannot exclude other members but usually exclude non-members. Rivalry is conceivable both inside and outside the group. Shared goods come about by way of contributions of the stakeholders

Private goods are goods held in private ownership. The right of ownership gives the right to exclude others from enjoying the fruits of the goods and, when a market exists for the good, transfer the ownership of the good to others. The ownership can be shared in the sense that several individuals have a legal claim to the ownership. The ownership is well defined legally in the sense that a court of law should be able to determine what belongs to whom.

Commodities are private goods in the situation of exchange. In such a situation, goods are for sale and for that purpose are priced.

Collective or collective goods are goods held in ownership by a collective, usually a state or another political entity. Their possession has a legal status. They are marked by non-rivalry in consumption and non-excludability. Their benefits are quasi universal in terms of countries, people and generations. Global collective goods benefit humanity in its entirety.

Common goods are goods that have no clear legal ownership. They are held in common by an unidentified group of people, countries or organizations. No one can be excluded from enjoying its fruits but there is rivalry between potential users: when someone catches a whale, another cannot catch that same whale.

Club goods are goods that can be acquired by becoming member of a club. We owe the identification of this kind of good to James Buchanan (Buchanan, 1965). Club goods are characterized by exclusion (non-members are excluded) and rivalry (there may be a waiting list).

The (creative) commons are a source, like an ongoing conversation out there. People can participate in it and draw benefits from it, but how and to what extent depends on the conditions of participation (or of membership).

We first distinguish goods on the basis of ownership. Some goods we own privately, others collectively, the important goods we share or have in common with others. And then there are the goods we simply enjoy, like a service, or a beautiful building. This division follows closely the definitions given above. Accordingly, when you and I trace the goods we possess, we will identify the following categories:

- **Private goods** include all commodities we have bought and of which we have the property right. I am thinking of my clothes, my computer, my car, my house, the shares I own, but also the electricity I buy, the haircut I received, the visit to the museum, my stay at a hotel the other week, and the (paid) advice I received recently on the mortgage for my house. This category covers the goods and services in standard economics.

- **Collective or public goods** are all the goods (or practices) that I enjoy together with the collective of which I am part. I am thinking of the clean air that I breath, the protection I get, the peace I enjoy, the democratic institutions of my country, the educational system, Dutch cultural herit-age and world heritage, the infrastructure of my country, and the highly subsidized public transport.

- **The (Creative) Commons** are all the practices to which I have access, possibly with some effort. I am thinking of all the art practices to which I have access, the scientific practices, street life in Amsterdam, and all kinds of local practices in my hometown (such as the weekly farmers market).

- **Club goods** are goods or practices that require membership. I am thinking of my soccer club, the philosophical society that I am chairing, the association of cultural economists, and the choir of my wife.

- **Shared goods** are the goods and practices that I share with others. For me they are my family, my friendships, my colleagues, my team in city hall, all kinds of knowledge and all kinds of art, some music so much more than other music, certain movies, Christian practices, soccer games that I played, all kinds of memories.

Another distinction focuses on the values these goods enable us to realize. The question to ask here is: "what is this good good for?" When we hold on to the four dimensions of values as articulated in the previous chapter, that is, personal, social, societal and transcendental values, than this suggest the four dimensions of "personal," "social," "societal," and "transcendental" goods.

The problem is that goods are good for a variety of values. An eggplant can nourish me personally, but it just as well can be good for a family meal and thus for social values. My philosophical practice serves maybe all four dimensions of values as it is good for my curiosity, for the community that it gives me, for its impact on society (awareness!) and for its transcendental significance. The following diagram collects a variety of goods that appear to fit, more or less, under the label "personal," "social," "societal," or "transcendental."

The criteria are that you can "possess" the good—legally or otherwise—, that you (can) partake in the practice that the good represents, or that you can enjoy its fruits or services. The listing should illuminate the immense variety of goods that we can distinguish as soon as we look beyond products and services.

Art is not for sale
Let me illustrate the preceding discussion by applying the concepts to a world that has preoccupied me for the last twenty years, that is the world of the arts. How to identify the notion of a shared good, a commons in that world? Here, too, we are up against a standard economic perspective.

One way to ruffle the feathers of standard economists is to assert that art is not for sale. It was fun to assert as much in a symposium with people of auction houses. After all, the art market is all about buying and selling art, isn't it? Sure, people can buy paintings, but that does not mean that they buy art doing so. "What nonsense," the auctioneers and the economists will respond. Having bought the painting, someone has ownership. Really? The problem is that they follow standard economic reasoning and therefore think in terms of private goods and property rights. If they were to recognize shared goods and the way a commons works, they might understand the point.

This is how I illustrate the point to my students. My question is what is it that they pay for when they buy a ticket for an art museum. Having other lessons in mind, they often mention "experience." They think that a museum sells an experience good, that is, the experience of art that they pay for. But they cannot pay for experience, just as they cannot buy the knowledge that the class conveys. So what do they pay for?

The answer is "access": the ticket gives them access to the museum and it allows them to do whatever they please during opening hours. People may choose to use the bathroom, to spend the entire time in the cafe of the museum or in front of a single work of art. That is completely up to them. What they pay for is "access."

The experience comes about only by the kind of work visitors are willing to do while wandering through the museum. When they walk around mindlessly, without making a serious effort, they will experience little to no art. Art requires an effort, such as looking, seriously looking, and some degree of reflection or exploration. Bringing in knowledge may help. Having the skill of looking and interpreting will contribute to the experience, too.

The visitors may subsequently become aware that art is a shared good. When they appropriate the art—by doing the work—they may realize that they share the ownership with lots of others. These co-owners are the curators, art historians, museum directors, artists, art critics and all those who are partially involved as art lovers or, like themselves, as casual visitors to an art museum. Art is a common practice. **Art is a conversation**.

Museums choose to exhibit certain paintings—and not most others— because they figure prominently in the conversation that is called art. Visitors will experience the art only if they are willing and able to participate in that conversation, when they gain some understanding of how and why an art object figures. That is their participation in or their contribution to the conversation that is art. Accordingly, experiencing art requires work, a contribution of some kind. It is not enough to just put money on the table. Art comes about in a process of co-creation.

Art is not a product. Art is not produced. Art is not consumed.

Art is a conversation. Art is a common practice. Art is co-created or co-produced.

Because art is not for sale, I am critical of directors of museums and theatres who focus all their energy and effort on selling tickets. Because the art that they exhibit and perform only comes to life when the viewers are willing and

TRANSCENDENTAL/ CULTURAL

AN ICON, A FLAG, RELIGIOUS CEREMONY SPECIFIC MUSICAL PERFORMANCES, SPECIFIC ARTISTIC PRACTICES, A SUBLIME EXPERIENCE, A HIKE THROUGH NATURE, YOGA PRACTICES, DANCE PARTIES, OBJECTS OF BEAUTY, TRUTH SEEKING ACTIVITIES, A PARTICULAR THEORY, EXPERIENCING SACRED SITES OR RITUALS

SOCIETAL

EXPERIENCING PEACE/SECURITY/SOLIDARITY/ LIBERTY/JUSTICE/EQUALITY/H ARMONY/DEMOCRATIC PRACTICES AND INSTITUTIONS/EDUCATIONAL PRACTICES AND INSTITUTIONS, ROADS, SEWAGE SYSTEMS, VARIETY OF SHOPS, CITIES, LANDSCAPES, VIEWS, SHARED HISTORY, NATIONAL HERITAGE SITES, SUSTAINABLE PROCESSES, A CIVILIZATION, A NATIONAL OR ETHNIC CULTURE, CITIZENSHIP

PERSONAL

A BREAD, A HOUSE, CLOTHES, A COMPUTER, VEGETABLES, A VACATION, BEING A FATHER/MOTHER/FRIEND/ARTI ST/COLLEAGUE/SCIENTIST, EXPERIENCING AUTONOMY, HAVING SKILLS, MASTERING A CRAFT, GETTING ADVICE, A HAIRCUT, THERAPY, A LESSON

SOCIAL

FRIENDSHIP, RELATIONSHIPS OF ALL KINDS, A COMMUNITY, A NEIGHBORHOOD, A CLUB, A COLLEGIAL ATMOSPHERE, A WORKING ENVIRONMENT, A CREATIVE ENVIRONMENT, EXPERIENCING COZINESS, A TRIBE, A GANG, EXPERIENCING TRUST/ LOYALTY/ RECOGNITION/ FAME/ REPUTATION/ STATUS/

Diagram 6-2 Four domains of (shared) goods

able to contribute, they rather should focus their energy and effort to get people to contribute somehow. They should ask themselves how to stimulate people to talk about what they have experienced, how it will be part of their life, as a shared good that they cherish. They then should develop a strategy that people are willing to contribute to financially or with their time and effort. It is in that way that they realize the values of their venue, rather than by selling tickets.

Intrinsic and extrinsic values of art

How about the **intrinsic** and **extrinsic** values of art? I touched on the subject in the previous chapter and announced that I was in need of other concepts to clarify the distinction. The main concepts that I needed are those of art as a shared practice, as a conversation, as a practice. Some values are intrinsic to the practice, in the sense that they have a meaning only within the practice that is art. You need to be in the conversation in order to appreciate those values or qualities. (The next chapter picks up this point and develops it.)

The conversation that is art is also good for all kinds of other practices. It can be good for edifying people, for strengthening communities, for national identity, for the work ethics in a company, for love, for a spiritual experience maybe. In all those cases art realizes values of other goods or practices, that is, external to its own practice. That is why they are called its extrinsic values.

Let me collect the arguments that warrant the statement that art is not for sale:

- The knowledge about art is shared, and has to be shared in order to be useful.

- The knowledge will be alive and active only if it is sustained in a conversation.

- The conversation is limited in the sense it is generated within a limited but usually not very well defined group of people.

- The conversation is owned by those who participate in it.

- Ownership does not imply economic rights like the right to sell, but rather social rights like membership, status, recognition and the respect of other participants.

- To participants the conversation is a good from which they benefit.

- Participants contribute to the conversation when they participate in it somehow.

- They "produce" the conversation jointly with other participants.

- "Consuming" the conversation, in the sense of drawing on—can also signify a production of—or contribution to the conversation.

- Intrinsic values are those values that are to be valorized within and by the practice that is art. Extrinsic are those values that the arts valorize for other practices.

When in the standard economic perspective artists who forsake an income in order to practice their art—who seem selfless in an unaccountable way—the identification of art as a conversation, or a commons, makes us realize that they gain a sense of ownership of the conversation with their sacrifices. In exchange for their generous gifts they gain membership and status as an artist, and that is apparently worth a great deal to them. But it should also be clear, that their work can only come alive when others are willing to participate and contribute to it. For art is not of the artists and it is also not of those who buy art objects. Art becomes art by being shared as art.

The life of goods
The example of art alludes to another characteristic of goods: they have a life (Appadurai, 1988). They come about in (co-)production, they are shared, other people join, and they may change hands by means of a transaction.

Where standard economics attempts to capture it all with the moments of production, distribution and consumption, the value based approach alerts us to the complexity of the processes and practices that constitute those moments. What indeed is consumption of an artwork, or an eggplant for that matter? One needs to know what to do with either one. Chewing on the eggplant just purchased is not consuming it. Cooking it with some kind of recipe works better. And then the question remains, with who will the dish be shared and with what kind of conversation. Likewise, buying an artwork is not consuming it, contrary to what is suggested in standard economic accounts.

The value of a good will be influenced by what happens in its life. When an artwork is sold at a high price at one point in its life, its life will be affected by that event. Sometimes its artistic value will be appreciated more because of the high price. In that case we speak of the **crowding in** of artistic value because of the high price. However, it is also possible that the artistic value will be appreciated less if insiders consider the artwork to have been commercialized by the high price and lose interest. Then the artistic value is **crowded out** (Frey & Oberholzer-Gee, 1997).

Contested commodities
It has been pointed out that various goods are ruled out for a commercial transaction (Walzer, 1983). Examples include body parts (like kidneys and

wombs), votes and children. Buying and selling of such goods would be immoral. The take away is the insight that markets are limited, that not all goods are to be commodified.

This chapter aimed to demonstrate that the most important goods cannot be commodified because they can only be acquired by means of contribution and have to be shared with others. The key insight is that the claim that all goods in our financialized world are getting commodified is a gross exaggeration.

Then again, body parts, votes and children are potential commodities because they can be priced and exchanged for a monetary amount. The ban on their exchange betrays a valuation, a condemnation of highlighting the instrumental values of such goods. Such condemnation is cultural. At other times and still in some parts of the world, pricing children is accepted practice, and so is buying votes and selling one's kidney or renting out one's womb for a price.

Why cooperative and social behavior is normal and selfish behavior less so
Listen to standard economists and you start to believe that we are all selfish people who are always out for personal gain. Even the warm, compassionate person turns through the glasses of standard economists into someone who is simply incorporating the utility of others into her own and subsequently tries to maximize her personal utility, just like every other normal egoistic person does. From a standard economic perspective, cooperative and compassionate behavior is an anomaly that is hard to account for.

Cooperative behavior becomes normal and easy to account for when we bring shared goods into the picture. In striving for a good life, people need to make contributions to a range of shared goods. They contribute to their family, to their friendships and show social behavior in order to sustain "trust," "collegiality" and other shared goods. In addition they participate in or contribute to one commons or another. Scientists will go out of their way to participate in and contribute to the commons that is their discipline; so do musicians, actors and visual artists. Furthermore, people make great sacrifices to be part of a religious practice, for example by becoming a monk, by investing a great deal of time, or by donating large sums of money. All this shows up as social and cooperative behavior. It is social because it is meant to realize a social or societal good.

Whereas standard economists are puzzled by so-called altruistic behavior, in the value based approach much of such behavior is understood as valorizing certain values by contributing to a shared good. Soldiers who are willing to sacrifice their life, do so because they want to do their part in sustaining "democracy," "freedom," "my people," "my nation" or whatever value they see realized in the territory or nation that they fight for. People who give up a career for the sake of assisting poor people contribute to the societal good "solidarity" or "justice."

The standard economic perspective is blind for social behavior because it only distinguishes private and collective goods. It is for this reason that it conveys the impression that people are mainly self-interested and inclined to free ride when and where they can. And sure enough, herdsmen may overgraze the common grazing ground and factory owners will pollute the air when they can. Then again, skilled people contribute to the development of open source software, correct entries in Wikipedia, join local political parties, serve on boards of sport clubs, volunteer as teachers in homework classes, organize neighborhood feasts and join the church choir. British and Japanese people queue at stops of public transport and Japanese people will not even consider dropping a cigarette butt in a public space. Social behavior is quite normal and that is because shared and common goods are common. They even make up a big part of our daily activities.

What motivates social behavior is a sense of ownership, to be able to say that the commons or a shared good is "mine" or "ours." The more intensely ownership is experienced, the greater the sacrifices people are willing to make.

Asocial behavior would be the shirking of social responsibilities. People may deny shared ownership to justify not contributing. Or they may think that they get away with asocial behavior. Whether or not they do, depends on qualities of the social environment in which they operate. The correction will be social and will come in the form of disapproval and social exclusion. American culture is such that people are frequently asked what they do for the common good. Having answered a few times "nothing at all" may be enough of an incentive to donate a sum to a good cause or join a board of a social or cultural organization. Most cultures reward social behavior by awarding distinction or reputation. The Dutch King hands out medals.

More importantly, ownership of social goods and being part of a commons give satisfaction and add to a sense of a good life. As we noted earlier, people mention shared goods as their most precious possessions. Realizing such goods must feel good. And the realization is only possible—so we found out—by contributing and participating, that is to say, by social behavior.

Here *phronesis* operates, too. We need to weigh the value of one good against another and we need to figure out how much effort is needed to sustain a sufficient sense of ownership. We can sacrifice too much, or too little. How much effort do we need to invest in order to sustain the respect and love of the others? There are trade-offs. When scholars put more energy into family life, they can contribute less to the commons of science and, in doing so, may lose out in terms of reputation and satisfaction as scholars. They have to weigh their options, may even make some implicit or explicit calculations, yet are cooperating and contributing either way. That is, they have to take others in the commons into account in order to know whether what they do constitutes a contribution.

To repeat: private and collective goods are instrumental

All this does not mean that the notions of private goods and collective goods, and the exchange in market places are of no consequence. The buying and selling of art objects, the pricing of paintings, the attribution of property rights, the selling of tickets, the claims and challenges of authenticity, they are all instrumental for the realization of good art. It is good that economists and legal scholars pay attention to that instrumental part of the world of arts. However, that instrumental side is just that: it is instrumental. Most important for the realization of the values of art are the conversations, or the commons, that constitute art. Most relevant is the way art is realized as a shared good. And that is not done by buying art, but by contributing to art.

CHAPTER 7

THE GOODS TO STRIVE FOR ARE OUR IDEALS

"I see us free, therefore, to return to some of the most sure and certain principles of religion and traditional virtue—that avarice is a vice, that the exaction of usury is a misdemeanor, and the love of money is detestable, that those walk most truly in the paths of virtue and sane wisdom who take least thought for the morrow. We shall once more value ends above means and prefer the good to the useful. We shall honor those who teach us how to pluck the hour and the day virtuously and well, the delightful people who are capable of taking direct enjoyment in things, the lilies of the field who toil not, neither do they spin."
(Keynes, 1963, pp. 371-372)

Keynes is a great economist. And he is a great writer to boot. His writings certainly belong to the sources that have inspired me in the current inquiry. He has led me to think about economics as a moral science, as a science that studies the realization of values. In the citation above, he appeals to "the most sure and certain principles of religion and traditional virtue" and longs for the day that we will "value ends over means." More than 60 years later the time has arrived to focus on the ends, or the goods that we are seeking.

In the preceding chapters we have already taken big steps in the right direction. The first step was to recognize that culture, or the content, is what our lives, organizations and societies are about. Income, production, wealth, profits and commodities are all instrumental. Culture is about values. We concluded, therefore that our actions and those of the organization and societies of which we are a part, are all about the realization of values.

In order to make values real we buy, receive or contribute to goods of all kinds. So we are privy to "conversations", "relationships," "public spaces," "knowledge of all kinds," "arts of all sorts" and a wide range of commodities. The questions that we must now face are: "what are all these goods good for in the end?" and "what purpose or end do they serve?"

The questions address the claim of Aristotle that all our activities are directed at a particular good (see chapter 1). In the current instrumental-ist mindset, the knee jerk reaction to the question is that the good to which Aristotle is referring is subjective and impossible to define. How could we possibly know? What you are striving for is your thing. I have my thing. End of discussion.

In the instrumentalist mode, this conclusion would justify the focus on the means, like economic growth, profit and such. I am not sure where the post-modernist conclusion takes us, other than to the realization that everything is complex. I propose instead that we take on the challenge to explore the goods that people strive for in order to be concrete and articulate what they might mean. It cannot be done, you say? Let's find out, shall we?

Aristotle takes us beyond the Maslow pyramid

The exploration starts with the presumption that some values are more impor-tant than others and that some goods or practices are worth more than others. Values and goods have a hierarchy.

One good leads to another, one good serves another. Money is good for all kinds of things, things like a car or a yacht. A car is good for all kinds of things, and so is a yacht. When a car or a yacht is good for impressing peo-ple than that must be good for something else, like self-esteem. Self-esteem is more important than the recognition of other people. It is a higher value. The question then is whether self-esteem is needed to realize an even higher or more important value.

Most goods and values are instrumental in the sense that their realization serves other goods and values. We want to be honest, courageous and loving as a means to some end. We acquire food, a house or a theatre ticket for other purposes than for the possession of such goods. We own a house in order to be able to create a home. The house is an instrument for the attainment of our goal, i.e. a (good) home. But the home in turn may be good for something else, like love and care. The food is good for a family dinner and a ticket is good for access and for a special experience. Aristotle suggests that we look for, or be conscious of, the ulterior purpose of whatever we do.

When I discuss these issues in seminars or lectures, it is inevitable that people associate what I am explaining with the Maslow pyramid. It is the hierarchy that they are reminded of. However, Maslow evokes a hierarchy of needs, not a hierarchy of values (Maslow, 1954). Starting at the founda-tion with basic needs such as food and shelter, we move up the pyramid by way of the needs for safety, social needs, the personal need of self-esteem to the ultimate need of self-actualization. The pyramid suggests that self-actual-ization is the ultimate. This framing must have had a great influence—I can only dream of having the impact that Maslow has had. Even students are influenced by it, so I learn in my classes. That is to say, they refer to Maslow. Whether they apply it in their daily lives, is another matter. I usually try to unsettle them with a few questions.

My questions are: "what does self-actualization mean?" and "When do I actualize myself?" The questions usually do not get any kind of answer. The discussion ends here. Self-actualization it is. But is it? If self-actualization implies the realization of some values or goods, surely we need to know those values and goods in order to be able to identify the possibility of self-actualization.

The same follow up question can be posed when people proclaim that they are seeking "authenticity," "personal growth," "utility" or "happiness" when asked about their goals in life. Even though those terms tend to make an impression on audiences, they are empty terms. They do not tell us for what goods or values they stand. An Adolf Hitler may have been authentic and happy; he may have actualized himself and may have experienced personal growth, but I doubt that people have a life like his in mind when they use these terms.

Aristotle presents a so-called teleological perspective on human action. We humans do things with a *telos*, or purpose. Whether we are chatting away, meandering, goofing off or playing a game, there is some purpose lurking somewhere. Maybe we are seeking company, or relaxing in order to gather the courage to begin an important task. Or perhaps we are engaged in a practice that is important to us in and of itself. The telos is the answer to the repeated question "what is it (the practice, action or good) good for?" The final answer is an expression of the ultimate meaning of actions and of lives.

The instrumentalist thinkers pur sang, standard economists, point at utility and welfare as the purposes of what we do. So apparently we as consumers are seeking the maximization of utility, or happiness, for that is considered to be a synonym. However, "utility" is an abstract notion with no content. If we answer the probing question each time with: "it adds to my total utility," then the answer becomes meaningless. Even if we add the notion of happiness, we do not say a great deal more. Am I going to a Shakespeare play because that adds to my utility and makes me a little happier? I have actually no idea myself if it will make me happier. Maybe I will be disappointed. Maybe Shakespeare will depress me with his somber message.

No, I rather think that I go because of values that I hold. To make those values real, I need to bring about goods, as we saw in the previous chapter. Some goods mean more to me than others. So you see me going to a Shakespeare play one evening rather than hanging out at home or working on this book. In that way, I make an effort to realize qualities that are important to me.

The same problem arises with "welfare" as a purpose. If it is the outcome of adding up all individual utilities, it is not only vague but also meaningless. If welfare consists of all those goods, the value of which can be counted in monetary terms, we still have to answer the question of what all those goods are good for. When we try to answer that question we inevitably end up with goods that cannot be quantified.

The teleological perspective that Aristotle invites us to take, encourages us to be explicit about our most important values and consequently about the goods to strive for in order to realize those values. The question to ask, then, is what is what you do good for? Another way of putting the question is "What are your ideals?" Or: "What is your contribution?" "To which end do you seek to contribute?" Even a simple "Why?" could do the trick. All of these questions are asking for the telos.

I have been asking these questions during the last few years whenever I get a chance. I pose them to leaders of artistic organizations, to bankers, to civil servants, to colleagues, to friends and to students. The question also came up during a session with the partners of a law firm.

Resistance at a law firm

It was Klaas van Egmond that posed the question, once a leading figure on environmental issues in the Netherlands, and now a professor. His actual question was: "What are you here on Earth for?" He used his entire body to add an exclamation mark to this question. The partners of the law firm, who had gathered to reflect on their business, looked at him as if he came from Mars. They were not used to being addressed in this way. Lawyers are known to resist discussions of their values and to object to big questions. Van Egmond repeated the question.

I know these partners quite well. I collaborated in a Ph.D. research into the cultural capital of the firm. My Ph.D. student and I already had figured out that this law firm struggled with what we had identified as a creativity gap. The partners sought more intellectual challenge and wanted more inspiring work than what they experienced. That did not surprise us. It is quite well known that firms of professionals grapple with the creativity issue. Yet what did surprise us, was that they were not really interested in dealing with the problem (or "challenge" as they prefer to call it). They were only interested in knowing how to increase their profit share. (As is common in law firms the partners receive equal shares of the total profit, regardless of the individual contributions everyone makes.) Each time we turned the conversation to some topic or another—the lack of cooperation, the need for more feedback, the improvement of acquisition, social responsibility or their childish behavior—their faces would darken after a while and the same question would pop up: how is this going to increase our profit share?

Before Van Egmond put his question to them, I had tried the same by asking what is most important to them. One of them responded without hesitation: my profit share. Others nodded. Nobody took exception. As I have explained before, profit cannot be an ultimate goal. It is certainly not what anyone is here on earth for. The question to ask is: what is the profit share good for? If the answer is "more profit" the next question is: what is more profit good for? This probing did not work, though. They diverted the question, as lawyers are trained to do.

We did not give up; we tried all kinds of strategies. We had them watch *The Return*, a Russian movie (by the director Andrej Zvjagintsev) about a father who goes on a trip with his two sons he has not been with before. The movie tells what it takes for the father to realize what the values of fatherhood are and, for the boys, what it is to be a son. The ending is dramatic and got them silent for a while. But when we tried to discuss the meanings, some of them objected. This is not a classroom, they pointed out. I pushed on and found out that most of them had identified with the rebellious youngest boy in the movie. How about the father? Isn't that the role they have in their firm? Isn't their problem—sorry, challenge—that they need to figure out what it means to have a leading role and to take on the responsibilities that resemble those of the father in the movie?

I asked them to read Aristotle, on the goods to strive for and on the virtues. The discussion was interesting, but I was not sure that it changed anything for them. We organized feedback sessions; those seemed to work. They especially appreciated to hear from colleagues about their strong points. And then we did a field exercise: we put them in cold weather in leaky tents with basic Dutch food to get them to tell their story. How did they become lawyers?

At first I was confused. Some spoke of how the law had struck them and how the law continued to fascinate them. But most had wanted to do something else and ended up studying law by accident or for lack of a better alternative. A couple even detested the law and found it boring. How would these latter people survive in the law, I asked myself? But as I listened to their stories, it struck me that they were lawyers for different reasons. Some of them were in it for the law. They were fascinated with the law and wanted to contribute to its advancement. A few were into the law for the excitement; they were like sportsmen who do everything they can to win, a case in their case. Most of these lawyers, however, respond to the archetype of the helper: they derive satisfaction from being able to help people in distress. They want to see their client satisfied with their advice.

Even while I doubt that we are at the end of the road with these answers, the experience convinced me that probing does get us closer to the ultimate goal. Keep probing is the motto. Keep asking what is "helping" or "winning" good for. Needless to add, profit is not an answer.

The goods to strive for embody the most important values

Is helping people a good in and of itself? What is the helping good for? What is the good that "winning" or "personal growth" —to take another frequently mentioned goal—good for? The probing has to continue. How far can we get?

I was visiting a Brazilian colleague and was introduced to his 14-year-old son. The kid looked pretty composed so I thought "what the heck" and asked him what was most important to him. He was quick with his answer: "money, history and my family." His father was sitting right there, so I let the "family" for what it was. His father was clearly pleased with that part of the answer. How about history? Well, he really enjoyed the subject and would want to do more with it. How about the money? What is that good for? "Oh, then I can travel," he replied. "So, it's not about the money, but about traveling," I continued. "And what is the travel good for?" "To meet different people." "Oh, so it's not about traveling per se, but about meeting different people." For a 14 year old this seemed good enough. We had moved already two steps away from the instrumental value that money held for him.

Another example: How about the goods that a school is to strive for? Does a school have ideals? I tried to determine them with teachers and directors of a high school. The directors told me that the good that they aim for is the satisfaction of their pupils. "And that of the parents," someone added with the approval of others. I began probing. How about the teachers? What might be the good they are striving for? They agreed with their directors that it is the satisfaction of the pupils and their parents. I suspected that they had previously done a workshop in marketing or something like that. Everything they did was directed at their pupils. I kept probing.

I offered alternatives. How about good teaching as a good in and of itself? After all, Aristotle mentions an activity as a possible good. The previous chapter identified practices as a good. Might a school be about great teaching? Is the practice of good teaching something to strive for? The directors shifted in their chairs, but I saw some teachers lighting up at the suggestion.

How about being a good school? Could it be that a school is a good in and of itself? (When directors start speaking of their school as a business, with parents and their kids as customers and with diplomas as its product, I am inclined to ask everyone to take a deep breath. Might a school not be just that: a school?) Maybe not, but what if we think of learning as a goal in and of itself? The school could be considered contributing to that goal.

But what is the learning good for? I suspected that I lost the majority of the teachers at this point. There were no reactions anymore. I had to do the probing myself. Might there be an ulterior purpose? Might it be that a school can aim high, and even should do so? Might it be that a good school contributes to the shaping of a good society, by empowering its students? And how about the idea that the school stands for the civilization? After all, with the help of the teachers, students get acquainted with all kinds of knowledge, works and traditions that our civilization has brought forth.

By then I had lost most of them. Would it make a difference, I wondered afterwards, with just a few interested teachers, to have civilization as a good to strive for? Would a shared awareness of that as a good affect the choices that the directors and teachers make? Would it affect the curriculum? We guessed that it would.

I am inclined to forgive the partners of the law firm for not realizing their goals. They can claim, after all, that they are just seeking profit. Yet, even they are in need of goals that go beyond the profit, so we found out. Yet it came as a surprise to me to discover that people of idealistic organizations also have difficulty articulating the goods that they strive for or the contribution that they seek. You would expect that the so-called nonprofits are clear about their goals, as they need to make clear what it is they strive for if it is not profit. They often are not. In the literature on the non-profit sector the question about the goal is a critical one. Economists see a goal as something that can be maximized in order to construct their models. Yet what non-profits are maximizing remains unclear. Is a theatre maximizing the number of seats filled? Is a theatre group maximizing attention? See for example Netzer, *Non-profit organizations* and Drucker, *Managing the Non-Profit Organization* (Netzer, 2011; Drucker, 1992).

In a project that is directed at the evaluation of theatre groups, I needed to find out the goals of a theatre group. What is the theatre group after? Making great theatre, maybe? So what? What is that good for? Once the probing begins, other possible goods quickly pop up. One theatre group I worked with wants to sustain the rich tradition of Dutch theatre. Another theatre maker ended up with justice as the good to which she wanted to contribute in the end. Very often theatre groups are seeking to challenge their audience. They are like missionaries seeking out lost souls to show them how much watching their plays can mean to them. The answer visibly pleases them. However, it provokes the inevitable follow-up question: what is the challenge good for? The answer is not obvious. Disturbing and shocking people or changing their minds are not activities that are good in and of themselves. Maybe the makers will be pleased to see their visitors shocked and disturbed for the remainder of their lives after having watched their play, but I doubt that they will get much support if that is the intended purpose. They must have something else as the contribution that they want to make in the end.

As a rule, cultural organizations want to do more than only sustain their art; they seek to bring about change in their art form—to do something that has not been done before—and they also seek to change the valuations of certain stakeholders (such as adolescents and students) by seducing them to appreciate something that they did not want to see or recognize before attending. Such organizations have lofty goals. Suggesting that they are about maximizing the number of tickets sold or the size of sponsor deals does not do justice to what they are striving for. Granted, they need to be specific about those goals also, especially when they want to get people to make donations or to contribute somehow. They furthermore need to be clear on their goals, or the most important qualities that they want to realize, in order to determine whether they are doing well, or not. Otherwise they risk that an evaluation focuses on instrumental values such as the number of performances, the number of visitors, or the percentage of total income that is earned income.

The probing for the goods to strive for also applies to persons, or agents, as economists are used to calling persons. Again, they may be striving to realize all kinds of goods. They may seek having a good family, and they may seek a personal good like dexterity. People like you and I like to do things we are good at. A musician wants to play well, an actor wants to act well, and a teacher wants to teach well. They all may seek to make contributions to something greater, like music, theatre, or education. People join political parties in order to participate in the striving for a good society.

I interrupted my writing to get a cup of tea, have a bite to eat, let out the dog, and fetch the newspaper. There it was on the front page: Nelson Mandela had died. This South African, black freedom fighter had become a living legend. People name him, along with Gandhi, when they are asked to name inspiring and good people. Mandela and Gandhi are both examples of individuals worthy of admiration for their goodness. I feel the same way about them, even if I am conscious of their less admirable traits. They stand for something important for me, too.

I read the coverage of the story and then the famous speech of his that he made during the trial that got him convicted to imprisonment for life. Then it struck me. This is what he said:

> *"I have fought against white domination, and I have fought against black domination. I have cherished the ideal of a democratic and free society in which all persons will live together in harmony and with equal opportunities. It is an ideal which I hope to live for and to see realized. But my Lord, if needs be, it is an ideal for which I am prepared to die."*
> *(Mandela, 1964)*

And this is what I wanted to express here: the importance of articulating one's ideals and to do so with conviction and passion. That is what Mandela did at the moment he was facing a life in prison or execution. His ideals of a democratic and free society, of a society in harmony, express the goods to which he was dedicated, to which he wanted to contribute everything in his power, and for which he even was willing to sacrifice his life.

Sometimes I ask myself and my students the question: what would we be willing to sacrifice our lives for? Is there an ideal for which I would give my life? Would a theatre maker give up his life in order to make his art—as the celebrated director Andrei Tarkovsky did when he decided to shoot his famous movie "Stalker" in a seriously polluted area? (He, his wife and the main actor died of the same lung cancer.)

I realized that I would have ideals to die for when I was walking with my family in the mountains of Montana the day after a bear had attacked a couple. What would we do if we ran into that bear? Running would be pointless, as would climbing in a tree. We agreed that we would have to lie down. The youngest would go first, on top of her the next child, then the next one, and then my wife. Guess who would have to use his big body to protect them all? That was the idea. It was me who launched it and it felt right. What I would have done in reality, we may never know. Yet I realized then that some "goods" are more important than my own life. They still are. (Although would I be willing to risk imprisonment or the intellectual death penalty that comes in the form of derision or, worse, indifference? I'm not sure at this point.)

Doing the right thing is presumably what makes people feel good about themselves and what is worthy of respect and admiration. When the economist wants to know how to model the striving for goods, I give up. Then again, why would that be the thing to do? Would a model help in figuring out what the right thing is to do? Is modeling the right thing to do when we want to make sense of the cultural sector? In the next chapter I will address the issue in more detail. The desire to do the right thing is what makes people and organizations look for the goods they are striving to realize.

During a class discussion a student pointed out that the question about what he would die for, disturbed him. People risk their lives for stupid reasons. Giving up your life for some idea, may be stupid, too. I sensed that he was speaking from experience. The student next to him helped me out. He suggested that the better question to ask is: "what are we living for?" The class gave a sigh of relief; we were back to the question with which we started: "what are we here on earth living for?"

We agreed though that living for one's ideals may require sacrifices. The first student agreed with the term "sacrifice."

(Economists may respond by pointing to the concept of welfare, or that of capabilities. They may be right in the sense that these concepts have a function in determining the right policy—although how that actually works is far from obvious—but they do little to help people like you and me or organizations such as a museum or a theatre company in determining what to do.)

So it is about purpose, telos or ideals.

A friend of mine, who practices Zen, keeps telling me that the purpose is not to have a purpose. His idea of a good life is to let go, to drop goals and desires. His remarks have an influence on me. The influence gets even stronger when I am reading Zhuangzi, Lao Tzu, and other great eastern thinkers, or the western mystic Eckhart or philosophers like Kierkegaard. In the end my friend is right. When we keep probing and press on asking "so what?" and "what for?" we all probably end up with the insight of wise gurus such as Buddha and Jesus.

In the meantime I have to teach classes, father my children, enter discussions about doing the right thing and I am doing so with a clear purpose, and with ideals in mind. I do need my moments of letting go, of silence and peace, of nothing. What are these good for? In my case, I still need those moments in order to gather strength to do the right thing, such as fathering and teaching well. Mandela needed to state his ideals to keep his faith during his time in prison and afterwards to be a leader in South Africa's time of transition. Even in the quest for a state without aim and without ego, I detect an ideal, a striving of some sort. It gets my friend to meditate, for example, and to have sessions with Zen masters.

The practice of Zen is helpful to keep in mind when we look for the qualities and goods that are most important to us. It is not said that the purpose is something out there, some dot on the horizon, something that we have to reach out for and never will grab. The purposes can also be a practice in which we are involved, like the practice of Zen, or the practice of art. The purpose is then intrinsic, that is to say, intrinsic in that practice.

Even when people are unaware of the purposes in their lives and organizations, it does not mean that they act without purpose or ideals. In a modern instrumentalist mindset there is no need to articulate the purpose or ideal. As Charles Taylor points out, the consequences of an instrumentalist frame is that we are allowed to eschew naming our objectives (Taylor, 1991). He calls it the ethics of inarticulacy (Taylor, 1989). Instrumentalist thinking is satisfied with goals like welfare, profit, or happiness. People of a commercial organization will say that profit maximization is their aim. When asked the question: "what is profit good for?" they will answer: "for the sustainability of the organization." The inevitable next question is "what is *that* good for?" And that may prod people to become aware of what is most important to them, of their ideals, of their most important practices.

The prodding may be thwarted by a lack of awareness; it may evoke resistance. People are good at discussing processes, targets, results, returns, means and instruments and not good at all at pointing out what their lives and their actions are all about, what they are good for. The lack of awareness of the ideals that people strive for shows in the mission statements of organizations. Usually they state what they do, or would like to do. They do not state what they do it for, what the intended contribution, or the goal is. The mission of a quite well known museum reads: "to show great art." That makes clear what it is doing. The question remains: "What is that good for?" Donors, for example, would like to know the answer. Mission statements have to articulate the ideals of the organization, the contributions it seeks to make.

The importance of articulating the goods or ideals to strive for

For the ancient Greeks honor was a good to strive for. Homer made that ideal patently clear in his epic poem about the battle between the Greeks and the Trojans. It was an ideal to die for! Plato wrote in the Republic: "in the world of knowledge the idea of good appears last of all, and is seen [...] to be the universal author of all things beautiful and right" (Plato & Jowett, 1941). In the Thomist tradition, that ideal became the life of the righteous. The Christian culture added also the ideal of salvation or entry into the paradise of God as the aim of the life of the righteous. The Buddha had articulated the ideal as enlightenment.

Questions linger. What is honor good for? What are salvation and enlightenment good for?

Taylor argues that those of us living now, too, are in need of articulating the goods to strive for: "articulation is a necessary condition of adhesion; without it, these goods are not even an option" (Taylor, 1989, p. 53). He also states: "A vision of the good becomes available for the people of a given culture through being given expression in some manner" (Taylor, 1989, p. 91). He thinks that if forced, we can articulate some of those goods. In the context of Western civilization we would come to articulate goods like

- freedom,
- inner depth,
- nature as source of good,
- authenticity and individualism,
- benevolence, and
- ordinary life. (Taylor, 1991)

All these strike a chord with me. Do they do so with you? "Ordinary life" may seem a strange item in this list, but when I think of the themes in the visual arts (Titian, Rembrandt, Vermeer and so on) from around the 1600s, it begins to make sense. And don't we tend to celebrate ordinary life nowadays? In my own country, the Netherlands, the dedication to ordinary life has a religious character, indeed. Authors who depict ordinary lives do well. With Keynes in mind, I recall the early 20th century philosopher G.E. Moore, who apparently influenced Keynes with his claim that the highest goods to strive for are personal relations and the contemplation of beauty. Personal relations are a big part of ordinary life.

Taylor calls the special goods *hypergoods*. They are goods that "not only are incomparably more important than others but provide the standpoint from which these must be weighed, judged, decided about." (Taylor, 1989, p. 63) The Roman orator, politician and philosopher Cicero coined the notion of the *summum bonum* to indicate the end that is an end in itself (Cicero & Gardner, 1958). In the term that I used to characterize the process of *phronesis* (see chapter 4), these goods are the *ideals* that people, organizations and societies strive for.

But is authenticity such a good? When are we authentic? And when are we benevolent? How would we determine that we are free? Taylor's list is, as he himself recognizes, not very helpful. Taylor sees its shortcomings, its vagueness, as symptomatic for the prevalence of the instrumentalist mindset. It would stand in the way of a clear view on the goods that people, organizations or nations strive for.

Getting to articulate the goods: some exercises.

Naming the ideals is difficult. That should be clear by now. Whether I am talking with lawyers, people of cultural organizations or people in general (economists are another matter), they may agree that the striving is for some ulterior goods, but when I ask what those goods might be, a deafening silence invariably follows. I am sympathetic as I experienced difficulties myself in naming the goods I am striving for.

In the case of individuals, it helps to ask what is really important to them. The question that I like to pose to people is: "What is your most valuable possession?" The answers are a good indication of the goods they strive for but quite often people still point at something instrumental like "health." Health is like money: it is good for all kinds of things but we do not live in order to be healthy. The question remains: "what is your health good for?" The suggestion is that being healthy enables us to do things that are important for us, to realize our real goals, that is.

However, also asking for the most valuable possessions provides only partial answers. People will most often mention their children (usually accompanied with the question "Can I call them a possession?"), their freedom, their mind, or their health. Is that all? How about their faith (for those with a faith), their society or their talents?

Another way to get an inkling of the ultimate goods is to ask people to design and articulate their utopia, or their ideal world. Our utopia tells us something about what we like to think away, or suppress, and what we long for. When my students articulate a world in which everyone loves each other or a world of tranquility and peace, they express their anxiety about the constant exposure to an abundance of information and the endless interaction by means of the social media.

I once used the latter exercise in a leadership program for people of a technical university. It had been difficult to get them to talk about their ultimate goods. When I spoke of transcendental goods they looked at me helplessly. They really had no idea what transcendental meant, and even less of a clue what transcendental goal they could be pursuing. They were too down to earth to be able to imagine anything transcendental.

When they shared their utopias I was struck by a feature that they almost all had in common. All their utopias had scientific research as a core activity. One professor of aviation technology had imagined a world of a small organization that was all about scientific research. The scientists constituted the core; everyone else was subservient to the goal of scientific research, including the managers and students. The latter were all curious and eager to learn from the scientists. There would be no grading of exams, as that would distract from the real work. Students would be like apprentices. Another colleague spoke of the perfect machine that would solve all his problems.

It suddenly occurred to me that absolute knowledge, or truth, is the transcendental good that these people are striving for. Even though their work is intended to have practical applications, it is the pursuit of some absolute truth or another, of the perfect machine, of the perfect solution to a technical problem, which is the highest good to them. Pursuit of that good accounts for the passion and dedication that characterizes their work.

Praxes are practices to strive for
Articulating merely a good to strive for may be too confining. At least, so I learned during the exercises. My Zen friend also already shared his hesitation. I see the point. After all, what do people mean to say when they identify "honor," "salvation" or "enlightenment" as the goods they strive for? What do craftspeople mean by saying that they want to be excellent craftspeople?

In the previous chapter I already suggested that the valorization of a good involves a practice or even multiple practices. Put differently, a practice stands for a good. In order to have a valuable friendship we do all kinds of things. The summation of all kinds of activities constitutes a friendship. Likewise, the striving for honor shows in all kinds of activities, like doing the right things and challenging, or even having a duel with people who have dishonored you. Striving for faith implies going to church, temple or mosque, meditating, praying, studying sacred texts and so on. Striving for truth requires endless hours spent in labs, at the library, in seminars, in the study at home and numerous conversations with colleagues. Striving for love calls for lots of relational work, doing good deeds, and battling one's ego. It is in the doing that the good is being realized. You do not have love, you do it.

I will call a practice that is directed at a good to strive for, at the realization of a hypergood, ultimate good, or summmum bonum, a *praxis*. That good is intrinsic to the praxis, generating intrinsic values. Of course, a praxis can be good for other things, for other values, but its defining characteristic is the ultimate good it stands for.

A praxis is a practice that contains the purpose in itself, and is, therefore, the good to strive for.

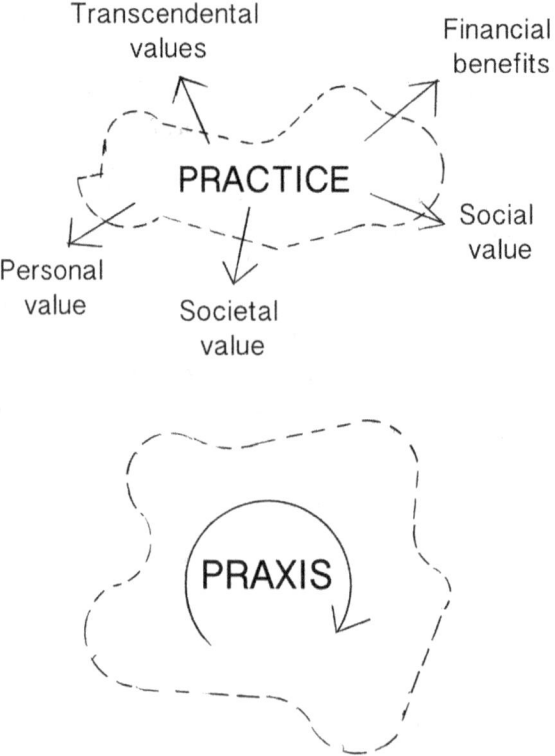

Diagram 7-1 From practices to praxes

Take the practice of excellent cello players, like Yo-Yo Ma, Mstislav Rostropovich or Jacqueline du Pré. Their play has delighted and moved many people; and it was good for generating an income for themselves and many others. Cello players play and do whatever is needed in order to play, including endless practicing, taking care of their body, listening to music, to other cello players playing, teaching and, yes, performing. Their playing cello becomes a praxis when the exercise of their craft, the perfection of the play, is a purpose in and of itself, regardless of the income. The true craftsman plays foremost for the purpose of playing right, regardless of the external effects (Sennett, 2008). Playing well, excelling in playing, is what gives the craftsman satisfaction. Craftsmanship is a praxis. So is religion, and science. Art, too, can be a praxis. And so might parenting be, I think. And teaching, ideally.

Thinking of praxes to strive for creates space for placing and identifying the goods to strive for. When engineers strive for the perfect machine, they do not need to define what that machine is like; they just have to recognize the range of activities that are geared to and constitute their praxis. Striving for the holy grail of whatever kind implies a certain range of activities, a practice that is a praxis because the ideal to strive for is inherent to it.

Four dimensions of goods to strive for

On the basis of endless exercises of this kind, I came to identify four dimensions of ultimate goods to strive for, or four praxes. The division concurs with the one I introduced earlier for the different kinds of values we hold and goods we possess. The diagram below provides a summary. The two dimensions on the top comprise lofty goods and praxes. They make for the grand gestures, the reaching out to the greater goods or the sacred goods. The two clusters at the bottom comprise the personal and the relational goods and praxes. The goods or praxes included are, so I postulate, are the ultimate answers to the question "What is this or that good for?"

The social domain is the lower right cluster. It comprises **social goods** to strive for or to contribute to. Social goods are usually concrete relationships and include a family, a relationship with one's children, a friendship, a close community and a strong team. In our striving we seek better qualities, as in a "better" family, a "better" relationship with the children, a "closer" community, and a "stronger" team. The goodness manifests itself in the realization of social values such as loyalty, collegiality, intimacy, coziness (to name a typical Dutch social good), status, social identity, membership of a club, recognition. A "good" family is a praxis with the "better" family as the good to strive for.

People, who say that their friendships and their children are most important to them, will do all kinds of things for the sake of these social goods. These goods must also be good in and of themselves in order to qualify as ultimate goods. If there still is a next answer to the question "what are they good for," then they are instrumental or subsidiary goods.

As social beings, social goods are common ultimate goods that people will name when they are being probed for their purposes. Although the idealist in me wants to continue probing, the pragmatist in me recognizes that social goods signify to numerous people ends in and of themselves. Maybe there is a good that having my children is good for, but that good is not what I need to consider. I would add that my desire is that my children will be happy and find a meaningful purpose in their life. I do not really care about what that purpose is, as long it is heartfelt.

Could a group of people, a community be a good in and of itself? Who am I to say? Who are you to say, for that matter? People tell me that they would do anything for a community to which they belong. Musicians who play together, care deeply for what they share, for their shared good, that is. They may be horrified at the suggestion that they need the group to distinguish themselves and to gain an income. They experience the group as an end in and of itself. As far as they are concerned, the probing stops at the group.

From Taylor's list of modern goods to strive for (see above) only "ordinary life" would qualify as a social good and even that categorization is not all too clear. He has missed personal relationships and, in particular, families.

The personal domain directs us to the **personal goods** that we as individuals can strive for. They are goods that are ends for their own sake. We may strive to be a good father or mother, a good friend, an excellent craftsman or professional, a great musician or surgeon, a wise or happy person or someone who is good at enjoying the good things in life or at helping or loving others. Being a good father or an excellent craftsman is a good since it requires effort to acquire the good and we risk losing it when we do not invest enough effort and attention. These goods may have a bearing on the social, societal and transcendental goods but they are personal because they are especially important for a person. Taylor lists inner depth, authenticity and individualism as personal goods. Maybe freedom could qualify as well if the freedom is strictly personal. Autonomy may be another term for such freedom. Experiencing autonomy could then be an ultimate good.

I would like to be a good father, a good spouse, a good teacher, a good intellectual, and I long for being a wise person. These are my personal goals because I do not share them with others. My wife appreciates my desire to be a good spouse and a good father but will say to you that my goals of being a good teacher and a good intellectual conflict with my wanting to be a good father and spouse. It is really a personal thing. My Zen friend tells me that his life is all about realizing inner freedom. I have difficulties imagining what that means but observe that he experiences this deeply. I myself observe that I do all kinds of things in order to realize these personal goals, and intense emotions are engendered by me either realizing or failing to realize these goals. When a lecture does not go right I usually feel lousy afterwards. And when a daughter tells me that I am a bad father, I feel terrible.

TRANSCENDENTAL GOODS OR PRAXIS

SEEKING THE TRUTH, BEAUTY, SALVATION, GRACE, ENLIGHTENMENT, ALL-LOVE (COMPASSION, AGAPE), SPIRITUAL FREEDOM, NOTHINGNESS, THE PATH (TAO), HARMONY, THE SUBLIME, FEELING WHOLE, ONE, EXPERIENCING GREAT ART, SACRED MUSIC, SEEKING THE PERFECT TECHNIQUE OR MATERIAL.

SOCIETAL GOODS OR PRAXIS

EXPERIENCING JUSTICE, LIBERTY, HARMONY, SOLIDARITY, PEACE, UNITY, DEMOCRACY, HIGH CIVILIZATION, COMPASSION.

PERSONAL GOODS OR PRAXIS

WISDOM, CRAFTSMANSHIP, PEACE OF MIND, AUTONOMY, BEING A GOOD FATHER/ MOTHER/ FRIEND/ LEADER.

SOCIAL GOODS OR PRAXIS

HAVING A GOOD FAMILY, BEING PART OF A STRONG/VITAL/INSPIRING/ SUPPORTING COMMUNITY

Diagram 7-2 Four domains of ultimate goods and praxes to strive for

Similarly, craftsmen derive the greatest satisfaction from exercising their skills well. My dentist derives great joy from getting my teeth right; the more difficult the job, the greater his satisfaction can be. Craftsmen have as a personal goal to develop their skills in such a way that they can be excellent craftsmen. An actor wants to act well, a musician wants to play at her best, and a director wants to direct a great piece of art. Excelling in one's craft is a praxis as the purpose is excelling.

Young people will say that something like having fun is their personal thing. But is it? I suspect that fun is rather something that they want to share with their friends, so I would call fun a social good. If so, fun cannot be a hyper or ultimate good no matter what people say. Then again, who am I to state so for another? A doctor, who was doing a course with me, resisted my pressing for his goods. He just wants to enjoy life and likes to eat well and spend good times with his family. At first I was taken aback. Then I wondered how he would be remembered by his children? Might it be as a man who was able to enjoy life? He thought so. Well, then enjoyment may be the personal good that he is striving for. (It would be a good goal for me, too, I realized.)

Could it be that the collection of personal goods that we are striving for, constitutes our identity? I will leave this question for now (but cannot resist implying that the answer is affirmative).

In the upper-right quadrant, you find the societal domain with the **societal goods** or **the common goods.** These are goods that large communities such as nations, or even humanity at large, have in common. People or organizations (like political parties and movements) can strive for world peace, justice, a sustainable environment or human rights and will do anything in their power to contribute to the realization of these goods. . When they experience peace, justice, a sustainable environment, or human rights, they can say that they have realized their ultimate good. Other people or organizations may want to contribute to societal goods such as "national identity," "patriotism," "democracy," "civilization," "political freedom," "equal rights" and "education." Taylor lists only benevolence as a societal good to strive for, although freedom could be included as well if understood as political freedom.

All such goods are different from social goods because they concern a society or the world. People do not need to know each other to share societal goods.

Artistic organizations are challenged to articulate the societal goods to which they seek to contribute when they apply for public funding. This proves not be easy. In the Netherlands, there was a period that they resorted to articulating the economic impact of their activities. But the economy is not a goal in and of itself; income and economic activity are instrumental to generate other goods. So the appeal to economic impact only suspends the question for the ultimate societal impact. Possible goals to strive for are a strong cultural quality of a society, or a rich civilization.

Politicians have the intent to contribute to societal goods, so are environmentalists, human rights advocates, soldiers, freedom fighters, and people who are conscious of being citizens.

The upper-left corner directs us to goods that transcend the social, the personal and the societal and are artistic, spiritual, cultural, scientific and other mental goods. I call them **transcendental goods** as they point to a metaphysical entity, to the mental space, to values that transcend the social, the societal and the personal. They are like the Holy Grail that we humans pursue without ever being able to get a hold of it. The search for meaning of life usually ends somewhere in this dimension.

Nature as a source of good, on the list of Taylor, could be thought of as a transcendental good if nature is a good in and of itself. But because nature is not a good to be realized as such, it might make more sense to think of it as a praxis, as all activities someone may undertake to experience nature, to be one with nature, to admire nature. This includes hiking, studying natural life and joining Green Peace. The same considerations apply to **cultural goods**, that is, goods with shared artistic, historical, or symbolic meanings. They are transcendental goods when they are good in and of themselves. You might say that in that case they have an intrinsic value. They constitute a conclusive answer to the repetitive question "what is this or that good for?" Cultural goods usually come about in practices that become praxes when they contain or generate the good to strive for.

In the end all probing gets us to name a transcendental good. Often such a good is not experienced as a goal to pursue. The experience of the transcendental dissolves all desire and makes each purpose purposeless. The lesson of Tao is that we are either on our path or not. It is not something we can aim for. The wise men and women will tell us to let go, to cease aiming, and to just be. Such way of being will show up as a practice, or praxis involving meditating, reflecting, being silent, showing compassion and so on.

I am experiencing myself a quest for spiritual meaning in my life, for the experience of the inner voice as I find them in the Deeds of Augustus and Etty Hillesum (a Jewish woman who accepted her fate of getting killed in the Holocaust and who wrote a most inspiring diary about her last years.) (Augustine, 1963; Hillesum, 1981). And I recognize the search for absolute Beauty and Truth in the work of artists and scientists. And when I read *The Chosen* by Chaim Potok, I recognize the total dedication of Talmudic scholars to the coming of the Redeemer, and to experience the divine light in everything and everyone. That dedication, realized at great expense and with major sacrifices, moves me to tears. So does the passion and dedication of Nelson Mandela, or those of a good craftsman or a good mother. You see: all this constitutes my transcendental praxis.

Priests, monks, nuns, imams dedicate their lives to the realization of transcendental goods. They do all they can, at least in principle, to contribute to the transcendental dimension in such a way that others can benefit. The same applies to some artists and scientists, musicians, healers, seers, gurus and so on.

Questions and issues
While writing and when laying out these four dimensions of goods to strive for, I am confronted with doubts, often my own, and with criticism, usually by others. I list these with my reflection.

- *No final truth here*
I have found these four dimensions useful to prod people to articulate their ideals, the goods to strive for. I still have to encounter a serious challenge of groupings. But I am far from sure that this is it, that these are the dimensions and that these are the only goods to choose from.

- *The probing can continue endlessly*
One objection that I often get is that with further probing, personal, social and societal goods may turn out to serve other goods anyway, and then especially so for transcendental goods. Indeed, I may wonder myself what having children is good for, or what social justice is good for. All these goods may be mere earthly distractions that dwarf by comparison to the importance of lofty pursuits such as Truth, Beauty, God's grace or Enlightenment.

I propose to be pragmatic in this. When people or organizations have a clear sense about the goods they are striving for, and feel satisfied with them as the final answer to the question "what is this or that good for?" then I would settle for such goods. Apparently, their pursuit provides guidance for daily activities.

Helpful may be the focus on praxes. When we can articulate a praxis, we may leave unsaid what the good is that such a praxis stands for.

- *No direct role for markets*
Ideals are not for sale and cannot be bought.

- *No direct role for states*
Ideals are not provided by states.

- There is no must involved
Nobody must define his or her ideals. There is no obligation. In some positions, in some situations articulating them can be a big help, for example when the position requires leadership.

- Articulation of the ultimate goods is therapeutic and edifying.
The therapeutic part is the questioning and the confusion that the questioning brings about. The edifying part is the offering of the four dimensions with the invitation to fill them in somehow, and the sense of direction that is the result. It works the same way when people in organizations undertake this exercise. It is basically the determination of the mission of the organization; the mission is the shared goal or intended contributions.

- Articulation of the ultimate goods can be instrumental, too.
Being able to articulate one's ideals or ultimate goods is good for the acquisition of funds. Donors respond to such an articulation.

- When the articulation of ultimate goods is merely instrumental, it is a lie.
When someone talks about love as his hypergood just to seduce another, he or she is dishonest. And when the people of an organization determine a mission for the reason that it sells well, they are lying to themselves and others.

- When you do not know what your contributions have been, just try to figure out what people would say about you at your funeral.
This is good question to ask yourself anyway.

- When you are not satisfied with your ideals or your contributions, you might reconsider what you are doing.

Appendix: the utopia exercise to determine the goods to strive for

By articulating your ideals first, then figuring out what you need to do to strive for those ideals (the design) and then doing so, you may improve your life! You may, for example, discover what satisfaction shared goods provide, or—as is certainly so for me—need to figure out which transcendental ideals are worth living for.

For that purpose I often apply the utopia exercise: *Articulate your Utopia*.

First I share a few utopias. I pick some elements from Moore's utopia, I tell about a Chinese utopia of a serene world with no change, I describe the utopia of Ayn Rand in *Atlas Shrugged* in which everyone is rational and honors quality and excellence, and I close with the utopian world of Julian Barnes in which he imagines what would happen should all our desires be met, immediately (see his *A History of the World in 10 1/2 Chapters*) (Barnes, 1989). I do this to tickle the fancy of the participants. I encourage them to use their fantasy and to radicalize the features that are important to them. So if they long for a world in which everyone loves each other, imagine a world in which everyone actually loves each other. How would that world look? What do those people do in case their interests clash? What if someone wants a world in which everyone is equal? Great, then imagine such a world. How do families look? In our world, inequalities begin with the assumption that the families in which people grow up are unequal. How to remedy that? How would the politics look? Would you have people be selected as governors in a lottery, as in Moore's Utopia. How is work arranged? How are the goods distributed? How about the role of the sciences and the arts? (In the Chinese utopia, there does not seem to be a role for them, in order to safeguard the serenity).

After these introductions I ask the participants to imagine their own utopia. I prod them to include issues such family life, work, distribution, politics, the arts and the sciences, the outside world, possible enemies and technology. And I insist that they illuminate their own role in their utopia (as many tend to forget all about themselves).

After they have designed their own utopia (that takes some time, and on occasion I make use of some time in between sessions), I make small groups of three or four people. I l ask each one describe his or her utopia and let the other two or three figure out what values and goals are becoming manifest in that utopia. What is most important for that person according to his or her utopia? Equality? Love? What else? Our utopias reveal our desires and those are usually informed by our values. The difficulty, so the participants will experience, is to distill the values and especially to characterize and articulate them. It is best to have one person keeping notes and give those to the author of the utopia. Then the next person gets a turn.

I like doing the exercise with people in organizations. Lawyers who insist that money is the only thing that counts, reveal in their utopia that they care about other things. They then imagine something like a small office in which collegiality is very important and that allows for meaningful relationships with clients. They imagine a good balance between family and working life, and turn out to be important to their communities.

When leaders of universities dream about the ideal university they invariably imagine small communities, intensive interactions among faculty and students, and an inspiring atmosphere. Why then, I ask, are you pursuing big universities and why are you focusing on increasing financial returns, and why do you care so much about the rankings? While they can readily cite economic and political pressures, it appears that they act in conflict with their own values.

CHAPTER 8

THE SOURCES FOR DOING THE RIGHT THING; ABOUT RICHNESS AND POVERTY

It had been a good event. More than 300 people had showed up to attend a lecture of my friend, among them a few colleagues and Ph.D. students. She had done very well and received a remarkably long applause. On the way home we discussed how privileged we felt. Here we are, doing the things we really love doing—thinking, writing and discussing ideas with others. In this instance, she was particularly blessed with all the interest she was getting for her ideas.

I was working on this chapter at the time and brought up the subject of our sources. What sources does she possess that enable her to have experiences such as an evening like this one? We quickly agreed on sources such as her stock of knowledge (she keeps amazing me with how much she knows, how much she has read), her strong skills in rhetoric including the repertoire of arguments, examples, anecdotes, jokes, metaphors and so on, her reputation (or ethos as the rhetorician would say), and her social network. She wanted to add "emotions" arguing that you need to have empathy, love maybe, to be able to do what she is doing. I was not sure at first, but maybe she does have a point, I now think. We also discussed the source "memories." Her knowledge is based on them but there are all kinds of other memories, such as the memories of hundreds of talks like this one that enable her to do so well. Memories constitute her experience. Then she has her talents, her intellect, her background with several gifted people in the family, including a father who was professor at Harvard, and a mother who was a talented opera singer and developed into a poet. They were gifts, you might say. Her *oikos* is a more delicate issue, as she is living by herself. Even so, she has a strong relationship with her mother and her siblings. And she has "homes" all over the world, places where she is always welcome. Like my home. These are important sources for her, too, as they give her the warmth and the emotional support that she needs as a base for her performances.

We paused a little and then I pointed out that we had not talked about her house, her financial assets, and other possessions that she has bought in exchange for money. This is strange, I wanted to say. She is an economist after all. She had just been preaching the virtues of the market. Yet for her performance, the sources of the market had been of little to no relevance. In a relaxed setting, sitting at my kitchen table, sipping tea, she could easily acquiesce. "I see your point," she said. And then she was ready to go to bed.

How rich are we? How poor?

In order to realize values we are in need of goods. That is what we noted in the previous chapters. Having a family enables us to realize the values of family, care and support. Having is a matter of owning or possessing. I do not think of our legal possessions only; I expressly point at all the goods we own that do not have a legal entitlement. My friend has no intellectual property right on her rhetoric, yet it is highly valuable to her.

Walking down this lane of values and goods we run into the question: how much are goods worth? What are they good for? If my friend has a great stock of shares and cash, she would be considered rich. But how about my "home," my "family"? They are priceless, I am inclined to say. How does "owning" a family compare with owning a pile of money? What makes someone richer? According to the standard economic definition the richer one has the pile of money, barring further information. But is she? She often remarks that she envies my household with all those wonderful kids, a good relationship, many visitors and so much going on. Would that make me richer? Then again, she is much more well-known than I am. Her lectures draw large crowds and her books get reviewed in the New York Review of Books. Would that make me poor by comparison?

How about the lawyer with whom I was in conversation? He is loaded, as they say. He has a large house and an even larger bank account. He drives an expensive car and has a second home somewhere. Yet our conversation was about his worry that he was missing out on some important things in life. In his youth he had wanted to live a free life as an artist and as an intellectual. He had wanted to travel to discover the world. His job now takes him all over the world, but that is not the kind of travel he had dreamed of. We came to this subject after I had asked him what he considered to be his most import-ant contributions thus far. The question had embarrassed him as it made him realize that he would not consider the big deals that he has made to be real contributions. It actually was starting to bother him that he works with and for people who are preoccupied with money.

"How rich do you feel?" I asked him. "You really want to know?" he turned to me, "I tell you, all that money, it does not mean much to me. What I really care about are my kids and my wife." When I pointed out, that he was doing everything to stay away from them, with all his travels and 18-hour working days, he sighed. I got even worried that he would become despondent. He was not doing justice to all that he possessed, I thought.

A few weeks before this conversation I spoke to an artist at the opening of an exhibition. We came to the topic of money. I asked him what he earns with his artwork. He could not tell me. His income fluctuated a lot from year to year. The last years had been tough. People are not inclined to buy art, he noted. He was not complaining, familiar as he is with the alternating highs and lows. "How do you do it with your family," I wanted to know. "Do you take vacations?" "Sure, we go on vacation," he responded and continued me to tell how they were celebrating their vacation with the little money they have. "You know, we visit these rich places, watch people hanging out at luxurious restaurants, being bored, and then go to the supermarket, buy us some wine, bread and cheese, and find a beautiful spot in a park or at the seaside and have a real feast." He laughed. "You know, we create our own luxury with the wine, the bread and the cheese and a wonderful spot. I actually pity those people who are spending a lot of money and remain bored."

So who of the two is richer, the lawyer or the artist? In terms of money, the answer is obvious. But that does not appear to be the right answer. I do not think that there is an objective standpoint from which we can compare both lives and determine that one has greater richness than the other. It all depends on what we value. The artist appears to be more authentic as he is living what is important to him while the lawyer seems to long for the life that he dreamed of in his youth. The artist "has" creativity as a source; the lawyer "has" his expertise and a large and powerful social network.

In the standard economic conversations, we learn to quantify all possessions in amounts of money. That enables a comparison. If we were to do so for the artist and the lawyer, we would have to conclude that the latter is worth a great deal more than the artist. But is that right? Do his quantitatively superior possessions enable the lawyer to realize a better life than the artist?

We can pose similar questions for organizations or communities (such as cities and nations). What does one university have that another does not? When we turn to the financial endowments of universities, we have to conclude that some (like Harvard and Stanford) are much richer than others. But what does that say? How to bring European universities into the equation? They do not have endowments, but have government support instead. Furthermore, large endowments are also the sign of an engaged and well-connected alumni community. Could that community be the real source of wealth? (Managers of European universities only recently have discovered this source; they may need it now that popular support for generous financing of universities is waning.) For a scholar the richness of a university rather shows in the quality of colleagues, the intensity of research seminars, and the curiosity and talents of students. It is the culture of a university that matters most, I would argue.

Companies like Google do not do so well because of their physical assets like factories and computers, but because of the reputation that they have. Reputation (or brand recognition as marketing specialists would say) accounts for attention, and attention is good for lots of income by way of advertisements. (Google offers attention space for other parties eager for attention to their offerings.)

Cities like New York and Amsterdam have sources that other cities do not have. Those sources attract tourists, intellectuals, artists, entrepreneurs and head offices of big firms. They have economic capital, economists would say, since they are able to generate income. But they have so much more than that. Amsterdam has, for example, the red light district, coffee-shops, the Anne Frank House, the canals and a few important museums. All those sources are good for large crowds of tourists. New York has "energy," an excess of virtually everything, from stores to jazz clubs, from galleries to dangerous neighborhoods, Central Park, and also quite a few great museums. Amsterdam lacks a "Broadway" and has not many important galleries. Does that make it a poorer city? I do not think a definite answer is called for. People will weigh the qualities and will decide one way or the other. The point that I want to make is that a city owns all kinds of sources and that many of those sources are immaterial, and impossible to capture in monetary terms.

The same point applies when we compare countries. Uganda does not have the infrastructure that the Netherlands has. At night the streets are dark and risky to walk on because of the many cracks in the pavement. It lacks a good health care and it is well endowed with civil servants and politicians that the Dutch would consider corrupt and unreliable. Yet, as the Ugandans will point out, they have rich local cultures, with a strong sense of tradition that the Dutch lack. In addition, Ugandans enjoy a much richer family life than the Dutch do. They consider all those senior Dutch people living by themselves to be a sign of poverty, social poverty that is. And yes, the income of the Dutch is ten times that of the Ugandans. Then again, how do the cultures of both countries compare?

Stocks and flows

All these examples point at an important element of the design in the actions of people and organizations. When doing the right thing, we do not only need to realize which goods to strive for, we also have to figure out how to do so. According to the scheme of *phronesis* (see chapter 4) this is a matter of design. The examples point at the importance of something like "stocking up," "accumulating" or "investing in" something like capital, power, resources or sources.

We do what the squirrel does, stocking up nuts in the fall in order to be able to make it through the winter. The stock of nuts provides a flow of nutrients throughout the winter. Robinson Crusoe invested his time and material to make himself a dwelling that could provide him a "flow" of protection and comfort for the years to come. He also stocked up seeds to secure a future flow of food.

The distinction between stocks and flows is the basic principle of accounting. Balance sheets report the stocks (including the debts that are negative stocks) and income-cost statements report the flows coming in and going out. The balance sheet shows the net wealth as the result of positive and negative stocks. The income-loss statement shows the profit (for organizations) and savings for social organizations, people and communities. This way of accounting for stocks and flows frames daily life. It makes us think of what we own and owe, and of the amounts that we receive and spend. It generates a fascination for the outcomes: net worth on the balance sheet and profits or savings on the income-loss statement.

Related to the distinction between stocks and flows is the distinction between investing and consuming. When the squirrel adds nuts to his stock, he is investing.When he takes a nut from the stock he is consuming. At least, this is the framing of accounting.

So when are you and I investing and when are we consuming? It all depends on what we count as our stocks. When we consider the examples above, we will quickly figure out that the stocks that usually appear on the accounts of accountants and economists are only a small fraction of the stocks that matter in the end. The reason is that they limit themselves mainly to the stocks that have been acquired by means of exchange. So they count **material goods** such as buildings, machines, computers and the like and **financial capital** such as bank accounts, shares, bonds and the like. Buying buildings and stocks should then be considered investments. Using a building, wearing it down in the process, should be consumption.

But what if a family is to be considered a stock, or the atmosphere in a town, or the culture of an organization? Then spending time with the family, organizing a festival in town, or having a company outing should be considered investments, too. Is reading this book an investment or consumption? It all depends on what you count as your stocks. If you think of your knowledge as a stock, then reading is an investment. If you are just passing time and enjoying yourself, you better think of this activity as consumption.

How to speak about stocks? Capital, power or sources? Source it is.
There is more to say about the words we use. Economists like to speak of
capital when they refer to stocks. So we speak of **economic capital** when we
refer to all those stocks that can generate a form of income, such as the stocks
of buildings, machinery and the like. We speak of **human capital** when
we refer to stock of knowledge and skills. Individuals can have such capital
but so do organizations when you think of the knowledge and the skills of its
employees. More recently the concepts of **social capital** and **cultural capital** have entered the scene. Social capital refers to the economic relevance
of social contacts and relationships, or the social network. Cultural capital,
as introduced by the French sociologist Pierre Bourdieu, refers to the cultural
baggage of people, including their diplomas, as well the stock of monuments,
museums, churches and other cultural assets (Bourdieu, 1977). Both forms of
capital are a form of economic capital since they are good for economic status
and income.

But the notion of capital obstructs the perspective that I want to offer
here. It is the identification with economic returns but also with the notion of
legal property that prevents us from seeing all the things that we own, including the stocks that really matter. I also find that outside the conversation of
economists, the notion of capital evokes the wrong responses. When I speak
of cultural capital, artists, for example, find reason to dismiss my argument as
a typical economistic one.

So I have been looking for another term. Power is a possible term to use,
as having a stock of some kind empowers the owner. Stock represents a power.
But "power" also generates associations that need to be sidelined before going
ahead. I settle for the notion of sources. A source is stock of something, nuts,
knowledge or skills that enables someone to realize certain values directly or
indirectly by way of certain goods. In the company of economists the notion
of source needs some clarification but in other circles it does not create as
much confusion as does the notion of capital. So, source it is.

Sources enable people, communities or organizations to realize their values. When Amartya Sen speaks of the capabilities of people, he presumes
that people have sources that make them capable, such as the source of an
education, or a supportive *oikos* and a stable society (Sen, 1985).

How to acquire the sources we need in order to do the right thing?
Before considering the wide variety of sources that people like you and I have,
I need to point out that the mode of acquisition matters. When we think along
with economists we are inclined to restrict ourselves to the sources that are
acquired by way of purchases, of (financial) investments. These are sources
like housing, buildings, machines and maybe even knowledge.

Yet there are other modes of acquisition. Some sources we have received.

They are a gift. Think for example of individual talents. We will say that the great violinist is gifted. But being born into a good *oikos* is a gift, too, as is being part of a strong society. Some of us may go much further to consider all we have as gift of God, Allah or nature.

Most important are the sources that we acquire by contributing to them. Think of shared goods such as friendship, art (or an artistic sub discipline), science, faith.

Accordingly, we need to distinguish

1. sources that have been bought and have legal ownership

2. sources that have been gifts

3. sources that are acquired by means of contributions and have a shared ownership

The first category usually receives most attention for the simple reason that its items can be measured reasonably well in monetary terms. I know the price of my house, but I have no idea how to pinpoint the value of my home that I have acquired by contributing to it. The CEO of a company knows the total price of its assets but when it comes to the culture of his company, he, or she, gropes in the dark.

How does culture come about? How can we do the right thing when we do not have a good idea of our sources? We need to know our sources in order to sense what we are capable of.

The Tree of Life: the sources for a good life

Later I will consider organizations, communities and societies. First I want us to think about the sources that enable us to live a good life. I have found the exercise useful for myself and when I do it with students, they often appear to be surprised. It gets them thinking for sure.

We cannot expect to come to a complete account and definite conclusions, but we can explore the sources that enable the realization of a good life.

The image that I work with is that of a tree. I happen to be fond of trees and have a special relationship with the giant beech tree in my garden. It must be standing there for more than 200 years. Just imagine. Its roots are deep and it reaches high in the sky. It carries huge branches that require a large space, crowding out the spurs that surround it. The other day, one of the branches broke off during a big storm. The branch was so heavy that I could not lift it on my own. In the fall it takes me a couple of days to rake its leaves. For me that tree is a source of magic that leaves me in awe. That gets me thinking of the tree of life.

Thinking through the tree of life is an organic process. We cannot gather the components and fit them nicely together as we would do with a machine.

The tree, so we will quickly discover, consists of a wide array of parts or sources, some more concrete than others. Measuring the parts, as we are used to doing in balance sheets, is pointless. Even so, we want to weigh the various parts somehow. How important is your cultural upbringing for the life you are living? Speaking for myself I would say that it is quite important as it introduced me to the world of literature (my family read together in the evenings), with the visual arts (we went to art galleries on Saturday afternoons) and the world of religion (my father was a Protestant minister). Is that upbringing more important than the gifts of the civilization that you can enjoy, including the institutions (schools and the like) that disclosed those gifts for you? Gosh, that is a difficult question to answer. Yet when confronted with the question, you and I are made more aware of the sources that enable us to enjoy a good life, or we are becoming increasingly aware of the impediments for a good life. Might it be, for example, that we are neglecting the gifts of our civilization, or the fruits of our upbringing?

The trunk of the tree of life as I imagine it stands for our sources. The branches and leaves that sprout from the tree are the qualities that make up our daily life. They consist of our realized values, but also our earnings, reputation, power, influence, experiences, sensations, emotions, pleasures and such that we owe to our sources.

Let us explore this tree of life.

a) At the base are the most essential sources: *oikos*, health, talents, basic skills

What would constitute the base of the tree? (I will get to the roots at the end.) I would say that the base consists of the sources that are most precious, most fundamental for a good life. Remember the question about your most important possessions? The answers constitute the base of your tree of life, at least so I suggest. The majority of people would fill in "family" and "friends," and some "freedom" and "health" (really? Are you sure?) and others "faith" or "love."

These sources are at the base because they are a) most important and b) feed other sources. Having a strong home usually enables people to participate effectively in networks, communities and societies. Home also stands for the environment in which we grew up, for our upbringing, for the knowledge, norms, experiences and social skills that we take away from our upbringing and that are so important for the rest of our lives. The home in which we grew up and our current home are sources of memories and remembrances, of shared experiences.

A home is partly a gift; that is especially the case for the home in which we are born. But for a large part, a home is the result of a great variety of contributions and investments. Just think of all the time, emotion and effort that are required to maintain a home. (If you are living by yourself, imagine what your parents have invested and ask people like me to tell you about what it takes. Who came up with the idiotic idea that time spent at home is leisure time?)

Not all homes are the same, of course. There are good homes, great homes and "poor" or "terrible" homes. A home with abuse or desolation, and a broken home can set people back; these may turn into a negative source. The better the home, the stronger it is as a source for a good life, at least so we may presume. (How would you assess your own home? Might it be a reason to put more effort into it, to give it more attention?)

Homes are good for all kinds of values and experiences, including the most important values like love, care and support, but also reputation, self-confidence, social skills and social networks, cultural knowledge and a religion maybe (showing up as offshoots and leaves).

Friendships are akin to home. This area of the tree of life contains the most intimate and important friendships. These are friendships that we have for the sake of the friendship. All the offshoots, all the outcomes are an extra. Even so, good friendships are good for all kinds of values, experiences and the like and are therefore important sources, as homes are. When a good home is lacking, good friendships constitute a good alternative source.

Every now and then I run into people who tell me that they have colleagues who are like family to them, only better. They share the deepest emotions, and have a cause in common and work together towards that cause, something that families are lacking. I have a few intellectual friends who are close to what I would consider family, so I recognize the sensation. Kinship is maybe not always most important; a shared cause or a shared experience (like having fought a war together) can form a bond that is stronger and more fruitful than kinship or intimate love.

All these sources will stand no chance if you and I do not have the basic skills and health for survival. Basic skills include basic social skills and skills like cooking and taking care of one's health, basic cognitive skills and skills that can earn the owner a basic income.

b) Social sources come next

At a slightly higher level I am inclined to locate a variety of social sources, such as the **social groups** I am part of, my **friendships**, the **academic network** that I can call mine, and the society I am a member of. From these sources I derive for example a social status, a social identity, recognition of my contributions, a sense of honor, and financial gains at times.

Social sources constitute what is also called **social capital**. It includes "ethos," the oh-so-important character factor that gives credence to what we say to an audience. I benefit every now and then from being a professor: in social settings it gets people's attention (but less so in political settings and not at all in my *oikos*). Reputation, "having a name," or "being a brand," is an important source, too. In the competition for attention it is crucial. (A bad reputation is counterproductive, of course. My experience is that a good reputation among some brings about a bad reputation among others: the trick is to get a good reputation with the right people).

An important element of one's social sources, or social capital, is the **social network**. Boy, how critical the social network can be. The other day a Japanese colleague told me that she was looking for assistance in a research project that involved Brazilian artwork. As it happened, I had an enthusiastic and capable Brazilian student who was just right for the job. That made the Brazilian student happy, my Japanese colleague happy, and me content because I had been able to put my social network to work. It is also great to land in Sydney and call up the friend with whom I studied some thirty years ago and spend a day with him, as if we had seen each other the day before. Social networks are good for all kinds of things. Some are better than others. How is yours? Does it contain the right people? Does it also contain bad contacts, contacts that can hurt you?

A couple may think it shares a social network. But that is not necessarily so as the remaining partner may discover after the death of the other: a big portion of the social network may have been mainly connected with the other partner and loses interest in the contact. I learn from such experiences that I should not leave the social networking to my wife and have to take care of my own. I will be in need of (intellectual) friends later in life—when the next generation has lost interest in what I have to contribute—so I should make an effort now.

Other social sources are communities, neighborhoods, clubs, societies, reading groups, political parties or any social entity that has a sense of "us." I now have neighbors who help me out from time to time, and whom I will help if necessary. But that has not always been the case. Thanks to a local soccer club I still can play soccer, and with a group of friends I can share hikes through mountainous areas.

c) Intellectual, artistic, scientific and spiritual sources
It is about right there that I place the **cultural sources**, including **culture in its anthropological sense, civilization and the arts**. Cultural sources constitute what is also called **cultural capital**.

We are part of a **culture** and we benefit from it, and sometimes we suffer from it. In the US I benefited from some, and suffered from other aspects of American culture. I benefited from its rich music scene, its fantastic sports, the rich and stimulating intellectual climate at its universities, and its entrepreneurial spirit and suffered from its lack of patience for long conversation, its materialistic culture and the death penalty. (That is my take on that source; yours will undoubtedly differ). Currently I am enjoying the fruits of Dutch culture and coping with its problematic aspects. I enjoy the qualities of Dutch personal and family life (with the emphasis on "gezelligheid" or coziness) and cope with a lack of an intellectual climate at its universities, a widespread disdain for reading serious books and its inhospitality (as experienced by so many foreigners).

An important cultural source is the language that we share with others. A shared language enables us to share experiences, ideas, values and feelings with others. When we have to speak to others in a foreign language a great deal tends to get lost in the translation. For a Dutchman it is difficult to be humorous in English, and Americans will have a difficult time with the guttural sounds of Dutch and to capture its subtleties. Having been raised in the West it is near impossible to be fluent in Japanese or Chinese; one can forget about ever passing as a native because of it, and also because of appearance. Language is a powerful cultural device and a rich source within the language community and a serious constraint for operating in the world at large.

Civilization is another source that is easily overlooked because it may seem to be self-evident. However, its richness is far from self-evident. Only will we benefit from its rich array of arts, texts, languages, histories and traditions when we are willing to put in the work. The bible, Rafael, Giotto, Plato, Darwin, Aristotle, Augustus, Zhuangzi, Confucius, Rembrandt and Rumi: they are all sources of great insight and inspiration. They require effort, time for study, discussion and time for contemplation to appropriate them.

As with culture, you will know how important your civilization is when you are outside of it, in a place where its richness does not resonate, where people around you have no interest whatsoever and are even hostile. We do not even have to travel very far to have that experience. I experience a lack of interest almost daily. Even at the university I run into indifference and neglect of all this richness. Too many scholars are not only ignorant to all the sources I have just listed, but also they are uninterested. The consequence is a deflation of their value. I, along with others who care about these sources, will experience their relevance less intensely. If this sense is shared widely, we are justified to speak of a decline of civilization and a loss of the source it represents.

The arts are an important source, of course. It is a source good for the valorization of all kinds of values. Do I need to elaborate? Each person will fill in this source differently. Bach's St. Matthew Passion moves my wife and me to tears, but leaves my children indifferent. Pink Floyd played loud gets me and at least two of my children going while my wife will shout in order to demand that the volume be turned down. A cello played well stops me in my tracks. I can't get enough of experiencing objects of visual art even if I do not understand them. But one of my daughters is even more into that art than I am. I often fall back on books that I have read and movies that I have seen. I did not even finish reading Musil's *The Man without Qualities*, but still the book inspires me while writing this book. The other day I found myself crying after finishing reading Potok's *The Chosen*. It must have been the father-son theme that got to me. Only recently, I discovered that the books of Karl May that I read as a 10-year-old boy had a profound influence on me. The intense bond between Old Shatterhand and Winnetou has made me long for a friendship that does not require words. In a way that is inconsistent with my fondness for conversation. Winnetou remains a hero. The fact that he is a fictitious figure does not really matter. I could continue but this is just to show how this source works for me in the hope that it evokes associations with you. How about your movies? How about dance? How about opera? Architecture? Fashion? Design?

Religion is a source, too. Churches, temples, mosques are among the places where people can experience the sacred, where they receive hope and inspiration for living the good life. Of course, many people have a negative experience with the church but the weekly services, the religious texts; the rituals continue to be a solace and an inspiration for multitudes. The bible is a crucial source for Western civilization. All kinds of common expressions and sayings are biblical and social values of solidarity and compassion are originally Christian values. It has been argued that the loss of religion would be the end of civilization as we know it. Buddhism is a source of a rich array of practices, such as meditation, throughout Asia and the Western world. And so are Zen and Taoism. Islamic religion has been galvanizing the Middle East.

Civilization includes **cultural heritage**. Cultural heritage comes in tangible form (monuments, manuscripts, art objects and such) and intangible form (music, traditions, rituals, craftsmanship, languages and such).

The **sciences** and the **humanities** are an immense source for knowledge, insight, meaning, research, teaching and technological and social innovation. Their products fill huge libraries. At Duke University, where I got my Ph.D., I liked to wander along the open stacks to be amazed and overwhelmed by the sheer amount, variety and richness of what people have produced thus far. There is so much to read, so much to study.

I like to think of civilization as a collection of all kinds of **conversations**. All these conversations are sources that invite us to enter and to which we can contribute. For me it is important that there are ongoing conversations on cultural economics, pragmatic and Aristotelian philosophy, sociology, the arts, classical music, theatre, the euro and quite a few more. I draw inspiration and insights from them. Just inspect my bookcase and you will know what I mean.

Memories are a source in and of themselves, although they are fed by other sources. Just imagine losing your memory. In that case, you do not remember those great moments of your youth, the love and support you received from your parents and others, your friendships, the books you read, the movies you have watched, your vacations, everything you saw and experienced, your study, your fights and the conflict situations you were part of, your achievements and your embarrassing moments.

Our memories enable us to be who we are. They constitute us. So much of what we do is for the sake of our memories. Vacations serve that purpose, for example. S   o do our visits to the theatre, social meetings and all kinds of efforts like giving lectures, organizing festivals, and meeting famous people. What remains of everything we do is a memory, at least so you may hope. For most things we do, if we are honest, is not worth remembering. The nice St. Nicholas party that I had with my family (a Dutch tradition that takes place on December 5) I will undoubtedly forget soon; it will become part of my memory of such parties in general. I will also quickly forget the meal I had yesterday or that great class. But those memories that I have, are precious for me.

Human capital is the knowledge and the skills with which the owner is able to earn an income. It is composed of a selection of the previously mentioned sources.

Just imagine how rich you are compared to Emperor Nero in ancient Rome or King Louis XIV in France in the 18th century. You can listen to a concert or any other music in a few clicks whereas they had to command large groups of experienced musicians to perform live for them. No pop, country or jazz for them. You can buy a mango around the corner that they had had to import—if they knew about its existence. And when you want to take a drive, you start the engine and speed away, whereas they had to get the horses ready for their chariot in order to get going at not even 20 km an hour. And then we are not even speaking of the health care you can have, the information you can access. Even if you do not have much money, you are in all these respects much richer than the emperors and kings of the past.

---

d) Societal or common sources

The **society** that you and I are part of, is good for all kinds of things. It includes educational institutions, public infrastructure, health care provisions, care of the elderly (for when we grow old), democratic or other political institutions, newspapers, media and good Internet. This source also stands for the degree of solidarity in a country, the sense of patriotism, a national identity and a national history.

I am reminded of the importance of the **societal sources** that I draw from when I visit other societies. Sometimes I notice how much better other societies function, but I confess that I often praise myself fortunate to have lived in the US and for living now in the Netherlands. I praise myself lucky for being able to benefit from the great universities that the US has to offer, and now recognize the benefits of a well-organized and well-functioning Dutch society. For an intellectual like myself, the fondness of the Dutch for discussion, meetings and lectures is a great good, good for plenty of invitations to speak and participate in debates.

But a society provides so much more. I enjoy the market in my local town, a few special shops, and the possibility to choose from a great variety of restaurants and cafes. (What shall we eat tonight? Italian, Spanish, Japanese, Thai, Indian, American, Russian, Greek, Indonesian, Argentinian, Vietnamese? African? Sorry, we do not have an African restaurant. We do not have a real Dutch restaurant either but that is because the identity of the Dutch cuisine is dubious.) The proximity of Amsterdam is a wonderful asset that I take too little advantage of.

Nature as part of societal sources is dubious but it sure is a crucial source. It generates the fruits, minerals and food of all sorts that we humans need to survive. But nature also provides landscapes, views and so much more.

e) Material and financial sources

The house, the car and computers are among my material sources. They are good for shelter, comfort, transport, information and a few more values, including status, I guess.

And then there is the bank account, and especially the number that it specifies, other accounts and their numbers, the value of shares and the accumulated pension. These are financial sources. We can exchange them for goods we need and appreciate. Financial sources, therefore, suspend the realization of values and are valuable for that reason.

Some of the material and financial resources we have purchased with the means that work, entrepreneurship and invention has generated. Others we receive as a gift, by way of an inheritance. Speculation may play a role, too.

f) The roots are faith, hope and love

What then are the roots of the tree of life? What sources secure everything else we own and make sure that we do not drift and get lost? Deirdre McCloskey (the friend with whom I began this chapter) suggested the answer to me: according to her, faith, hope and love are the most important of all sources. They are fundamental for a good life.

"Faith" stands for "trust." Having self-confidence, having a source of inspiration and having a firm faith: they all contribute to a good life, at least so we may surmise. The question is "what feeds a source like faith?" A strong *oikos* could be a contributing factor, but quite a few people will mention a religion, a spiritual practice or a passion of some kind.

When people have lost hope, all sources lose their meaning and their power. Without hope everything we do becomes pointless. There is no purpose, no direction. It is the condition at risk when cynicism takes over or when people fall into a mental depression.

Love is most important of all, as the Buddha and Paulus (in the letter to the Corinthians) declared. It is the source that enables us to connect with all living beings, to experience empathy, this most human sentiment of all, and thus to do the right thing.

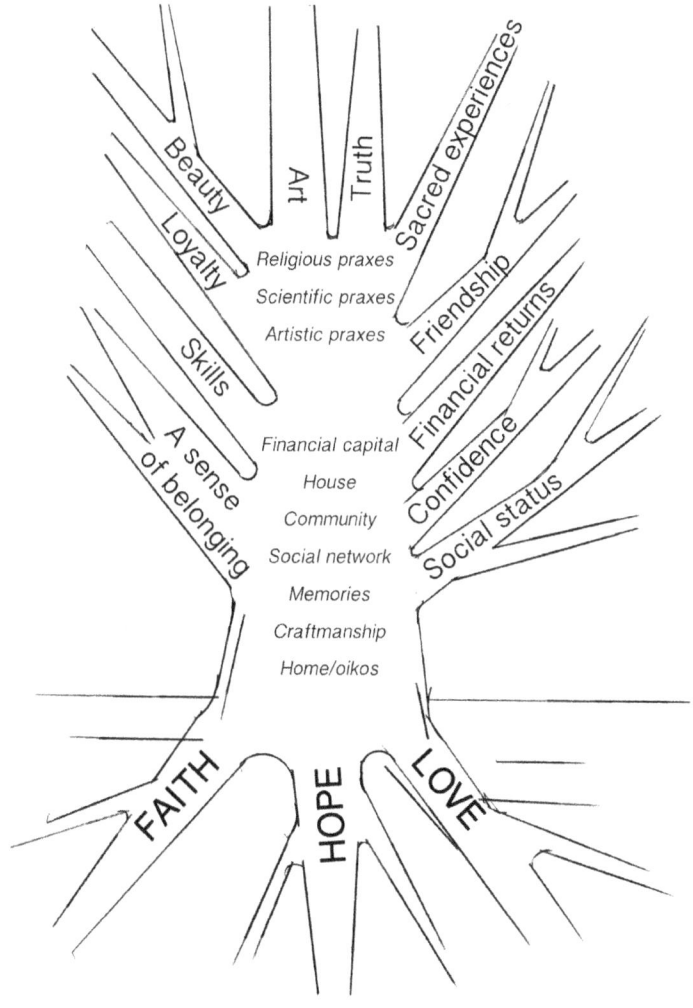

Diagram 8-1 The Tree of Life

So what?

Have you formed a picture of your tree of life? Can you distinguish the most important sources? Are there sources that I have not mentioned (or thought of)? Do you recognize the roots as I imagine them? Or would you do them differently? What do you make of your tree of life? Allow me to make some suggestions, speaking for myself of course.

- The wealth of nations? The book by Adam Smith carrying that title got people to think about the economy, physical wealth and markets. That was not the common perspective at the time— at the end of the 18th century. Religious values still prevailed and richness had to do with faith and God's blessings. If one dared to think of material wealth, one thought of gold and silver. Nations who were able to accumulate large stocks of gold and silver were considered wealthy. Adam Smith upset this conventional wisdom by claiming that the wealth of nations has more to do with how much the people of that nation produce, and how much they are able to trade with people of other nations. It is by labor and industry that nations become wealthy. Such has become the conventional wisdom up till now.

The tree of life is to upset this conventional wisdom. It generates another concept of wealth by including sources that cannot be traded in markets, and are not produced by labor and industry. We generate our most important sources, so we have figured out, by way of social and cultural activities, by sharing goods with others. It makes for a picture that is quite different from the one that Smith adumbrated in *The Wealth of Nations*.

- The richness and variety of sources: once I got started I began to realize how many sources I draw from almost daily. I was not aware, for example, of the importance of my memories. Were you aware of how much you owe to the civilization you are part of? Or of your society and its institutions?

A British artist, Michael Landy, methodically destroyed all his material possessions in 2001. He did so in an art gallery using a big machine. Among Landy's possessions destroyed was a Hirst painting, which at the time had no insignificant economic value, a Saab, his passport, his pictures and his clothes. At the end he was left naked. He owned nothing anymore. Did that mean he did not possess anything anymore? Certainly not. For one thing, this performance earned him quite a reputation and led to a well-sold book. He also could not crush his skills, his knowledge, his social network, his memories, his society, his culture or his civilization. Even with nothing to his name, he remained well endowed with sources that enabled him to continue a good life.

- The limited role of the sources we have paid for directly: the relevance of our financial sources and economic sources pale in the presence of all the other sources we draw from. How curious it is then that we pay so much attention to those sources. Might that be because we can measure them, or does this bias have a cultural cause?

- Tell me again why you deserve that income? When people justify a high salary on the basis of their productivity, or contribution to a financial or other result, their tree of life will compel them to reconsider. How much do they owe to everything that they received, like talents, their social and cultural upbringing, and their society and its institutions? And how about the luck factor? Desert or merit becomes dubious when we become aware of the richness of sources that back us up. It makes me, at least, modest and grateful.

> The star player on a soccer team earns an extravagant salary these days. The argument is that he is worth it because of the contri-bution he makes to the team's success and, with that, to the revenues from tickets and television broadcasts. But what would this player have achieved without a) his teammates, b) the organization of his club, c) the soccer infrastructure and the soccer culture that is good for popular interest, d) his upbringing and e) the talents he has received? Might it be that if he were aware of all the sources that enable him to do so well in this game, he would be grateful and more modest? Could it be that he has a sense of being indebted to at least some of those sources—and happily pay his taxes?

- The importance of neglected or overlooked sources. The exercise of imagining and composing one's tree of life compels us to realize sources of life that we might not think of otherwise. The result might be a heightened awareness of all the sources that enable you to live a good and full life.

- Who is rich, who is poor? When we survey all that we own and possess, we gain quite a different perspective on richness and poverty. In general, richness stands for owning a lot of money, as in material and financial assets. Poverty stands for owning all but nothing of those things. That is different now. When we take into account all our possessions, distinguishing richness from poverty becomes harder. Who is richer: the lawyer with all his money or the artist with his art of living? You tell me. And who is richer: the one with little money but with dear friends and a strong family or the one with lots of money and no friends to speak of and an alienated family?

How rich are we with our civilization, health care and welfare? Or are the Ugandans better off with their strong and extended families and their deeply-rooted local cultures?

The problem with the conventional statistics of wealth and poverty is that they measure what can be measured and leave out the most important possessions. Maybe the distribution will remain more or less the same if we were to weigh in those possessions, but I doubt that it will. At any rate, comparing qualities makes even less sense than comparing the quantities.

Different types of inequality

When I was working on this book, a French economist, Thomas Piketty, made a big impact with his book (Piketty, 2014). He showed, on the basis of extensive calculations, that the distribution of wealth was rapidly growing more unequal. I quickly checked out what he meant and my suspicions were confirmed: he limits his calculations to those assets that are measured in monetary terms. He showed, therefore, the increasing inequality of financial wealth, that is, merely instrumental wealth as defined in this book. Other forms of inequality he does not even mention. Let me do so here. I base myself on the tree of life.

- **Cultural inequality** is the inequality in the distribution of cultural sources, such as civilization, art, spirituality or what some people would call a meaningful life. In this case it is not financial capital that is unevenly distributed but cultural capital, or the ability to inspire or to be inspired. This is the most substantive form of inequality. We have no clue what it is. As far as I know, no attempt has been made to develop a measurement or indicators to get a sense of the magnitude of cultural capital and its distribution. Perhaps it is even senseless to try. Even so, we could say that those who are deprived of cultural sources are poor in a substantive way. A monk without any financial wealth whatsoever would end up dirt poor in Piketty's account, but may be richer than most of us in terms of cultural accounting.

- **Societal inequality** is the inequality in the distribution of societal goods. The kinds of societies people value will depend on their values. People who value freedom will appreciate some societies more than others. The same applies to people who value stability and security. So it will be difficult to develop a monitor for societal inequality, unless we focus on specific characteristics. That societies are unequal is apparent in the flows of refugees, immigrants and fortune seekers.

- **Social inequalities** refer to the distribution of social capital, that is, the ability to function socially. Social capital depends on factors such as the social network, status, recognition, memberships and the strength of communities. People who suffer a lack of financial sources often have a low social capital. Yet that is not always the case. Rich people can be lonely and financially-poor people may have a strong social network. The question is, when we want to fight poverty, whether we can ignore the social inequality by focusing solely on the financial aspects. Raising the question already hints at the answer.

- **Personal inequalities** refer to the uneven distribution of personal talents, skills, health, roles and functions that individuals have. No matter how equal people are, they are not the same. Some people simply are better equipped to deal with certain situations. In modern societies people with strong cognitive skills tend to do better than people who have physical skills; in wartimes practically-minded people are better situated than the intellectuals. The inequalities show up at schools, in the world of arts, at universities, in the world of chefs, in sports and in any world where selection on the basis of skills and aptitude takes place.

How about the negatives?

The recognition of additional sources, of the most critical sources, serves as an antidote to the fixation on financial wealth. It encourages us to reconsider the nature of poverty and richness, and to focus on substantive qualities that we own. The value based approach breaks the discussion about these issues wide open.

I anticipate that those who fight poverty are troubled. Their fear is that poverty will be relativized and as a consequence disappear on the agenda of urgent issues. I doubt that the argument here will have such a big impact. Furthermore, as a politician I actually benefit from the observation that poverty is as much a consequence of social inequality as of financial inequality. It motivates me to focus my policy on strengthening communities, on social work that aims to get "poor" people engaged in local activities, to get people out of their isolation.

A more serious problem is the lack of measurements of all inequalities except for the financial inequalities. That makes them difficult to work with, especially for politicians. That may be so. I would like to point out that measurements of financial inequality remain problematic and even if they are produced, for example by Piketty, this does not mean that politicians are quick to respond. At this point it is more important, I would argue, to widen the discussion and to raise awareness of inequalities on different grounds.

What follows? Taking stock

Firms do so at the end of the year, individuals do it occasionally: they take stock. They then count what they own and what they owe. The result is the net wealth. However, taking stock only concerns the financial and other stocks that can be valued in monetary terms. We still need to work on the total picture of organizations but the tree of life shows how narrow a picture given by the usual stock-taking is. There are so many more possessions, some so much more important than the ones usually accounted for.

What if we were to take stock of all our possessions, and basically compose our tree of life. One result would be greater awareness of all the sources that we need and that enable us to live a good life. What is needed next is the evaluation of those sources in order to be able to determine lacks and shortcomings. What would be the cause of a life not going too well? What is missing? Or what is the reason for feeling good about life?

How to do so? Usually we do so using *phronesis*, our practical wisdom, weighing qualities of the various sources. We figure out that we have neglected friendships, need to invest in our spiritual sources, or may take another job to increase the financial capital. Measurements play a limited role in this process of *phronesis*. It really is a matter of practice and experience.

New, mostly qualitative, methods are needed to assist people in organizations in this process of *phronesis*. I will introduce later the quality impact monitor. However, I will dare to postulate here that such methods will never replace the daily practice of weighing and assessing values, of deliberation, of evaluation, of correcting mistakes and of generally muddling through. It is the process that makes us human.

Exercises

In order to determine how important a source is, imagine what it would mean for your life, organization or society if you or it would be without? What would you be without memories? What would an organization be without those?

What would your life be if you were to lose your family? What if your organization would lose its network (for example, by moving, or by merging with another organization.)

In order to determine the relative importance of a source, ask yourself questions like: what is worse, losing all your money or losing all your friends?

Would you consider accepting 20 million euros or dollars when that would mean you are going to lose your family and friends?

CHAPTER 9

REALIZING VALUES IN FIVE DIFFERENT SPHERES:

INVOLVING OTHERS

We need to acquire or produce goods in order to make values real. Scientists need to write papers to realize their knowledge or research, artists need to generate a piece of art to realize their art, and shoemakers make shoes to display their craftsmanship. We form friendships, start a marriage, develop collegiality with colleagues and work on welfare programs in order to realize values that are important to us. Goods are the way to something of importance.

In order to be able to acquire or produce such goods, we are in need of sources, as made clear in the previous chapter, and a great variety of sources, at that. We make use of our talents, benefit from a stimulating culture, apply our skills and are glad with a loving family and caring friends because they support and encourage us.

The question that we need to address now is how we can acquire all those goods and sources. Put differently, the question could be why we find it often so difficult to realize the important goods? Why do we so often end up with the wrong things? Why do we so often experience a lack of one thing or another, like money or love?

Here we have reached a critical juncture. Up till now, we could reason from the perspective of the individual or a group of people seeking the right thing to do. We could more or less ignore other people. Only when we came across the notion of shared goods, we saw the need to involve others. But when it comes to the valorization of our values and goods the "other" becomes critical. Valorization is inevitably and necessarily a social process; it requires that others recognize a value in what we do or offer.

Our inquiry into what it takes to do the right thing takes us now out in the open, to involve the "other." We need to get others interested in the goods we generate. That is obvious in the case of a good like friendship because what is a friendship worth if no other person is interested in it? We have to make friends to have a friendship. The same applies to an idea: for what is an idea worth if only one person has it? An idea gains value when it is shared with others. An artist may be full of his own work, but what does that work mean if there is no one to appreciate the work?

The necessity to get others interested in a good is obvious if the owner, or creator, wants to realize other goods with that good. The shoemaker is in no need of the shoes he makes but needs bread, clothes and such. So he has to figure out how to swap his shoes for those other goods. In that case a good is a means to generate other goods. His challenge will be to get the owners of those goods willing to give them up in exchange for a certain number of his shoes.

Getting others interested in your goods is what valorization is all about. Valorization of a good requires that others recognize that the good is good for them. A pair of shoes could be of use, for example. It possibly could be good for more things, like social or esthetic values (I am thinking of the Uggs in chapter 5). Valorization of an idea may require a certain kind of conversation, usually as part of an existing conversation. Others have to get interested in the idea, in what it means, what it implies, what its applications could be, for such a conversation to come about. They must recognize the value of the idea.

Valorization is a matter of design, or strategy. You and I have to figure out how we are going to go about making our values real, whom to get involved and what we can expect from them. Will they be willing to pay? Or is it more important that they participate in a conversation? Where to go? With whom to speak? In what way? What to do? What are the options? What is the right thing to do?

The standard picture

When people are under the influence of standard economics, they will automatically think of the market as the main option for the valorization of their goods. The idea here is that you and I go to a "market" to offer our good for a price in the expectation that other people are willing to pay the price in exchange of that good. Valorization in that case implies the realization of an amount of money (the price) in transactions with others. At universities the managers currently speak of valorization when they want us, the scientists, to sell our ideas or to get sponsors for our research. Valorization would then be equivalent to "selling." An alternative option is to get a government grant.

This gives the standard picture of the market and the government as the two options for valorization. In the market prices rule, the government is all about rules and standards. Standard economics is fixated on exchange in markets, on the forces of demand and supply, on the role of prices, on products. Governments have a role where markets fail or turn out to be unstable or unjust.

Markets or governments: that is the question that motivates most discussions in economics and policy. Should there be more market, or should the government step in? Should the government control more, or should the government let go? Laissez faire, laissez passer.

We can depict the standard perspective as follows:

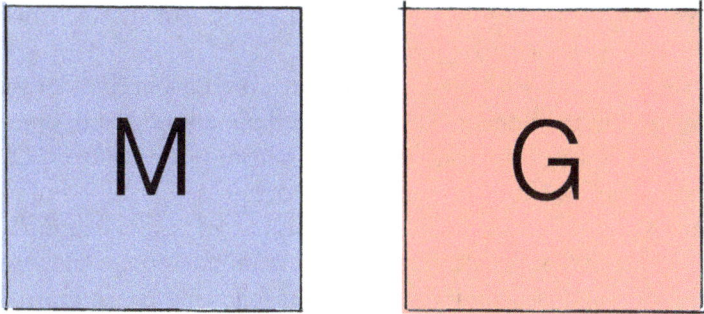

Diagram 9-1 The two standard logics: Market and Governance

M stands for the market and G stands here for the government (later we extend the meaning of G to stand for governance, or governmentality). Economists know a great deal about how the market works. In order to understand how governments work, you better consult those who study public administration and legal scholars. The market is where private goods are traded. G provides public goods.

The conversation that motivates the standard picture makes us think about issues like the efficiency of markets, the possibility of a general equilibrium in a system of markets and about the effectiveness of government interventions. We are made to wonder about the workings of the market and get sucked into discussions on the pros and cons of economic policies, of the need of intellectual property rights, or not, of government subsidies of the arts, or not. In the discourse of standard economics all this makes perfect sense, of course. But step away and consider your own experience. How much sense does the talk about markets and governments make? Does that tell us how we realize friendships? How about a home (versus a house)? And can it tell managers how they realize trust in their organization? Can it account for valorization of political ideas in the society? Does it tell us how people realize art, scientific knowledge or religion? I would say it does not.

The following anecdote should make clear why the picture of M and G is incomplete and is in need of other dimensions.

How an artist involves others to realize the value of his art

A befriended artist who teaches at the art academy in town had asked me to talk about art and money with a group of his students. They all were involved in a project about the highway as a special kind of space. Apparently they had weekly discussion evenings to which they invited guests. I was surprised by the number of students present, and then detected a few people who more or less looked like me: older and dressed up, that is. Later I found out that they were representatives of the Transportation Department that was financing the project. I sat down next to them.

A 35 year old guy—the age I was guessing, but he looked older than the others—was doing the talking. At first I had difficulties figuring out what it was about. Slowly I put the fragments together and determined that it was about an art project of his. Apparently he had designed an algorithm for the exploration of a city. By applying the algorithm, as seemed to be the idea, you would discover a city in a totally different way from how you would see it with a tour guide in hand or as a local inhabitant following the habitual routes. The presentation triggered an animated discussion about the technique of the algorithm, the personal and the political ramifications, the artistic qualities and about what it is to experience a place—or should we say space? It was a discussion that is quite typical for a gathering of artists.

At one point during the discussion the befriended artist invited me to comment. I asked the question that might be expected from an economist: "How much have you made with your project?" Artists can be direct; these certainly were. "What a stupid question," one student with a braided hairdo yelled. Another joined in: "Why is that important?" "Yeah," added another, "I really don't care." Having the advantage of age and function, I insisted: "No really, what did you make so far with this project? I am interested to know what others have been willing to contribute to it or pay for it."

The guy muttered "300 euros." He sounded like he was exaggerating. "How long have you worked on it," I asked him then. "On and off for half a year, a couple of months work so far, I guess. "How then do you support your family?" (I had picked up that he has a kid.) "Well, I have a small administrative job and my wife works."

I could think of all kinds of other options for him. He could sell his algorithm, to a tourist agency maybe, to Lonely Planet or another alternative tourist guide. He could have an app for the smartphone made. It might be a hit and make him a rich man! He could also approach the government people next to me, so I thought at the time, to find out whether his project could qualify for a subsidy. All these seemed to be obvious ways for him to realize the values of his project. Yet, they were not his options. So what is he doing to involve others and to get others interested in his work?

My task at the meeting was to point these students towards various options that M, the market, has to offer them to valorize their art. Much of what I said, seemed new to them. The resistance remained strong, though. A tough crowd they were. Yet with all their resistance they showed me that I was not doing justice to their practice. They were actually telling me that they had other ways to valorize their art, even if they were not explicit about those. Those other ways were obvious to them. It was the spheres of the market and the government that were elusive to them.

The ways that are so obvious to the artists are lost in the standard perspective simply because they are not included in the framework. So to do justice to the ways of artists we are in need of more dimensions. On the basis of this experience and many others in the course of time, I have concluded that the framework needs at least three more dimensions that artists, and ultimately we all, use to valorize our goods.

First is what I call the social sphere.
Note that the artist was sharing his work with a group of enthusiastic and ambitious future artists. He got them to take his work seriously and even got them to talk about it. Why is this noteworthy?

Millions of artists are making art and only a small fraction of all that work is being considered and even a smaller fraction is talked about. All these artists aspire to be in the conversation, to get other artists to pay attention to their work, but only very few make it big. This artist got his project at least in this conversation. The teacher had invited him, so apparently he was interested in the work. The students were willing to engage in a discussion. The work might even influence them in their own work. (It actually had an impact on me as it got me thinking how I approach foreign cities and made me realize how habitual I am in my ways in my own city.) For this artist, being able to present his work that evening is important. It is an achievement. It valorizes his work in some way.

Getting in the conversation and getting recognition for work is something he accomplishes in the **social sphere**, that is, in the sphere where people socialize and are in conversation with each other. In this sphere they get others interested and involved, they persuade or seduce others to contribute with their time, emotion and intellect, and maybe even money (in the form of gifts). For that purpose they develop networks and have various relationships with others, some of which are professional, others more intimate. For this artist, this sphere is crucial.

The cultural, or artistic, sphere

In having the discussion about his work, the students and he are practicing their art. They use the terms that are meaningful in the conversation that is called art, they appeal to shared values ("innovative," "political," "interdisciplinary," "cliché," "interesting," "authentic," "critical") and use the codes for that conversation (like the mentioning of certain names—Marcel Duchamp, Joseph Beuys, Vincent van Gogh—while avoiding others and using exemplars from the field—in this case other action-oriented art). If we had been in an academic seminar, the discussion would have been entirely different since academics engage in another kind of conversation with other terms, values and codes.

For the artist, the conversation that constitutes action-oriented art—a sort performance art—is a source. Within the context of that kind of conversation, his work stands a chance to become valuable. So he needs that conversation to valorize his art.

Then there is the sphere of the *oikos,* or home.

Often overlooked, especially when the standard economic perspective prevails, is the *oikos,* the home. (It is included in economics, *oikos* nomos, meaning the law of the household.) I didn't see it at first either. For the artist, the home plays a critical role in the valorization of his life as an artist (less so for a piece of work). His home is his life with a family, with himself. He first has to convince himself to do his art and to make sacrifices doing so, like taking a meaningless job and forsaking a larger income. That is part of the valorization of his art, convincing himself. Then he needs to involve his significant other: he has to convince his wife to support him in doing what he is doing. Imagine the discussions at the kitchen table. "When are you earning some money with your art." "Give it some time. Van Gogh also needed some time before his work became successful." "Yes, but I am not his brother, and we have a kid to take care of." "I know, I know. I also am not happy with how it is going. But you know how important this work is for me. Next week I am going to talk about it at the academy. Who knows what is going to come out of that." She sighs, and lets the issue rest. And off she goes, to earn the income that they need to pay the rent, the basic livelihood and a family vacation from time to time.

Home stands for *oikos.* And as I already pointed out, the *oikos* is a crucial sphere for the valorization of all sorts of goods. It is not that the family needs to appreciate the works and ideas of its members but it sure helps if it supports them in doing what they are doing. Most people start the process of valorization at home, among family. Kids seek approval for their artwork from the parents, or make sure that they get fed and sheltered while doing their thing. When they grow up they may make sure that they have their *oikos* as a last resort to turn to when everything else fails. At the end of our lives, when we lie in our grave, we may find out that the most appreciation for all we did comes from those with whom we shared our *oikos*.

In the experience of this artist each sphere is significantly different. The sphere of the *oikos* and the cultural and social spheres are obvious to him. He knows all too well that he needs support from his wife, that he needs to work in order to get other artists to pay attention to his work and that he needs to participate in the artistic conversation appropriate for him. It is the spheres of the market and the government that are difficult for him to grasp. He had no idea how he could market his concept and earn money with it. Whom to approach? Which organization might be interested? He had no clue. And he had not even considered the options that the market offers. It took some serious persuasion from me to get the students interested in the market. It was not the sphere where they fancied themselves. If they could choose, most of them would opt for the *oikos* and the social sphere to valorize their art. Interestingly, the two options depicted in the standard perspective—coming to all of them as an afterthought—are the options that they need to have pointed out to them.

Getting the artist to see the option of the sphere of the market:
The artist could consider getting other people, or organizations, to pay for his algorithm. In that case he would seek an exchange: the use of the algorithm or even its ownership in exchange for something that has value for him, like food or clothes or gas or an amount of money that allows him to buy all that. When he seeks an exchange, he enters the sphere of the market.

Practically, that means that he has to approach individual people or people in an office, in a gallery maybe, and tell those people about his idea, convince them that the idea is of value to them and then agree on a price.

An exchange occurs when the other is **willing to pay** or, to put it differently, is willing to give up some other goods in order to acquire this one. The question here is: why should someone else be willing to pay for his art? The artist in this anecdote appears to have no clue of the answer and that is why he ignores this option. That shows that participation in the market calls for imagination and some creativity: the artist, or some intermediary, needs to imagine someone else, a stranger maybe, and then imagine his or her values in order to propose a deal. He might imagine, for example, that an organization like Lonely Planet, could be interested offering the algorithm to its customers and would therefore be willing to pay for it.

The exchange is instrumental, at least in principle. The exchange serves the goal of acquiring other goods; the price that another will pay is good for money with which he can pay the price of goods that he is in need of. The exchange is not so much about the relationship with the other—it could be, but it is not necessary—but about the possibility that the good offered has value for the other.

And then there is the option of the government or governance.
The artist can also apply for a subsidy or a grant. He can download the appropriate forms from a government website, or talk with government officials to discuss the possibility of support. He then enters the sphere of the government. When he approaches foundations for a grant, he more or less gets into a similar process. In both cases he involves others, not for what they may value themselves, but for the function they have and the system they represent. When he deals with governments and foundations he needs to take into account the procedures, the criteria, the rules and regulations. He may need an accountant to help him to account for his expenses. And he will be dependent on the judgment of committees.

He could also subject himself to the governance of an organization. That may happen when he offers his creative skills to a firm or gets to teach at an academy or another school. In that case he valorizes his skills by persuading people of the firm or school that he is worth a salary. The firm or school will have application procedures, functions, salary scales, conditions of sickness leave and the like. The firm may claim the rights to whatever he creates as an employee. The academy will have requirements about his art production. A high school wants him to show up in time or may have requirements as to his teaching skills to boot. In all such cases he subjects himself to the logic of G, that is, of governance. He will get a secure and stable income in return.

So now we have expanded the standard economics frame consisting of just the market and the government—or better, governance—with the social sphere, the cultural sphere, and the sphere of the *oikos*. I draw it as follows, with the *oikos* as the base and the social sphere in the center holding all spheres together. The cultural sphere could be a third dimension; I draw it to encompass all others to suggest that everything that is done in either of the five spheres, is embedded in a culture (as I suggested in chapters 1 and 2).

Someone saw in this picture a bicyclist riding a unicycle while keeping the market and the government in the air. She noted that the S is the back of the person; that back has to be very strong in order to maintain the balance between all spheres. So right she was, as will become clear.

M stands for the sphere of the market, G for the sphere f government, or more general, the sphere of governance (as I will clarify below), S for the social sphere, O for the sphere of the *oikos* and C for culture. Each sphere has its own characteristic logic, that is, a collection of rules, norms, institutions, relationships and values that makes certain actions meaningful and renders others strange, unheard of or objectionable, that is, illogical.

The M is the sphere for exchange. It is where the logic of the quid pro quo rules, where goods become products, or commodities, with a price attached, where people or organizations buy and sell, where money functions as a unit of account and a means of exchange. It is the sphere of commercialization, of profit seeking, of interest, of competition, of efficiency, of entrepreneurship and of free choice. It is the sphere in which people become sellers, buyers, customers, consumers, traders and merchants. It is sphere in which goods get valorized as private goods, that is, as goods that are privately owned.

G is the sphere of governance. It is where governmental logic operates, which is a formal logic based on rules and regulations, standards, accounting procedures and laws. It is the logic of bureaucracy. Governments work with this logic, but so do all organizations, some more than others. Foundations work with this logic and so do commercial organizations of some size. In this logic, people become functionaries, managers, employees, subordinates, civil servants, clients, patients, subjects and citizens. It is good for the valorization of collective goods, that is, goods that are collectively owned.

S is the social sphere. Its logic is social and therefore informal. Prices do not figure, neither do rules and regulations. Social logic is the logic of reciprocity, of contributions, of gifts, of participation, cooperation and collaboration. It is the logic of relationships and of networking. In the social sphere people are partners, friends, acquaintances, colleagues, members, comrades, contributors, donors, supporters and participants. In the social sphere people generate shared goods such as social and cultural goods. In the social sphere (creative) commons come about and conversations take place.

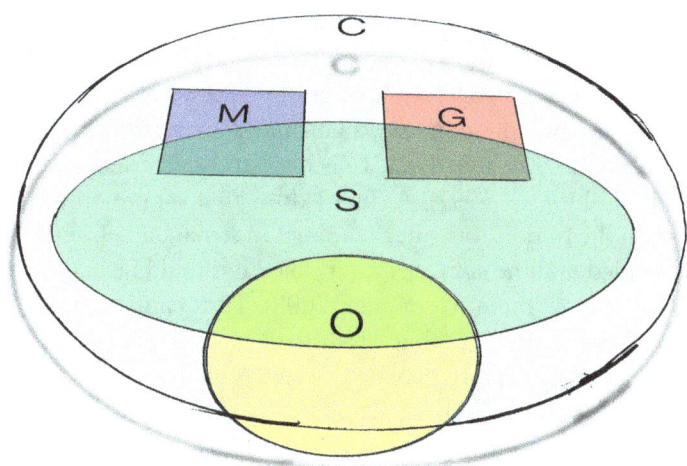

Diagram 9-2 The Five Spheres: Market, Governance,
Oikos, Social and Cultural

The logic of the *oikos* is akin to the social logic but it is different because it presumes kinship or a shared fate. It is the logic of interdependence, of loyalty, of family ties, of intimacy and of love. In the *oikos* people are parents, children, uncles, aunts, nephews, cousins, family members, soul mates, close partners, friends of the family and intimate friends. The *oikos* is good for social and intimate goods.

The logic of the cultural sphere is cultural. In the cultural sphere we transcend all other spheres, relate to the Good, the Beautiful, the Truth, to God or to Karma, harmony, the Sacred, or whatever suggests transcendence. It consists, among others, of religious, artistic, and scientific conversations, or practices. In this sphere people relate to their cultural values, celebrate rituals together, honor sacred objects and share a common history. This is also the sphere where people tap into the sources of the civilization in which they partake.

The following two chapters will probe the spheres further and deeper and will provide a more complete picture. They will discuss the overlaps, the encroachment of one sphere upon the other, the phenomenon of crowding in and out, and a few more of those matters that are relevant when people or organizations are determining their strategies in order to do the right thing. In the remainder of this chapter I will show how the model came about, how it makes sense of historical developments and how it can affect our worldview.

Becoming aware of a need for this model of five spheres

The idea to distinguish spheres came many years ago when I worked with P.W. Zuidhof, then a Ph.D. student, on a paper about cultural heritage. We needed a sphere for gift giving and called that the third sector because that was the common nomenclature at the time for the philanthropic sector. When I presented the paper at a conference of cultural economists, Michael Hutter referred me to the work of Luhmann, a German sociologist (with the warning that he might be too much for what I needed) and suggested I add a sphere for the family (Luhmann, 1997). At first I drew that sphere on top, with the social sphere in the middle, but after reading Gudeman, a befriended anthropologist, I decided that the *oikos*, as I then called it, should be at the base of all spheres, that is, below them (Gudeman, 2008). That came as an insight and caused a revolution in my thinking. From then on I taught myself to use the *oikos* as the point of departure of whatever train of thought. You must have noticed the effects in the preceding chapters and will continue doing so in the remaining chapters. So much of what people do is for the sake of the *oikos*. Life starts at the *oikos*, involves significant others—spouses, parents, children, close friends—revolves for a great deal around them, has often a good *oikos* as a major goal and usually ends there as well.

Later I began to recognize the need to express the cultural dimension. When I teach the culture of economics, a course that I taught already for fifteen years or so to students of philosophy, I discuss the social and rhetoric aspects of economics. My argument is that scientists need to operate in a social setting using a social logic and that that setting may affect the way they practice their science. That is the sociology of science and clearly connects with the social sphere in the model here. But it is not just that logic that applies since scientists use special scientific terms, follow scientific codes and respect scientific values, that is, they practice a particular rhetoric. All that does not show in a model with just four spheres. I was in the need of another sphere. Because I imagine that sphere as transcending the social, I could draw it above the other four spheres, in a third dimension. When I connect the anthropological meaning of culture (C1) with the meanings of culture as civilization (C2) and art (C3) I see the sphere of C as encompassing the other four.

The model of the five spheres serves various purposes, as I began to realize when using it. It will gradually become clear in this and especially the next chapter that it not only helps to account for a great variety of phenomena, but it also encourages an analysis of the characteristic practices in each sphere and of their differences. Gradually it has shaped my worldview. I present the model in almost all lectures that I give and make use of it in my political function to motivate my policies.

The differences between the spheres are crucial for the model to make sense of and to signify what we do when we realize our values. I have found that they can help make people aware of alternative options, of different strategies, when they recognize the differences between the five spheres. Our artist could benefit if he were to step out of his comfort zone in spheres C, S and O, and recognize the opportunities that G and M have to offer him. The differences are also helpful to account for the hostility that the art students demonstrated towards M, or me, when I brought up M. Apparently they were focused on S, the social sphere; the practices of M and the values that they associate with M, clashed with the social practices that they value. That made them feel hostile. Hostility is incidentally also the response of M lovers towards G. Listen to free market economists speaking about governmental practices such as taxation, regulation and laborious decision making, and you can notice the disgust vibrating in their voices. There is more hostility around. Quite a few artists I have run into seem to have a thorough dislike of the *oikos* and it's, in their experience, suffocating and suppressing practices. They are more comfortable in S.

Hostile feelings are a clear indication of important differences. The model should make sense of all such sentiments, and I think it does, as chapters 10a and b will show. We will see more need for the model when we try to figure out how we generate shared and common goods. We will not be able to make sense of those if we stick to a model with an M and a G only. We are in need of an S, a C and an O to understand how we realize the goods that are most important to us. We also need S to understand how creative commons such as those of the arts, religions and the sciences come about and how they function. The "M and G only model" blinds us to the realization of social and cultural goods.

All this is not to say that it is easy to get people to see the merits of thinking in terms of five spheres. The pull of the framing in terms of M practices is powerful. Especially economists are inclined to apply the instrumentation that they have developed to comprehend the practices of M to any other practices. Accordingly, they propose that politicians are striving to maximize votes and that partners in the *oikos* are entering a kind of exchange when dividing chores (Becker, 1976). Such an economistic perspective annihilates the differences between the spheres and makes everything look basically the same, as if everything is subject to the logic of M.

A similar tendency I detect among sociologists. In their case social processes are all that count. They see, for example, the socializing of traders in the market and the role of social factors in markets, such as status and the need to belong. Politics is for them a social process and so is family life. For them the S covers all.

I will not deny that overlaps among spheres occur, that the logic of M may operate in S and O, and that S works in M and G. They actually can be most significant and I will deal with them in the next chapter. However, first we need to be clear about what makes the spheres different, and why those differences matter when we are realizing our values.

The spheres through times

The differences may become more clear when we take a quick run along the course of history. For all we know, human life started out in the *oikos*. The first people moved in small and tightly connected groups. They were entirely dependent upon each other (Sahlins, 1972). They shared what they gathered and hunted, and respected clear lines of authority based on age and skill. Their realization of survival, of a sense of belonging and spiritual life all occurred in these small groups. The ties were close. The others were all well known. Dealings with other groups were rare or non-existent. These groups operated first of all in O.

Yet, humans are cultural beings. Equipped with the faculties of language and imagination, they have to articulate expressions and design symbols that give meaning to their common experiences. Cavemen began drawing on the walls of their caves, developed rituals to cope with the vagaries of fate, and developed the method of the narrative to render their actions meaningful, to give them continuity through time. Accordingly, the activities in the *oikos* were embedded in a cultural sphere.

The groups evolved into tribes in which we notice the beginnings of social practices next to those of the oikos. In S, members of an oikos relate to members of other oikoi and do so socially, on the basis of reciprocity. The S constitutes the public sphere, a sphere in which all people have access but where they do not relate on basis of kinship of family values. Tribal members created rituals together, collaborated and swapped goods and services. Yet, there was no need for money as a means for interacting; no need to keep count of the what for whom. The elder usually ruled on the basis of phronesis. There was no need yet for governmental practices with rules, regulations, enforceable contracts and the like. A tribe operated in O, in C and in S. It even did so when it interacted with other tribes. As the French anthropologist Marcel Mauss describes in his famous book The Gift, the Trobriand tribe entertained an intricate gift exchange to maintain stable relationships with other tribes (Mauss, 1967).

For all we know, market practices emerged quite early on. Strangers might come by offering wares of interest to the people in the tribe, or local community. And here something remarkable happened, something that children still experience when they go out of the home with a few coins in their little fists. Instead of asking someone of your *oikos* for something you wish, you now go up to a total stranger to ask for something of value to you to discover that the stranger, an unknown other, is willing to accept something from you in return, something like a few of those coins in that fist. How can that possibly work? Why not attack that stranger and take the goodies away from him by brute force? Why not take the goodies when he is not looking? How can you tell what is needed for getting a deal done? Why does that amount of coins suffice and not another amount? What is the worth of those coins anyway?

For many people these questions might seem silly, as the answers seem so obvious. But they are not necessarily so obvious. The artist in the opening anecdote had no idea what he had to offer and what to ask in return. The possibilities of M continue to elude so many, especially those working in cultural organizations.

The social sphere was getting more diverse and more elaborate in Athens at the time that Aristotle wrote down his reflection on the polis. Where people gathered in cities they came in need of the goods and services of so many other people, so many that they could not get to know them all very well. And they needed other people to make a living for themselves, to bring about a full and meaningful life.

According to Aristotle the *oikos* was still the pivot around which practical life revolved. The *oikos* was to provide for shelter and as much of its food and other necessities as possible. Autarky was the objective. And the position in one's *oikos* and the wealth of that *oikos* determined the position someone had in the public or social sphere. Heads of well to do households clearly did much better than, say, slaves and women, who had no public position.

The men were supposed to partake in political life that took place at the agora, the central square of the city. Political life is social as it involves discussions and arguments with fellow citizens. The polis (city), therefore, had quite a rich C and a developed S with plenty of social interactions. The G showed up in the form of governmental structures and institutions that the Athenians had put in place. Athens had a sphere of governance. Some citizens had governmental functions and there were laws to regulate daily life and the interactions among citizens. The S was needed for the philosophizing that made these Greeks famous, for the realization of theatre and artwork, that is, of the C. Athens must have had a highly developed civil society, that is, a strong S outside the *oikos*, with a great variety of intense and intensive conversations going on in order to produce such everlasting beauty and insight.

Problematic for Aristotle was the trading that took place in his Athens. He named it *chrematistike* and considered it unnatural since the exchange of goods with complete strangers for a price conflicts with what he considered the natural way of doing things. To him the *oikos* was meant to provide all necessities. That had to be the natural state of affairs. Exchange did not seem natural to him. He had problems with the idea that people use other people as instruments for the realization of their own values and that they reduce the nature of goods to a quality that they are not, that is, a price expressed in monetary units. Even so, he grudgingly admitted that *oikoi* were in need of the goods to be acquired by means of chrematistike.

The G becomes more important when we move closer to current times. Governance was central for the mercantilists in their picture of the world. Strong governments with powerful armies and warships could amass great wealth, so was the idea (and still is albeit with different attributes of power such as size, large domestic markets, innovative power, ownership of vital sources and yes, also military power). Governments stood for central authority, rules and regulation, taxation, control and the law.

We credit Adam Smith for the distinction of M as a distinct sphere with its own practices and its particular importance for the realization of values. He articulated practices that were anathema for Aristotle and so many thinkers and religious scholars after him. How could the pursuit of self-interest be justified? Does the prioritization of profit not corrupt social interactions? What good could come if the interactions between people were left to an invisible hand, without the intervention of governmental authority?

Historians such as E.P Thomson and Karl Polanyi narrate the impact that the emergence of M as a common practice had on traditional communities (Thompson, 1991 and Polanyi, 1944). Just imagine what it means for people growing up in a farm, expecting and being expected to farm in their own *oikos*, to face the breaking away of some members in order to work for an outsider for a monetary payment. It must have meant a dramatic change in the lives of *oikoi* at the time. E.P Thompson narrates the revolts that occurred in the 18th century when locals would attack the miller on his way to the market with the flour that he had grounded from local wheat. The locals perceived this action of their miller as a "selling out to strangers". Their social logic clashed with the logic of the market (where selling to strangers for a good price is perfectly normal).

In his narration Polanyi is in need of a distinction of spheres, too. He distinguishes four spheres, one of exchange (the M here), one of redistribution (the G here) and one of reciprocity (the S here). In addition he addresses house holding, the O in the model here. He needs especially the S to indicate that market type interactions are not "normal" as a run of the mill economic analysis would suggest and that other, social, interactions once overwhelmed market exchanges. The latter started to grow more dominant only in the 16th century. (My good friend Deirdre McCloskey tends to fume when the name of Polanyi comes up as he, according to her, grossly distorts the history of markets and underestimates their role; she is probably right--she usually is on such matters--but the more important point here is not the timing, but rather the very phenomenon of frictions that occur when the emphasis shifts from one sphere to another.)

In the last two hundred years or so, the market has acquired a strong presence in the collective mindset. People in the modern world grow up in awareness of the importance of markets for earning an income and acquiring goods. We all learn how powerful M is when it comes to the exchange of private goods and the size of economic capital. The widespread resistance against the dominance of M corroborates the point.

An important factor is the increasing capacity of modern societies to measure market outcomes. Turnovers, profits, the value of assets like machines, buildings, shares, bonds and bank accounts; they all come in numbers. The financialization of our world means that we can count an increasing number of transactions and possession in financial or monetary terms. And that conveys a sense of hardness and concreteness to M. For it is a strong belief in instrumentalist thinking that numbers are factual and therefore concrete and hard. It makes one belief that all that cannot be counted in monetary terms is "abstract" instead of "concrete," "soft" and thus not "hard." That makes anything that comes about in O, S, and C "abstract" and "soft," at least in an instrumentalist way of thinking. The value based approach turns that worldview upside down or inside out.

Even so, the impressive accumulation of economic and financial wealth that the modern world has witnessed in the last two hundred years attests to the great impact of M and the innovative and entrepreneurial practices that brought about all of that. The M is a crucial sphere for us to valorize our value as workers (in the labor market), to buy computers, houses, clothes, therapy, vacations and all kinds of other goods that we need so much, and in order to acquire the means to buy. People in most parts of the world do not know any better than that they have to engage in practices of M in order to get what they want.

However, we also learned that the practices of M can be destabilizing, can even bring about crises and can have unintended consequences such as inequalities and injustices. The Great Depression of the thirties continues to linger in the collective memory (in Western countries at least) as an episode of grand market failure. I doubt that the recent recession (2008-2014) —or shall we continue speaking of the financial crisis?—will have the same impact. At the time the answer to the crisis was sought in boosting G. Communists in the Soviet Union had already embraced the practices of G as a way to outwit M and bring about more welfare for everyone. They sought a scientific solution to the problem of allocation and perceived governmental practices as essential in the implementation of such a solution. Socialists and social democrats looked for a solution in a combination of M and G. John Maynard Keynes propagated government expenditures to compensate for a fall in domestic demand. Jan Tinbergen took a more systematic approach with models to show that governmental policies can influence economic outcomes. But for the government to be effective it had to grow bigger.

Accordingly, governmental practices increased dramatically in the decades that followed, with increasing budgets for welfare programs, and, in the sixties and seventies, in waves of rules and regulations. In most developed countries, governments grew in size to claim up to half of Gross Domestic Product. They ran utility companies, took care of education, healthcare, telecommunication, the post office and cultural activities such as museums, theatres, and libraries; they subsidized cultural and social activities as well as entrepreneurial activities. They protected companies against foreign competition and prosecuted violators of the anti-trust laws. In the eighties governments began to embrace M as a governing logic and the process of privatization and liberalization began. Even so, governments continue to contribute between 40% and 55% to the total of national income.

Governments signify bureaucracies and bureaucracies make up G. Every private party seeking gain, profit or pleasure in M will have to deal with governmental bureaucracies. Just try to get into India or the US as a tourist or businessperson and you will notice.

The sphere of G becomes even more dominant when we take business organizations into account. Although the inclination is to relegate them to the sphere of M—since they buy and sell—they actually operate internally in accordance with governmental logic. They also, after all, have bureaucracies assign functions to their employees, maintain a system of accounting and operate by way of all kinds of rules, procedures and contracts. They all stand for what could be called a managerial culture. Such a culture came about in the second half of the 19th century when feudal and paternalistic practices no longer sufficed for complex organizations like the railways, and it took flight in the thirties of the 20th** century, when MBA schools shot up (Chandler, 1977). Management is about organizing, guarding and implementing a governmental logic and for that, advanced education was deemed necessary. The emphasis on management in the business world also gave plenty of opportunities to consultants to assist managers in being systematic, structured, and evidence-based in their strategies. When consultants got hold of institutions like universities and hospitals, those, too, became subject to the managerial culture.

When we imagine G as the sphere of all organizations, public and private, it may be possible to realize that G involves us more than M. Most of our interactions take place within organizations or with organizations. A great majority of workers receive their paycheck from organizations; transactions within large multinationals constitute the greater part of international trade. The influence of governments is pervasive. We are ruled and regulated by them, receive income or benefits, pay taxes and fines. So although in the collective mindset M is dominant, in their daily lives most people depend more on forces in G than on those in M. The bias probably occurs because transactions in M are measured and most interactions within G are not.

Throughout the 20th century, the logics of the market and governance have received most attention in public and scientific discourses. Economists made everybody else believe that the market logic is all that matters, whereas business economists discussed the shaping of governmental (or managerial) logic to profit optimally from the market logic. Lawyers and public administrators were focusing on governmental logic as it functions in governments. The social sphere and the sphere of the *oikos* all but disappeared from sight. Sociologists did a valiant attempt to keep their logics in the public picture, but in the eighties their discourse became increasingly marginalized.

Spheres of regulation, coordination and discipline

The historical perspective makes clear that the five spheres have distinctive principles of regulating, coordinating and disciplining human actions and activities. No matter how much freedom we have or desire, we are in need of (outside) correctors, of signals that tell us whether we are doing the right thing, or not. As children we are in need of some serious disciplining from time to time, and even as adults we need to hear from our spouse, the police, a judge or a manager that we have to do something about our conduct. For politicians and governors one of the key questions concerns what mechanisms are best to get people to do the (politically or commercially) right thing. How to prevent them from abusing welfare provisions? How to get people to be entrepreneurial? How to get them to be efficient and productive? How to motivate people to do right?

The inclination, once again, is to focus on the disciplinary and regulatory mechanisms that M and G provide. The picture of the five spheres calls attention to the regulatory and disciplinary forces of the three other spheres.

The cultural sphere is good for intrinsic motivation. A cultural setting stimulates and gives meaning to certain actions and makes other actions senseless or even bad. In C you find out whether your beliefs make sense, or not; whether your idea is meaningful; whether a contribution or action resonates with the prevalent culture (as in C1 and C2).

The sphere of the *oikos* appeals to loyalty and the norms of kinship; when you violate them other members may get mad at you and in the worst case you risk exclusion. The Amish *oikos* will ban members who choose to join regular society. In the *oikos* parents have a stern talk with their children, will ground them if necessary, and otherwise may correct them all the time. ("Close your mouth when eating." "You are not going out before you have done your homework.") Children may do the same with their parents, at least in some cultural settings.

The social sphere provides mechanisms of social control, of approval and disapproval, of shaming, of teasing and revering, of attribution of guilt, of reputation and recognition, of exclusion, and of authority, power and hierarchy. Social mechanisms are probably most pervasive in daily life. When I injure the feelings of someone, that person or someone else, may let me know in such a way that I feel badly about it. When I am aggressive in traffic, my wife usually yells at me. When I am too full of myself, a child lets me know. When I give a bad talk, I will not be invited again. When I treat a colleague badly, I will pay for it later, for example by her support of a measure that is bad for me.

The market regulates by means of prices and financial rewards: a high reward is a sign of doing well. In the market some profit and others lose. The market punishes bad ideas and bad products, and rewards good ones. Markets make good entrepreneurs rich and throw others in poverty. As economists like to say, the market provides incentives to do the right thing. And it does so without the involvement of any authority. Accordingly, it does not restrict the freedom of those who participate in it.

That is different in G. The governmental sphere regulates by means of rules, programs, accounting procedures and monitoring, that is by restricting actions and activities of people. Bureaucracies punish and reward by way of rules, judgments of committees, or decrees of authorities. Governments apply the law and make use of the judiciary if necessary. In G we get speeding tickets, may be thrown in jail, disallowed to build as we please, cut trees at will, or merge with another company.

The mechanisms of M and G are widely acknowledged. This model of five spheres expands these two with three other mechanisms of regulatory, coordinating and disciplinary mechanisms.

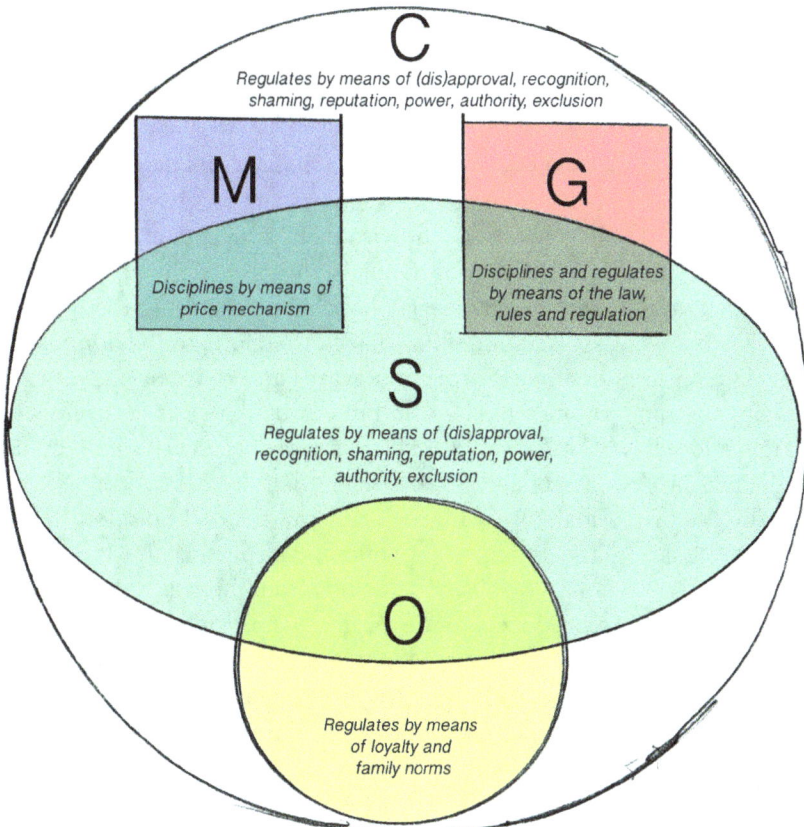

Figure 9-3 Five systems of control and regulation

Worldviews

Others have pointed out the need to differentiate between spheres beyond those of the market and the government. Mostly they do so to call attention to the existence of a society, of social processes, that is, and sometimes to remind us that we operate in an *oikos*, too (although that is not the term they use). I refer to the philosophers Hegel and Habermas , the sociologists Paul DiMaggio and Viviana Zelizer, the anthropologist Stephen Gudeman and the historian Karl Polanyi. Most of them do so in order to explain things better, to give a more accurate picture of the real world than the one-sided pictures in which M, or G, dominates.

My objective is a moral one as it is my purpose is to figure out what is the right thing to do. What is the right strategy for the realization of values? I offer the model of the five spheres to inform worldviews of people and organizations seeking the right thing to do. Yet if we can use the model for individuals, groups of people and organizations, then we can use it for politicians as well; the only difference being that politicians are in need of a strategy to realize societal values. Main political movements turn out to stress one sphere or another, as I will show.

The model may be used to counter the idea that M is all that matters and to argue that there is such a thing as a society (as the former British prime minister Margaret Thatcher, a fervent advocate of M, once famously denied) (Thatcher, 1987). The issue that got us going in the case of the artist was the outright rejection by the art students of my appeal to M logic. To them selling an artwork is not what art is about. They object, therefore, to the dominance of M logic. They are not alone. Suspicion towards and resistance against the market logic is strong. I notice it all around me. A book that is critical of the market tends to sell well. *What money can't buy: the moral limits of markets*, by the Harvard ethics professor Sandel was a bestseller (Sandel, 2012).

Usually the discussion stops with the criticism. A good question to ask, I would suggest, is why the criticism is so loud and so persistent. Markets are clearly operating all over and we all are benefiting from them as they enable us to valorize the goods we produce and the services we provide, and we acquire goods and services that are useful for us. So why all the criticism? One reason for this is that markets do not always work very well and generate unwelcome outcomes, like pollution and inequality. Another reason is that people do not recognize all what they do in the sphere of the market. Whether it is their intimate interactions, their friendships, their social activities or their conversations about art, they cannot make sense of those in terms of the market. When people see the spheres of the social sphere and the *oikos*, at least some of their criticism is resolved when they perceive that they are justified in surmising that there is life beyond the market. In the case of the artist the social and the cultural sphere as well as the sphere of the *oikos* help to make sense of his behavior and show that he was valorizing his work even if that was not in the spheres of the market and the government.

Additionally, having a picture of the S, we can more easily recognize movements that occur in the social sphere. Especially the digital environment thrives on social initiatives to which people contribute without monetary compensation and which operate with a minimum of G. Think of open sources, of Wikipedia and the like. S is also the domain of the share economy in which people share cars, machines, homes, rooms and so on. S is the domain where communities are active, where people start cooperatives and use social money. It is also the sphere where colleagues support each other, where scientists share ideas and research findings, where musicians make music together and where people pool resources to help each other out. The more you explore S, the more you will see.

The purpose of the picture with the five spheres, therefore, is to make sense of all possible strategies that people follow when they valorize their values. When you make it your own, you may find out that it will affect the way you perceive the world around you. You will still discern markets working and governments operating but you will probably pay more attention to what people and organizations do in the social sphere and, as far as people are concerned, in the *oikos* in order to do the right things. It will get you interested in the possibilities as well as the limitations of each sphere, of the frictions that occur when people switch spheres, and the misunderstandings that result when it is unclear in which sphere someone is operating. And you may wonder, as I do, whether the spheres as they function now in current societies are sufficiently in balance or whether some kind of correction is called for.

You will also notice that the model of five spheres enables us to address all kinds of other questions. For example, when the question comes up why the level of trust is going down, we might consider processes in S besides what happens in M and in G. The S factor, incidentally, was generally recognized as problematic when the former Soviet countries embraced the M; it was surmised that they lacked the strong civil society that is needed for a good functioning market and an effective government. The inclusion of S and O furthermore indicates that other coordinating mechanisms are at work besides the pricing mechanism of M and the regulatory mechanism of G. I refer to the socializing and moralizing forces in S and O. And when the discussion turns to the qualities of life, to issues of meaning, to the question of civilization ("are we experiencing a loss of civilization, or not?"), we need to distinguish a distinctive cultural sphere.

Those forces are not always recognized. A while ago I addressed a large audience together with a well-known and eloquent Dutch economist. I presented the model. He thought it was all "nonsense"—he likes to be provocative. His example was the traffic. "Listen," he said to the audience with a dramatic tone in his voice, "when we regulate traffic, all we need are rules and prices. Because of the rules people drive on the right side of the road, or the left in some countries, and stop for traffic lights. The price of cars and gas prevents overcrowding of the roads." And then he turned defiantly to me. That was an easy one. "Arnold," so I responded (I was prepared this time!), "ever driven in Iowa City, Naples, Mumbai and, say, Amsterdam? Did you notice how different the traffic is in those cities? In Iowa City people drive slowly, they are considerate of other drivers, stop for stop-signs and traffic lights and they yield to others. In Naples you have to ignore those behind you and forget about looking in the rear-view mirror—and take whatever space you can, to notice that the Italians are gracious in defeat. Mumbai is just one big chaos where it is not clear on which side of the road you need to drive, where no one seems to care about what the others are doing, where you better ignore traffic lights if you want to keep going and where it is perfectly normal to get stuck in a massive traffic jam. In Amsterdam there is a continuous war between cars and bicycles, with the latter violating all possible traffic rules to beat the cars. In all cases, the official rules are more or less the same, and in all cases, prices operate. Yet the traffic is dramatically different. This shows that the most important regulating forces are social, or cultural, in kind. People are socialized in the way they manage the traffic." Arnold decided to ignore the point and barged ahead with another point. This confirmed my impression that economists have a hard time seeing the spheres of S, C and O, even if you point it out to them.

Not only economists have a problem perceiving the workings of S, C and O. My guess is that most people do. When it comes to their worldview, most people will mainly see a world with M and G. After decades of belief in G, M appeared to become more popular. Whereas in my student years the discussions were about what the government should do, nowadays the discussions are about what the government should not do. At least that was the case until the recession that started in 2008. It was believed that governments had grown too big and too bulky, that taxes were too high and welfare programs too generous. Ever since the late seventies free market ideologies are back in vogue and free market ideologies such as Milton Friedman and Friedrich Hayek were once again widely read and discussed. The trend was to withdraw governments from all kinds of activities. This resulted in the privatization of all kinds of government organizations (such as in telecommunication, utilities, maintenance, health care, transport and education) and the liberalization of various markets from government control, the financial sector being a prime example.

In the model, this shows up as a shift from G to M. As noted earlier, the Great Depression had motivated a move towards G. Keynes advocated more and bigger governments, a larger G, that is (Keynes, 1963). They saw in a large G a counterbalance to an unstable and too powerful M. However, they did not go as far as communists who advocated the abolition of the M logic altogether. Accordingly, developed, non-communist countries moved first from M to G, then moved back to M, to return to more G during the financial crisis of 2008-2014.

You would expect liberals (the European label for free market advocates) to celebrate the embrace of M by politicians from the eighties onwards. But that is not necessarily the case. The reason why I could figure out with the help of my model and the dissertation about neo-liberalism by Zuidhof (whom I mentioned earlier in the chapter). Neo-liberalism is a commonly used term to characterize current policies. It is said that current social democrats have turned into neoliberals and that the policies of the EU are neoliberal as well. The definition of neoliberalism, however, remains usually unclear. Most people I ask can't tell its difference from liberalism. They come as far as identifying neo-liberalism with Chicago economics and its emphasis on selfish behavior and free markets. The model creates clarity. Zuidhof helped me by making a connection with Foucault's notion of governmentality that I subsequently adopted (Foucault, 1975).

Governmentality is what characterizes neo-liberals. They are people who operate in G, or think in terms of G, and adopt the logic of M as a strategy in their politics. Neo-liberals, therefore, are governors, or people who identify themselves with governors, who advocate free markets and entrepreneurship, as managerial solutions for societal problems (such as high unemployment, inefficiencies and high prices). They are the politicians who want to liberalize markets and privatize government organizations. Yet because they are governors, they also seek ways to somehow stay in control. That is why we have witnessed a surge in supervisory institutions, regulations and accounting procedures. All those are anathemas for true liberals who prefer to minimize as much government as possible and safeguard the autonomy of individuals, especially of entrepreneurial individuals.

Typical was the response to the financial crisis starting in 2008. Instead of propagating laissez faire, as a true liberal would do, politicians as well as people on the street called for massive government intervention. The logic of G had to come to the rescue of what was perceived to be a failure in M logic. As a consequence, governments rescued banks, even nationalized them, and formulated a massive set of new rules and strengthened the supervision of the sector.

In the academic world I see a similar trend. Even where academic governors speak about the importance of valorization of research in markets, and where students have become our customers, the number and influence of rules and formal procedures are only expanding. In recent years European universities have suffered greatly under time- and money-consuming accreditation procedures. It is all about control and accountability, that is, values of G. In that area of my life, I experience G indeed as a capital G. A colleague of mine speaks of a Soviet system. I am reminded of Kafka, since nobody can give me the rationale of the procedures and everybody tells me that we have to do it whether we like it or not. (I can't help revealing my bias here. I would argue that universities should focus on S, on the fostering of academic communities and experience G practices as undermining the S in the academic world.)

Whereas conventional wisdom would probably state that the M logic is dominant nowadays, I would argue that G logic rules in everyday and public life. When something goes wrong, like an airplane crash, a large fire, high unemployment, a failing bank or personal misfortune), most people look to the government for a solution. When journalists ask for the solution when someone has discussed a problem of any kind, they usually imply asking what the government should do about it. Bring a politician on stage together with any other citizen, and everybody wants to know what the politician has to say. Only pop stars may succeed in drawing the attention away. When people or organizations are in trouble, they expect the government to help them out. This is certainly the case in northern European countries, but such a mentality is also strong in countries like England and the US. In southern European countries people customarily whine and complain about ineffective and corruptive governments, but that practice betrays rather a longing for strong and effective governments than for no government at all. Advocates of mere laissez faire, laissez passer may have a large audience but find few followers when it is time for action.

Of course, it is a matter of political belief to stress one sphere over another. People recognize their values more in one sphere than in the others and will be inclined to advocate strategies pertaining to that sphere. The model is not going to determine who is more right than others, although I surmise that the final conclusion will be that there is a need for some balance. That still leaves room for discussion as to what the perceived imbalances are and how to correct for those. Politics is the working of *phronesis* at the level of societies and beyond. People apply it in cafes, in classrooms and in public squares. It is in the corridors of power that *phronesis* is really at work, with consequences for all citizens.

The model allows for rough characterizations of political movements, based on their faith in or valuation of one sphere above the others. The table on the following page provides a summary.

In conclusion

The model of the five spheres provides a picture of the world in which we all operate in order to realize our values. It directs our attention to the others we need to involve in order to do so. Also, it points out to us that we have various options, various strategies that we can follow. It is not that one strategy excludes the other, but we need to be aware of the consequences of choosing one strategy rather than another. The choice may matter for the values that we ultimately succeed in realizing.

The model provides a set up for a view of the world. It inspires us to look beyond market and governmental practices and to recognize the role that social relations have in daily life. The social and the cultural sphere and the sphere of the *oikos* are essential for the generation of social and cultural goods, for all the goods that we need to share with others. Without a clear view on those spheres we cannot make sense of social and cultural goods, and will fail to get a clear understanding of how artistic, scientific and religious practices, among many others, work.

Having the overall picture, we can now turn to the intricacies of each sphere and to the interactions among and between them.

Simple characterizations:

Liberals (in the classical sense) celebrate the forces of M and are critical of the actions of G for the sake of freedom.

Keynesians or **the liberals in the American** sense argue that a strong G is needed to compensate for failures of M for the sake of stability and justice.

Socialists argue that G should dominate M for the sake of justice and the power of the people.

Neo-liberals are governors (that is, they are positioned in G) who see practices of M as solutions for their problem.

Communists seek to displace M with G; in communism all goods are state owned.

Communitarians stress the importance of S, of social arrangements, and downplay the role of M and G.

Corporatism stresses cooperation between organized labor and organizations of enterprises with secondary roles for the market and the government.

AN EXPLORATION OF THE FIVE SPHERES: LOGIC, RHETORIC, VALUES AND RELATIONSHIPS. THE OIKOS AND THE SOCIAL AND THE CULTURAL SPHERES FIRST

The main message of the value based approach is hopefully clear by now. In order to do the right thing we need to reach beyond the practices of exchange (M) and governance (G), beyond private and collective goods. To valorize our social, cultural and whatever other goods we have to operate in all five spheres. To realize an idea, we do best in the cultural sphere. Is it a family we need to realize, or something like care or love? Then we do better in the sphere of the *oikos*. Reputation, recognition and trust are best realized in the social sphere. For selling tickets and advice, the sphere of the market is probably ideal, and when an organization needs to be in order, we have to be in the sphere of governance.

And what if you are just trying to survive? In that case any sphere will do. Get welfare benefits if you can in G, sell whatever possible in M, find support in S, or plead for help from family members in O. C may not be a very useful source, though.

The picture of five spheres will broaden the perspective of people who are in the process of planning their life. Quite a few of my students express a preference for work in the commercial sector. They think of M and the logic of exchange and the values of ambition and financial security. The picture warns them that if they seek employment in a commercial organization they will have to deal with the governance in that organization, that is, with G.

Would they fit in a bureaucratic structure? They furthermore have to answer to how they are going to operate in S and O, that is, in the social sphere and their *oikos*. What kind of *oikos* are they striving for? Is a family life important to them? How about close friends? And then there is the cultural sphere. How will they bring about meaning in their life? What kind of relationship do they seek with the transcendental? Will they seek contact with the Muse, with Nature, with the Divine? What kind of practices, or praxes, do they seek to appropriate? All these questions together are too much to answer when you are, say, twenty-one But they will cross your path sooner or later.

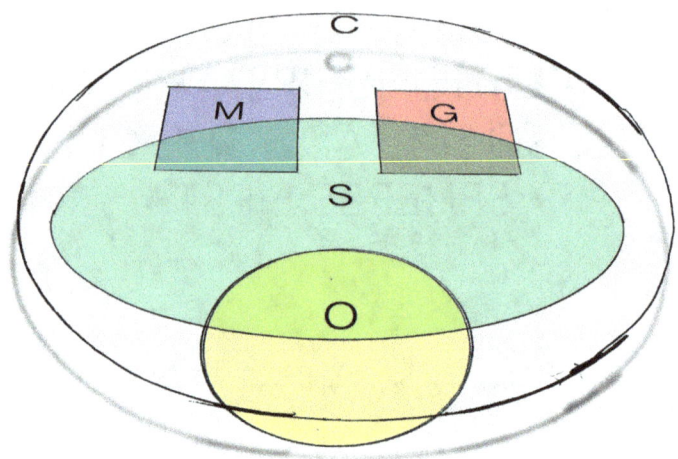

Diagram 10A-1 The Five Spheres

Awareness of the five spheres is a practical matter. A director of a museum better knows the differences when she is planning her financial strategy. Might she respond to the values that people seek to realize in S and C? How would she do that? When she is seeking donations, she is likely to engage with the logic, rhetoric and values of S, and possibly O as well. Likewise, leaders of a business firm are well advised to take notice of the cultural setting in which they operate (C), and the way social goods like trust, collegiality and a creative environment come about (and get lost) in S. They, too, may ponder how their goods can appeal to the need to realize social and cultural values or to feed an *oikos*. Political leaders who fail to recognize the workings of S, O and C are at least partially blind.

People like yourself as well as politicians and governors have another reason to consider all five spheres with their logic. Their reason is that of guidance, control or regulation. As an individual you are in need of (outside) correctors, of signals that tell you whether or not you are doing the right thing.

For politicians and governors one of the key questions is what mechanisms are best to get people to do the (politically or commercially) right thing. How to prevent them from abusing welfare provisions? How to encourage people to be entrepreneurial? How to get them to be efficient and productive? How to motivate people to do right? As we saw in chapter 9 each sphere generates a distinctly different system of regulation, stimulus and discipline. The five sphere model brings out the importance of social and cultural systems next to the regulatory systems of M and G.

The previous chapter introduced the five-sphere model and also showed how the model can inform one's worldview. This chapter will explore the characteristics of each of the five spheres of the *oikos* (O), the social sphere (S), the cultural sphere (C), and in chapter 10B the market (M) and the sphere of governance (G). It addresses questions of *how*, *what* and *why*. The *how*-question contemplates how best to valorize certain values and how to strive for certain purposes. The *what*-question reveals in which sphere what goods are to be generated, acquired, given, or shared. And the *why*-question examines why certain strategies are failing and others succeeding.

For starters

The five spheres represent ideal types. Each of the five spheres stands for a stereotypical interaction with others.

Real interactions usually involve aspects of more than one sphere. Take the visit to the local grocery store whose owner you happen to know. You walk in and chat some with the owner; you exchange some niceties and you make a few jokes. That interaction takes place in the social sphere as you do things to affirm the relationship that you have with the other, the owner of the shop in this case. Then you get the carton of milk, the cookies and the coffee that you need, go to the cash register and pay for the goodies. That interaction is a market transaction and pertains to the sphere of the market. The value added tax that you also pay is an interaction within the sphere of governance. Then you go home and make yourself and your housemates some coffee. That you do in the sphere of the *oikos*, or the social sphere (in case you are not that close with your housemates). The cultural sphere is responsible for the cultural setting in which you, the people in the store and the people in your *oikos* operate. For example, in an Asian setting the carton of milk would be an unlikely item, and the jokes made in Central Africa will be quite different from the jokes made in a Dutch provincial town.

Similarly, people working in an organization are switching between the different spheres all the time. When they talk with each other, share experiences, make plans, talk about what is going on in their lives and in the world in which they are interacting socially, in S, that is. When they appeal to, work with and enforce rules, contracts, functions, standards, protocols and the like, they are in G, the sphere of governance. When they discuss the content of their work or whatever makes their work meaningful, they operate in the cultural sphere, C. When they sell their goods to other people or to other organizations they take advantage of the sphere of the market, of M. They may wish to be an *oikos*, being close to each other and all that, but the claim of having a true *oikos* in an organization will be highly dubious (for example because of the risk of getting fired).

Even so, it is important to be aware in which sphere you are operating. It probably would not go over very well if you were to go up to the grocery owner with a sad story and then ask him to let you just have the goodies for free. It would be also weird if you were to say something like "Hey, I feel really at home here" and walk away with the goodies without paying, as though you were grabbing stuff out of your refrigerator at home and taking them up to your room. And your colleagues would look strangely at you if you suddenly ask them for money for the advice you just gave them: it's alright to charge outsiders, but it's not what you do when helping out colleagues. It would be illogical.

The following exploration, therefore, is about raising the awareness of what it takes to valorize values and goods in the right way, how to involve others rightly. It is meant to be edifying and tries to influence your worldview—it has already done so for me. It adds content to the picture of the model of the five spheres that may affect the way you design the activities in your life, organization, community or society.

Many of the examples in the following exploration I have taken from the cultural sector. The reason for this is that I regularly advise cultural organizations and frequently talk with artists. When the issue of valorization comes up and—what it often boils down to—the financing of their practice, I use the model. But the model applies to any kind of activity that is meant to be the right thing.

As I keep saying to people in the cultural sector, the sphere in which you valorize your art matters. In the heat of the money game, however, the message is easily lost. When people are badly in need of money—or when they think they are—they easily forget to what end it is that they are doing what they are doing. Not all money is good. The source of the money is important. Selling more tickets is fine, but if the sacrifice for doing so is the forsaking of ideals, then it is not so fine anymore. Likewise, acquiring money from a sponsor with a dubious reputation (shall we say from a rifle factory, or a Mafia organization?) could be disastrous for a cultural organization.

This is where the process of valorization must begin: the ideals, that which an organization, a person or a community articulates as the goods to strive for, the goods that define the purposes, the mission. Is that good something artistic, social, societal or personal? Without articulation of those goods, the subsequent actions are aimless and without meaning. If someone wants to create art, he better look for a group of people that are able to appreciate his art. If fatherhood is the good to strive for, then the *oikos* is clearly the sphere to look at. If justice is the good to strive for, then the governmental sphere is probably the best choice, although certain parts of the social sphere might qualify as well (e.g. for the bringing together of people interested in the same goal).

How about production for profit, or status? It is possible, of course, to articulate an instrument as an intermediate goal, such as profit or social status. Although, as we saw in chapter 7, that triggers the question of what such an intermediate goal is good for. What is the profit good for? If the ultimate purpose is having a good family, or a more just world, or a better quality of work and products, then a single-minded pursuit of profit may not be the right thing to do.

With the set-up of chapter 4 in mind—going from ideals via strategy and practice to evaluation—the five-sphere model informs of the next step: the determination of the best design, or strategy. Is the market the best option, or should the sphere of governance be the main focus of the valorization process? How about the possibilities that the social sphere has to offer? How about the *oikos*? Accordingly, the model gets us thinking about the design of activities, an organization maybe, financial strategies and the like.

The main characteristics to look for in each sphere

1. *The kinds of relationships.* The design of activities concerns first of all the way in which to involve others. It is a matter of the kind of *relationship* that best suits the purposes at hand. A social relationship that is somehow reciprocal is good for the realization of social goods. An exchange in the market with a merely instrumental relationship is good for the generation of financial means that, in turn, are good for other things. The government can also be good for financial means but requires a different rationale ("Does the proposal meet the criteria?"). If the idea is to sustain certain activities, some kind of organization is called for and that requires the formalization of at least some aspects of relationships with others. Then there is the option of fostering intimate relationships in the *oikos* with specific requirements for the design to allow space for such relationships ("work-life balance"). The relationship with the transcendental is not a social one. Even so, we can say that we relate to Nature somehow, to a (national) Culture, Art, the Truth or the Divine. Such relationships constitute the cultural sphere. Accordingly, the types of relationships are one of the characteristics to look for in each of the spheres.

2. *The logic.* The second characteristic to consider is the *logic* of a relationship and the sphere in which it functions. The logic refers to the way of doing something, the types of interactions, and the norms that makes sense for that kind of relationship, in a particular sphere—and what would fail to make sense (be illogical) in the other spheres. The logic includes institutional practices, norms and (implicit) rules, and the kind of currency that mediates and regulates the interactions. (The currency in M is money; in S it comes in social forms like favors, reputation, credits, and blame.)

3. *The rhetoric.* The particular way of speaking that characterizes a sphere is its *rhetoric*. It represents persuasive strategies that are particular to that sphere and would not make sense in the other spheres. By calling it rhetoric, I want to alert you to the types of metaphors at work and the narrative (the kind of story) that makes sense.

4. *The values.* Then there are the *positive and negative values* for which each sphere stands and that the practices in that sphere valorize. The positive values are what people generally appreciate in a particular sphere, what makes them propagate that sphere. Negative values are usually the values that are attributed to a sphere from the point of view of other spheres and will motivate moves away from that particular sphere. For example, the positive value that people attach to M is freedom to choose; a negative value is greed, a value that emanates from the vantage point of the social sphere.

Let us now explore each sphere in turn for each of these characteristics. We start in the sphere where life begins, and usually where it ends as well: the *oikos*.

1) Oikos

It all starts at home. It does so for all of us. At home we realize important values of all kinds by way of goods that are particular to O. These goods are all shared goods, such as a good family, intimate relationships, cozy evenings, vacations, conviviality, trust, love, and memories. All of these are answers to the what-question: what goods do we realize in the sphere of the *oikos*?

Another set of answers to the what-question is the virtues that we hone by partaking in an *oikos*, virtues like being honest, loyal and loving. At home we seek to be all of that in some way or another (and that is not to say that we actually behave accordingly).

The *oikos* can be a purpose in and of itself. In that case it is a *praxis* (as defined in the chapter 7.) Many people value their *oikos* as their most precious possession for which they are willing to do anything to protect, from hard labor to even sacrificing their own life. The *oikos* can also be good for the realization of other ideals, such as the ideal of being a good father or mother, and of love.

The *oikos* is instrumental in satisfying a variety of wants and needs. A home can be good for shelter, children, grandchildren (I would love to have some myself), home cooked meals, companionship, cozy evenings, interesting experiences (vacations and the like), education in art and music, religion, craftsmanship, attention, support, and care. In addition the *oikos* can be a production unit as in a farm, a shop or a (family) business.

Products and services that economists call "consumption" are instruments for the *oikoi*, to realize themselves and for their relevant values and goods. The apples that I buy are an input into my *oikos*.

Dysfunctional families fail to realize some or more of these goods and values. Some families do not succeed in providing support, love, affection, cozy evenings and fond memories and instead generate bad experiences of suppression, loneliness, and exploitation. They demonstrate that the realization of a good family is tough and requires skill, lots of effort, and a bit of luck.

Realizing a good *oikos* is about getting *relationships* right, respecting the proper *logic* and adhering to its *values*. Let us take a look at what these characteristics involve.

The kinds of *relationships* that the O encourages us to generate and sustain are family relationships, as well as intimate and sexual relationships. The latter are the basis of a new *oikos* that members of two different *oikoi* will form. (Note that *oikoi* are changing all the time, by death, divorce, marriage, birth, tragedy, and romance.)

The relationship with the *other* that we need in order to valorize our goods is in the *oikos* a family, kinship, or an intimate, close and loving relationship. We get the other involved because of that kind of relationship. The other will support us out of love, loyalty or duty ("it is the family duty to back each other up, and to do so unconditionally").

Through the O we sustain relationships with parents, siblings, partners, children, grandparents, nephews or whoever is inalienable for us. The Germans express the idea well: your home consists of people with whom you share a "Schicksalgemeinschaft"—a community that is based on a shared fate. One characteristic of such a relationship is that it is very hard, and in some cases impossible, to sever. Even when children break with their parents, or vice versa, the parent-child relationship does not cease to exist. (Think of the biblical story of the prodigal son who is welcomed back by his father, even though he made an elaborate effort to make such a welcome unlikely.) Divorce or separation, however, is a good method to break up an *oikos* and sever the relationship of a couple (though it will usually not sever the ties with children).

One's *oikos* is usually based on kinship, but it is not necessarily so. A partner, for instance, does not have a blood-relationship to you. Marriage is about connecting different *oikoi*. An intimate friend could be part of your *oikos*, too. An *oikos* can be extended, as in tribal communities, or consist of extended families as in the Chinese societies. In Western societies the *oikos* is usually small and consists of only a few people. Even so, it is possible to experience an *oikos* in a particular place, or in one's own country. People, who have been away from the country where they were born for a long time, may experience that country as their *oikos* and anyone they meet from that country as a member of that *oikos*. (Imagine yourself in a dire and desperate situation far from home. You feel helpless and hopeless. Imagine now how you feel when someone comes up to you, introduces himself as someone from the embassy of your country, and offers to help since you are a fellow citizen. I imagine that it feels like coming home.)

My students do not always recognize the relevance of the *oikos* and neither do quite a few artists I talk with ("I can be at home anywhere, with anyone."). This is understandable as the students have often just left their original *oikos* behind and still have to make up their mind about whether or not they are in need of their own. And the artists resist the *oikos* for all kinds of, for them good, reasons. Yet, even they, at least most of them, have a place that they can call home; it is the place where a parent or friend prepares the food, where they have a bed, and where they can take refuge when in trouble. Home is what people fall back on when they have experienced a disaster, where they seek solace in troubled times, and where they can "let their hair down." Home can also be a feeling or a sensation.

When you are so clear on what your home means to you that you hardly have to think about it, just imagine what it would be like to 'lose' your home, because of violence, a divorce, or death. It happened once to me. The feeling of loss is tremendous.

Within an *oikos* a special kind of *logic* is at work. One distinctive characteristic of this logic is the sharing: families share the evening meal, some members share their bed, and they share vacations and memories. Another characteristic of this logic is the *contributing*. Members chip in somehow, by doing chores, bringing in goodies, providing financial sources, taking care of others, telling stories, cooking meals, cleaning, and so on. Small children tend to get a great deal just by being small, cute and naïve. When children grow older they learn that they have to contribute something somehow ("You do the dishes tonight"). The *oikos* logic is also one of interdependence. Because the members share goods and need to contribute to the family, they depend upon each other.

How families are organized, how their hierarchies are established, how they work, and how they deal with the frictions, quarrels and conflicts that are typical for families, is partly a cultural matter. In some families the father is the head, in others the mother leads. Members of traditional Chinese families defer to the will and decisions of the elder of the family. In such families aunts and uncles have also a much more important role than in most Western families. The typical Dutch family tends to negotiate when differences occur, with children having a voice (and at times even seem to dictate what the parents do); an Italian family will shout and gesticulate a great deal when something needs to be done (at least that is my impression).

The currency that families use is usually hard to pinpoint. Members build up credit when they have contributed a great deal; the father who is never home and neglects his chores may lack the credit that he needs when he gets into trouble. Charm may attract credit and a bad mood may deter it.

Families develop their own values and norms, and therefore have their own specific culture (C1 as defined in chapter 2), as usually becomes painfully clear during wedding ceremonies.

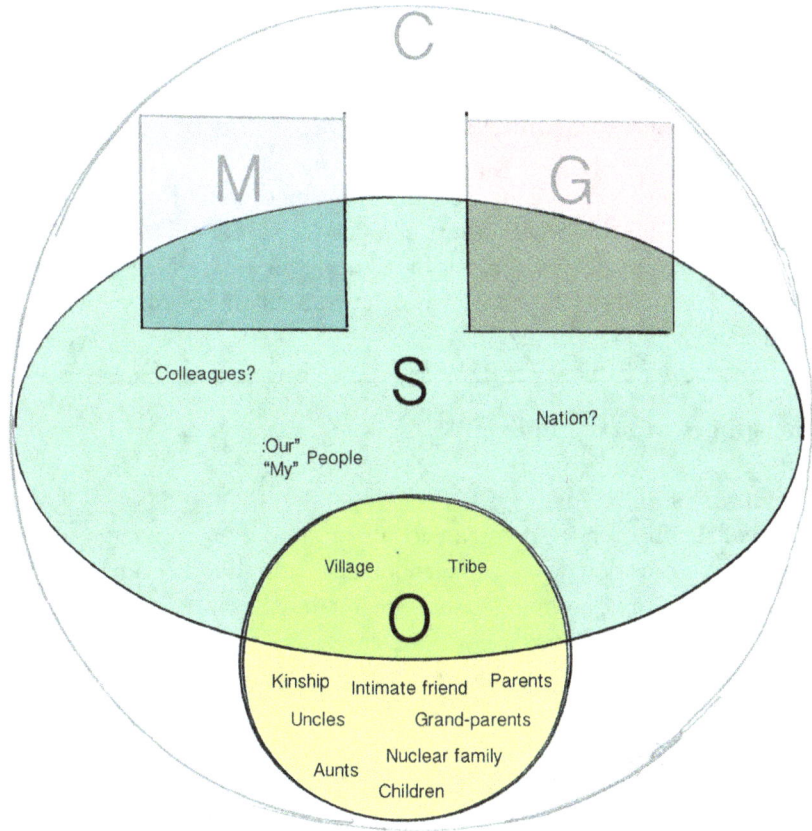

Diagram 10A-2 The sphere of the oikos

Families represent and reproduce overarching values as well. Families foster the values of loyalty and trust. (Emblematic is the way Francis Ford Coppola's movie *The Godfather* portrays the working of such values in a mafia family.) Families stand for the values of care and love: members care for each other and may love each other.

An *oikos* needs boundaries. Families close the doors of their homes to keep outsiders out, and have special hospitality rituals when outsiders enter. (But what to do when you run into a young stranger in the kitchen one morning, waiting for your 18-year-old daughter to serve him breakfast?) That is why an *oikos* is a shared good or, even better, a shared practice.

All these characteristics have consequences for the realization of values and goods in the *oikos*. They work well to realize values such as care, intimacy, and love for the nurturing of healthy and well-behaved children and for getting attention, recognition, support, and a sense of belonging. Yet they work less well, and often not at all, when you want to become a good artist, contribute to science, practice a religion, start a revolution or set up a business. An *oikos* is unlikely to satisfy the desire for fun, excitement, adventure, justice, and great wealth. In order to realize all that, people must venture outside their *oikos* into the other spheres. People usually figure out in their adolescent years that they have to leave their original *oikos* in order to "make it in the outside world."

It may be possible to create great art or a sanctimonious life within and through an *oikos,* but that may require the development of a very particular *oikos,* such as an artistic community or a monastery. The idea is to create an intimate community of people who share the same ideals. The Jewish Kibbutzim are a good example.

The sphere of *oikos* in brief

The *oikos* is good for:
The realization of an *oikos* as an ideal—a good *oikos* can serve as a purpose in life, as does love, motherhood and fatherhood, intimate and sexual relationships, companionship, shelter, meals, shared experiences and memories, attention, support, and care.
Oikos can also be a source of income, a possibility for work (farms, family businesses, child care).

The *oikos* is less good for:
The realization of great art, science and religion (unless an *oikos* is specifically designed for such purposes), worldly success in working and

political life, all kinds of goods (the *oikos* rarely produces computers, cars, meat and vegetables, clothes, entertainment, music, and counseling)—those have to be acquired in other spheres.

Logic
The logic is one of interdependence, sharing, and contributing. The logic involves respecting the culture of the family, the established hierarchies, positions, and roles. The currency is social; families work for example with credit and blame.

Values
Positive values fostered by the *oikos* are loyalty, trust, love, and care. Negative values associated with the *oikos* (at least in Western cultures) are dependency, paternalism, suppression, and discrimination.

Relationships
Involving the other in a process of valorization requires persuasion with an appeal to the values of loyalty, care, dependency, kinship, connectedness, love, and intimacy. The others will share or give what they have (like attention, care, food, and money), or contribute somehow (chipping in, cooking a meal, cleaning, listening, or giving advice).

Rhetoric
The rhetoric of the *oikos* gives expression of its logic and values. It uses the family narrative and series of topoi (Greek for commonplaces) with expressions such as:
I love you.
What's mine is yours.
We share equally what we have.
You are a great dad. Can I have a raise in my allowance?
I'm hungry.
I take care of you. You don't have to worry about anything.
Why? Because I am your father and I say so.
I am happy when the kids are happy.
I hate you.
Because you are my wife, I will support you no matter what.

These characteristics are particular for the sphere of the *oikos*; they generally will not make sense in other spheres (there are exceptions, though).

There are good reasons why people resist the *oikos* and even abstain from any involvement. Developing and sustaining an *oikos* requires a great deal of effort, time, and resources. Disappointment and failure are almost inevitable. There are plenty of stories in circulation in the form of novels, movies, and gossip to highlight the dark side of the *oikos*. Moreover, we know that an *oikos* can in some cases be stifling and suffocating, inhibiting personal freedom, and suppressing desires and ambitions. The *oikos* can furthermore fail to deliver a wide range of goods that we need and want. All of these are reasons for us to venture outside the *oikos* and operate in the other spheres. Yet, people who have turned their back to any kind of *oikos*, will often find out sooner or later that they are in need of some form of *oikos*.

2) The social sphere

When we venture outside our *oikos*, away from the kitchen table, we will first enter the social sphere, by walking into the street, going to the public square, playing with other children, going to school or by joining a club, a church, a synagogue, a mosque, or maybe even a political party. When we do so, we engage with people to whom we do not feel connected in the way that we do with those belonging to our *oikos*. The social sphere is the sphere of informal social relationships. It is the sphere where we find commons of all kinds.

While S does not appear in economic texts, the social sphere, S, is a dominant presence in real life. In S we realize relationships of all sorts, we join clubs, become members of communities, we are in conversations with others about sports, the weather, religion, art, science, and relationships of course. It is the sphere of co-production and co-creation, in the sense that it is where we co-create social, cultural, and symbolic goods. It is in S that the sciences and the arts come about; in S religion and politics happen; in S open sources are generated and maintained; and in S creative commons come about. A great deal of market transactions are intended as inputs for the realization of social goods, like when we pay for meals, drinks, rooms, concerts, performances, and other such goods. Suppliers of those goods do better when they are aware of the social purposes of their goods.

S is varied and comprises social settings, the society at large, all kinds of social organizations like clubs, societies, political parties, ensembles, orchestras, and groups, as well as a great variety of commons, or shared practices. In a further development I can imagine that a differentiation of the S is desirable. After all, participating in a crowd is quite different from being in a friendship. The political S is quite different from the S of sport clubs or academic departments (although... academic departments can be quite political). For this exposition, S is considered to be one entity.

Once you see S clearly, it becomes hard to comprehend why standard economics overlooks it altogether. When you overlook this sphere, you do not see all the work that S requires; you will not notice all the goods that S generates. Once you picture S, so much of what keeps people occupied every day suddenly makes sense. It will make, for example, cooperative and even altruistic behavior seem normal.

To answer the *what* question, the social sphere is good for social goods—that is for goods that we need to share with others for them to have social value. Friendship is such a good, and so is a sense of belonging, collegiality, community, political relevance, reputation, identity, recognition, collegiality, trust, solidarity, membership of a club, authority, power, and so on. The social sphere is good for relations and conversations of all kinds.

As we noticed in chapter 6 conversations are commons or shared practices. In the US you can join an ongoing conversation about topics such as baseball and American football, but such a conversation is all but absent in Dutch society. That society, in turn, has unique conversations about ice-skating, the battle with water, and the Dutch monarchy (tulips and windmills do not make for much of a conversation in the Netherlands).

The social sphere is crucial for the realization of values. When you want lots of people to wear your hats, watch your movie, savor your art, enjoy your music, know what you know, or share your faith, you have to make sure that your good is part of a conversation, that it is talked about. (In business this is called word-of-mouth advertising.) All that takes place in S.

The social sphere is also the sphere in which power has to be realized, since power is the force to influence or determine the activities of others. Power is a relational thing. So is trust. It is in the social sphere that trust comes about, or is lost.

The how-question concerns how we involve the other in assigning value to our goods. The answer in the social sphere begins with the *social relationships* that we form. The objective in this sphere is to befriend people from other *oikoi*, to develop close and weak ties with a variety of people, to develop networks. We need these relationships in order to generate goods like friendships, networks, and conversations of all kinds. Some of these goods are goods to strive for, like friendship, others are instrumental for the generation of other goods (you need to have team members in order to play soccer or baseball, but you can also play baseball for the sake of friendship, to share the game with friends).

The next part of the answer to the how-question is the *logic* of the social sphere. That logic is social. It is the logic of informal relationships, of participation, collaboration, donation, and contribution. In order to play soccer, the social logic dictates that you befriend some people to play with you and that you then convince another group of likeminded people to play a game. To be part of a team you must be willing to contribute to the team effort. When you play all by yourself, never passing the ball, you are likely to lose the team (unless you are exceptionally talented).

The social logic is informal. Unlike the formal logic of the market, it does not use money as a unit of account. And unlike governance logic it does not rely on rules, standards, protocols, contracts, or laws. Social logic is qualitative, not quantitative. (And that makes it hard to capture in mathematical models and empirical statistics.)

The logic of social relationships relies on the *logic of gift giving*. The gift is an important instrument for the initiation and sustenance of social relationships. Gifts have been the subject of a great deal of scholarly research. Often referred to, is the book *The Gift* of the French anthropologist Marcel Mauss (Mauss, 1967). From this research we learn that gift giving is about reciprocity: when I give you something, I expect something in return. It is tempting to identify a form of exchange as it takes place in the market, but the logic of exchange is fundamentally different from the logic of gift giving. The big difference is that the terms of trade are made explicit in case of exchange, but are left ambiguous in the case of gift giving. When you give a friend a present, support, or your undivided attention you will expect a gesture in return but when, how, and even to whom remain undefined, undetermined, and usually undiscussed at the time that you give your gift. A thank you from your friend may suffice, but for good friends that would be even too much (you do not thank a good friend, since giving each other is what good friends do). It is even not determined that you are the beneficiary of the gesture in return. If your friend is doing a favor for your child, or for another friend, then that may be good enough for you.[2]

The *logic of contributing* is another major component of the logic of S. It is related to the logic of gift giving. (See also the discussion in chapter 6.) When you want to be part of a conversation or to share a good such as friendship or community, you need to contribute somehow. Friendship and a conversation are shared goods that require contributions to be part of them, to share in their ownership. You contribute by making a gesture, giving attention or a piece of your mind, showing interest, doing some work, and so on. A contribution needs to be recognized by the others to count towards the establishment of co-ownership of the shared good.

The logic of contribution is also what brings about so-called creative commons, or conversations. It underlies the co-creation and co-production

---

2   If you want to know more about the logic of gift you can consult apart from Mauss, an extensive literature including Klamer, Gift Economy (2003) and Komter, The Gift. An Interdisciplinary Perspective (1996)

of the commons. Co-creation or co-production is what is needed to generate a shared good and a claim to shared ownership. A creative commons comes about in the digital environment when people add content, respond to that content, and share the content with people in their network. All such activities are contributions. Without them the creative commons would not exist. As a rule, contributions do not have any reward other than the satisfaction of being part of that conversation, of sharing in its ownership.

In chapter 6 we already discussed how art is being realized in S as a common or shared practice. We concluded that while you cannot buy art, you could contribute to the common practice somehow in order to appropriate art, to make sense of it. The same social process applies to the practice that is

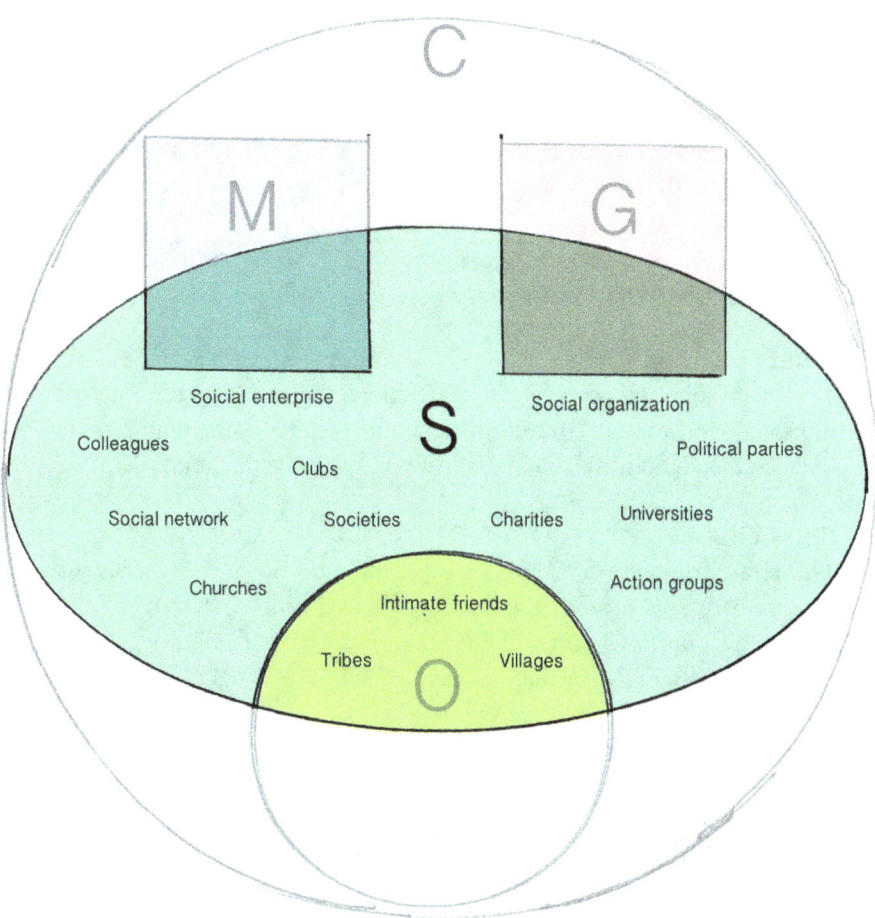

Diagram 10A-3 The social sphere

knowledge or science. You have to do it in order to "have" it. And the doing implies participating in some social setting or another, such as a lab, university environment, or discussion group on the Internet. In all cases contributing is a critical part of the logic concerned.

Knowing what to contribute, what to give, or how to give or solicit a gift is a matter of *phronesis*. You have to be able to assess what is called for, what is appropriate, whom to approach and how. You also have to take into account the cultural context. Americans are more used to being asked for contributions than the Dutch (except for members of a church) and the Japanese are most sophisticated in their gift exchange (foreigners are well-advised to consult natives before they engage in a Japanese gift exchange). You may contribute too much or too little.

The social sphere is filled with clubs, neighborhoods, communities, societies, schools, churches, mosques, and social organizations (also called non-profits to indicate that they do not follow the logic of the market). We have to be careful, though, since the organization of clubs, schools and social organizations, often requires introducing the logic of G, of governance. The social context with informal relationships and the logic of reciprocity and

---

The social sphere in brief

What is it good for?
The social sphere is good for the realization of shared goods like friendships, conversations, communities, clubs, teams, colleagues, movements, parties, an atmosphere, culture (C1), and civilization (C3).

Relationships
The relationships in S are informal, usually do not involve money or governance, and serve the purpose of generating a shared good or serving a common interest. The other is a partner, member, friend, donor, contributor, associate, colleague, helpful stranger, comrade, or neighbor (but not a customer or client).

Logic
The logic of S is the *logic of reciprocity*, as in the circulation of gifts, and the logic of contributing.
The logic of reciprocity stipulates that a gift, a gesture, an offering of whatever kind gets reciprocated, that is, it calls for a counter-gift, gesture or offering. However, and this makes for a fundamental difference with the exchange in the market, the terms are left informal

(no contracts and monetary measurements) and inexplicit; the what, how and for whom of the counter-gift are ambiguous. *Phronesis* in the social sphere applies moral and social forms of accounting, taking into account environmental, historical, and cultural conditions.

In the logic of contributing, we provide attention, knowledge, interest, labor, time, and money for the sake of a shared good, of gaining a share in shared ownership. A contribution counts when others somehow involved in the shared or common good recognize it.

Values

Positive values: community, friendship, solidarity, social cohesion, social inclusion, status, a sense of belonging, and membership.

Negative values: discrimination, exclusion, exploitation, power, nepotism, favoritism, provincialism, unprofessionalism, and chaos.

In S we **involve others** by persuading them to acknowledge a common interest, to form some kind of informal relationship, to realize a shared good like a conversation, and to contribute somehow to the valorization of our good.

The **rhetoric of S** dictates that we use the language of partnership, of social exchange, of reciprocity, of social exchange, of reciprocity. When we address the relationship with others we speak of partners, friends, contributors, donors, participants, members, associates, colleagues, soul mates, and comrades. We are part of a team, a club, a community, or movement. When we articulate our actions, we contribute, participate, cooperate, collaborate, donate, co-create, and co-produce.

Rhetoric

Expressions that make sense in S, the social sphere:

I would like you have this. No, I do not ask for anything in return.
I do this because I care for this community.
Let us do this together.
I really like your ideas. I want to do this and that to get it realized.
I am hungry. Can you help me?
This is my idea. What do you think?
Great idea of yours. It could be even better if you use this idea of mine.
I am willing to sacrifice my life for freedom and democracy.
We would like to invite you to give a keynote speech at our conference....No, there is no fee.

contribution will remain, but certainly in the case of larger organizations, governmental logic will crowd out at least some of the social logic. (When people call for professionalization, they usually have concluded that S logic has to be limited and checked by an expansion of G logic.)

The social sphere is good for the generation of shared goods of all kinds, but it may fail to generate legal order, and to procure sufficient (financial) resources or the variety of goods that we need. In poor areas people have access only to the social sphere beyond the *oikos*; in developed areas they have access also to a developed M and G.

The social sphere is good for the propagation and reproduction of social values such as the values of community, friendship, solidarity, social cohesion, social inclusion, status, a sense of belonging, and membership.

In a negative sense the social sphere can be the sphere of discrimination, exclusion, exploitation, power, nepotism, favoritism, provincialism, unprofessionalism, and chaos. Accordingly, people can have plenty of good reasons to take recourse to the spheres of the market and governance.

3) The cultural sphere

This is the all-encompassing sphere, in which all other spheres are embedded. I imagine it to hover above the other four spheres to suggest the vertical or transcendental relationships that constitute the cultural sphere. It is the sphere that gives meaning to the actions in the other spheres. In this sphere we all realize ourselves as cultural beings.

When we go through daily life, living our *oikos*, interacting socially, trading and respecting governing structures, we may not be aware of the cultural sphere. Yet when we engage with art, religion, or science, then we have to. Also when we change environment, by moving to another country for example, we may discover the cultural values (as in C1, see chapter 1) that have influenced so much of what we did and thought.

It is in the cultural sphere that ideals are realized. It is there where we distinguish the ideals of Goodness, Beauty, and Truth. It is where people find and experience faith, grace, the sacred, compassion, the Holy Grail, and other such transcendental goods. It is the realm of artistic, spiritual, religious, and scientific practices. It is in such practices from which people derive—or hope to derive—meaning for their life, with which they try to make sense of their world.

So when we want art, religion, or science in our life, we need to reach out to the practices that constitute the cultural sphere. This will involve a social component as we seek the company of kindred spirits, as we do in the S, the social sphere. However here, the content of such practices comes about at the cultural level. In a Platonic interpretation we will try to see transcendental ideas, ideas that are beyond what we can see directly. They are metaphysical

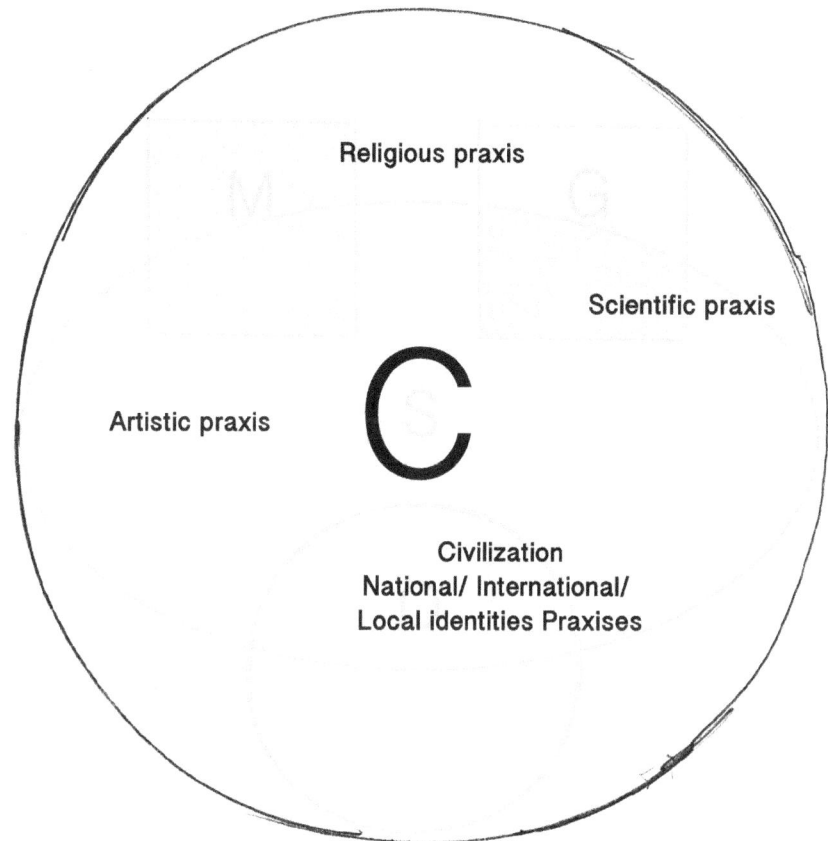

Diagram 10A-4 The cultural sphere

in the sense that we cannot grasp them or hold onto them. They are transcendental because they transcend the social and the physical.

In the cultural sphere we relate to abstract entities. Religious people will say that they seek contact with the divine, naturalists may try to feel one with nature, and artists are passionately involved with their art. We all relate somehow to the (anthropological) culture that we are part of, or to the civilization that has formed us.

The logic of the cultural sphere may differ for each practice. What is logical in the arts may not be logical in science, or in religion. Each sphere's logic includes rituals, norms, and rules. In a religious practice bowing one's head may make sense, but in scientific and artistic practices it does not. Reading sacred texts—the thing to do in religious practices—is a taboo in most scientific practices.

The cultural sphere in brief

What is it good for?
The cultural sphere is good for the realization of cultural values (C1), civilization and transcendental practices such as art, science, and religion, as well as transcendental goods such as faith, truth, beauty, and moral rightness.

Relationships
In the cultural sphere we relate to ideas, to abstract entities. The relationships vary from being intense to being superficial and incidental.

Logic
Logic is that which makes sense. The sense-making process follows rituals, respects an idiom, and heeds norms.

Currency
The currency comes in the form of meanings. Meaningfulness is the reward and may be experienced as feeling inspired, passionate, blessed, humble, enlightened, uplifted, in awe, knowledgeable, or connected. The other side of the coin shows a lack of meaning, a sense of loss, emptiness, shame, stupidity, or superficiality.

Values
Positive values are curiosity, dedication, authenticity, inner freedom, and humility.
Negative values are blind faith, one-sidedness, fundamentalism, obsession, impracticality, and abstraction.

Rhetoric
Each practice in the cultural sphere has its own idiom, metaphors, and narratives that are usually manifest in exemplary texts or works (like the sacred books, canonic works, the classics). The language of economists, to take one obvious case, is dramatically different from, say, the language of musicians. It takes a long period of education and training to fully master the one or the other.

Most people grow up in a cultural idiom (as in "Dutch" or "Chinese"). After the age of sixteen, or thereabout, it is nearly impossible to fully master another cultural idiom.

The cultural logic in the sense of C1 follows cultural values and becomes noticeable in contrast with other cultural logics. While being direct is considered "logical" in a Dutch setting, doing so in Asian contexts would be seen as insulting, rude and uncivil.

The currency in the cultural sphere comes in the form of meanings. The reward is the experience of meaningfulness, of a sense of connection with the ideal, of feeling blessed, enlightened, inspired, fulfilled, uplifted, knowledgeable, or spiritual; punishment comes with a lack of meaning, confusion, feeling stupid, feeling lost, empty, superficial, sinful, and the like.

The cultural sphere provides content, or least the resources that enable us to realize content in whatever we do. That is why the notion of civilization (C2) is important for us. Civilization stands for the great variety of resources that enable us culturally, or to realize cultural values. It provides us with a sense of history, a narrative that makes the present meaningful. It constitutes civility as the outcome of a long evolutionary process.

As soon as these three spheres are spelled out, it should become obvious how pervasive they are, how much they are a part of our daily lives. Not only our *oikos* that we know best, but also the social sphere is so present that we are left wondering why it is left out of legal and "economic" practices. I hope it has also become clear why it helps to distinguish the cultural sphere separately, certainly when trying to make sense of artistic, religious, and scientific practices.

We now turn to the spheres that figure so pervasively in the instrumentalist approach, that is, the spheres of the market and governance.

THE MARKET AND GOVERNMENTAL SPHERES, AND THE SPILLOVERS, OVERLAPS AMONG THE FIVE SPHERES

For the valorization of the important values and goods, the *oikos* and the social and cultural spheres are most relevant. Social as people are, they will forever seek out social situations in order to partake in shared goods. It is in our nature, Adam Smith would suggest, that we emphasize with others and seek their attention when we are in need of their good will. At least that is what he stresses in *The Theory of Moral Sentiments*, his first major work (Smith, 1759).

Adam Smith is, of course, also the moral philosopher who got us to imagine the market. Achieving this at the end of the 18th century, he earned the title "father of modern economics." In *The Wealth of Nations* he led us to imagine the market as follows. First he observes that

> "[man] has not time, however, to [get the attention and the good will of others] upon every occasion. In civilized society he stands at all times in need of the cooperation and assistance of great multitudes, while his whole life is scarce sufficient to gain the friendship of a few persons."

Notice the reference to the social sphere and the suggestion that the social dimension comes first and has our preference. However, the social dimension does not suffice. Therefore, he continues,

> "he will be more likely to prevail if he can interest their self-love in his favor, and show them that it is for their own advantage to do for him what he requires of them. Whoever offers to another a bargain of any kind, proposes to do this. Give me that which I want, and you shall have what you want, is the meaning of every such offer; and it is in this manner that we obtain from one another the far greater part of those good offices

which we stand in need of."

He follows with the most often cited sentence in the economic literature:

"It is not from the benevolence of the butcher, the brewer, or the baker that we expect our dinner, but from their regard to their own interest."

All these citations are from Adam Smith, The Wealth of Nations, Book I, chapter II (Smith, 1776). The Wealth of Nations came out in the year that the US declared its independence.

I refer to Adam Smith because he puts the sphere of the market in its place, that is, not as some sort of ideal arrangement, and not as the dominant logic but as necessary when the social sphere falls short for the realization of goods. Where Aristotle still idealized the *oikos* as sole provider of food, shelter and all kinds of other goods, and Smith concurs by acknowledging the importance of social relations, Smith acknowledges that modern life calls for a sphere of the market. Accordingly, the claim that Smith puts the market on the central stage is unwarranted.

Accordingly, following Smith we should now put the market first, and prioritize it over any other sphere. It is what economists like Ludwig von Mises, Friedrich Hayek and Milton Friedman instruct people to do. It is what conventional wisdom dictates. It is what politicians and journalists usually do. But is it right to continue now with market? I do not think so. I, however, will continue our exploration of the various options for the valorization of value with the sphere of the government.

4) The sphere of governance

The reason to begin with the governmental sphere is simply the realization that in our daily activities we have more dealings with the sphere of governance than with the market. We work for organizations, we run organizations, we deal with organizations, we are member of social organizations like clubs and political parties, and we are subjects of governmental organizations that make us pay taxes, pay out benefits and subsidies and that employ quite a few of us, including myself. Sure, we enter a few exchanges every now and then, but most of our interactions are with organizations of all kinds. Apparently we are in great need of using the sphere of organizations, of governance, that is, for the valorization of our values. So we better be aware of what organizations are good for, of their logic, their values and of the way they make us talk and think. Dealing well with organizations is an inevitable aspect of doing the right thing.

Note that the sphere of governance comprises all types of organizations, not just the government. The following elaboration should make clear why that is.

What for?

First the what-question: what are organizations good for? Alternatively put, why would you deal with an organization? The reason is that organizations serve a purpose of some kind. The local grocery store aims to sell the groceries you and I need, which is a sufficient reason to frequent it. The organization of Facebook makes it possible to share our news with "friends." The multinational law firm provides very expensive legal advice that we may need when we happen to work in a large firm with serious legal issues. In short, private organizations deliver the private goods that we need or want (mind you, as instruments or inputs to realize the really important goods).

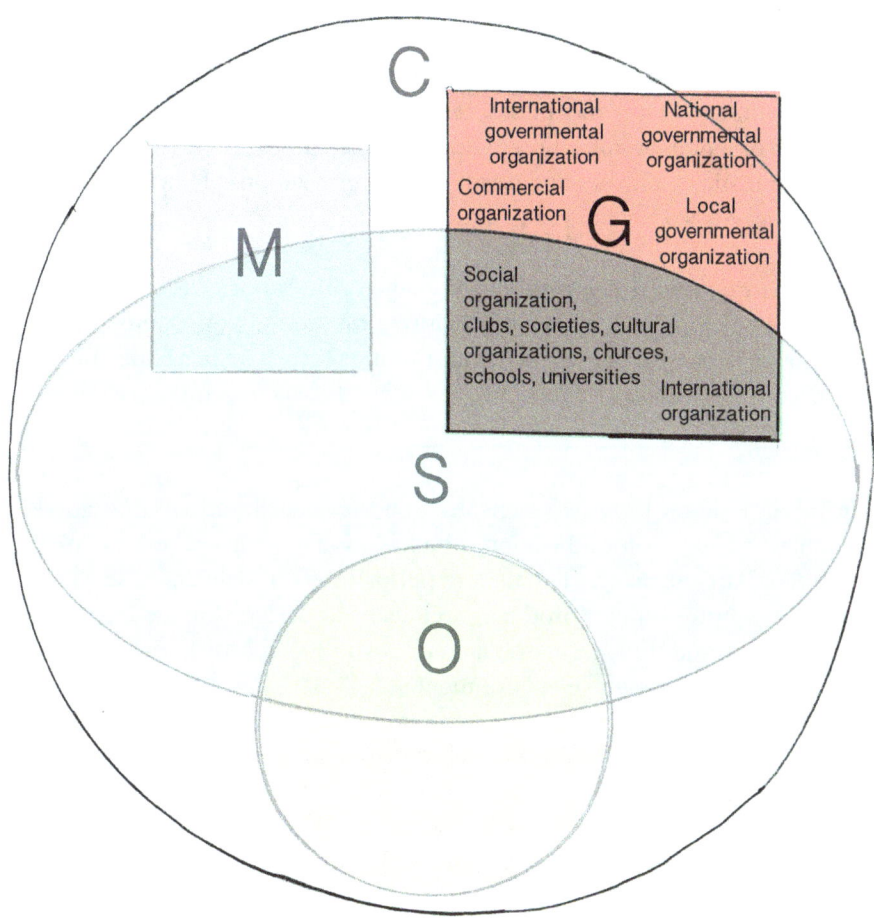

Diagram 10B-1 The sphere of governance

Types of organizations

Governmental organizations serve a public or societal purpose; their actions aim to improve the qualities of life in S and O and for that purpose regulate transactions in M and organizations in G. They procure collective goods.

Commercial organizations focus on M; they supply (private) commodities to anyone who is willing to pay the price. Their purpose is instrumental in the sense that they seek maximal financial gain for work, great products, and social returns).

Social organizations aim to realize social or societal goods for their stakeholders. They include the so-called non-profits and NGOs (non-governmental organizations). Sport clubs, societies, foundations, aid organizations, universities are all social organizations. They rely on the willingness to contribute by the stakeholders.

Cultural organizations aim to realize cultural or artistic goods for their stakeholders. Think of theatres, museums, pop bands, dance groups, orchestras, design firms, and architectural bureaus. Stakeholders need to be willing to contribute to realize their goal values.

Social and cultural organizations are good for social and cultural goods. A school wants to provide education, which is good to realize when you are a kid in need of an education. The theatre performs art or delivers entertainment. An architectural bureau produces architectural designs for the building you may need. Amnesty International enables you to support human rights and Greenpeace, a sustainable environment.

Governments are good for the provision of collective goods. A national government provides, hopefully, safety, social security, laws, schools, and a great deal more. Local governments provide welfare to people with little to no income, maintain the sewage system, and collect garbage. The United Nations stand for world peace and collaboration of national governments on international issues.

Most organizations are also good for jobs. People seeking challenging jobs greatly benefit from organizations such as universities that can give them the necessary credentials and other organizations that provide a challenging work environment. Organizations are employers or, as the Dutch word accurately describes them, "werkgevers" (work-providers). Whether it is the local grocery store, the school, the theatre, the multinational law firm, the national government, Greenpeace, or the United Nations, they all provide work and, with that, income. Consequently, organizations are **instrumental** for the generation of financial means, and hopefully for meaningful work as well.

When you want to realize a particular good, such as a performance, or a consulting advice, or a new type of car, you will most likely need an organization and will have to deal with other organizations. When you want to make a career, you probably do so by way of an organization. When you want to fight for human rights, animal rights, or a crime-free neighborhood, you can either make use of an existing organization or set up your own.

Is it possible to valorize goods without the mediation of organizations altogether? I doubt it.

How and why?

Organizations are an answer to **the how-question**. When I am seeking radical reform in academic education, as I actually do, I can work within existing academic institutions or, when I decide that those institutions do not really work for that purpose, I can found an entirely new institution, as I actually tried. When setting up an organization or working within organizations, we operate in G.

Therefore, the sphere of governance can provide the means—a strategy—for people to realize what is important to them. When someone wants to become a ballet dancer, she will first go to one organization—a school—and then try to join another organization—a ballet company. When you value the environment and nature, and want to valorize those values, you can set up your own organization, join the World Wide Fund for Nature, or become a politician to attempt to steer governmental organizations in the right direction. You face similar choices when you want to make true on your personal ambitions concerning your career, or on your societal or transcendental values. Whether you join a society for artists, a church, or a temple, you become part of an organization. Most of us will be in need of one organization or another. Working with or working for an organization or setting up your own organization is part of your design, or your strategy.

Why do people organize? Members of tribes organized all kinds of things but they did not work with or for organizations in the formal sense or for the type of organizations that fit in G. They worked in S, using S logic. Governmental organizations were needed when taxes had to be collected and armies had to be formed. Bureaucracies came about, with clearly defined hierarchies; within them rules dictated actions, and actions were accounted for. In the Middle Ages workers organized themselves in guilds in order to limit competition among each other and with outsiders. The church is a deliberate attempt to organize religious practices. The Roman Catholic Church is called the first multinational dealing in real estate, setting up franchises first in Europe and then all over the world, developing a bank and running all kinds of "businesses" providing not only services such as religious performances, festivals, concerts, confessions, and absolutions, but also goods like beer.

Business organizations as we know them now only came about in the 19th century (Chandler, 1977). The first modern organizations were railway companies. They were necessary to coordinate complex logistics and coordinate itineraries that covered long distances and different time zones. For the sake of efficiency, specialization was in order and a clear hierarchy became necessary. Later it became clear that a similar organization also worked well for the production of cars, steel, electricity, and more of such commodities.

Nowadays, the need for such large organizations is called into question as new technology makes small-scale production efficient again and more and more people prefer to be autonomous in their work. So maybe organizations will become smaller. In the Netherlands, an increasing number of people are self-employed. They mostly work for organizations on a freelance basis. In the Netherlands, 9,500 care workers have organized themselves into small teams; the central office has only 34 staff members. Organizations do change.

The size of governmental organizations continues to be a subject of dispute, too. Free market economists advocate minimization of such organizations, whereas socialists consider big governmental organizations to be the only way to secure all kinds of societal goods. However, even in times when cuts in government spending rule the political agenda, governmental organizations maintain their dominant presence in most countries.

Relationships in G

The shapes, sizes, and appearances of organizations vary enormously. They are usually housed in buildings, small or large, and often have a logo. Other than that, they are mainly abstract. They are formal entities with a legal status, represented in legal documents. We relate to organizations in a formal way. Of course, people associated with organizations will address us and interact with us when we seek employment or work in a governmental organization, but they do so in their formal capacity, as part of the organization. (When they use small talk and address us in a personal manner, they apply social logic, not governmental logic; there is a great deal of that in everyday life in organizations.) My relationship to the university comes in the form of a contract, the description of my function, and a series of rules and regulations that articulate the constraints for my actions and interactions within the organization. (When a colleague once remarked that the university does not appreciate him, I asked him what he expects: does he really think that the university buildings will bow when he passes by?)

I combine governmental and private organizations in the same category.

Their legal status is different, of course, and they differ in many other ways, as we will see. Nevertheless, all organizations have in common that they are instrumental and formal, implying that our relationships with them are also formal. The government, too, is abstract to its subjects. It presents itself most directly in the form of envelopes that contain information about the amount of taxes owed, and through offices, windows, forms, and websites where we learn about our rights, programs, procedures, and so forth. People working for a governmental organization are civil servants with well-defined functions and explicit contracts.

The formal character of internal relationships is expressed in the hierarchal structures of most organizations with formalized lines of authority and concomitant titles (CEO, CFO, director, president, vice president, department head, supervisor, team leader, account manager, secretary general, project manager, and so on).

Although most social and cultural organizations have formalized positions and functions (with artistic leaders, directors, supervisors, board members, chair people, and team leaders), their formal character will often be less pronounced because a) they tend to be small and b) their social or cultural objectives require plenty of social interaction. Recall art is a collaborative activity and therefore does not suffer a formal embeddedness in formal structures easily.

An interesting issue is the **ownership** of organizations. I already established that universities do not approve or disapprove of the work of its people. But to whom does the university belong? Who are the owners? In the Netherlands, the government could be named the owner. Yet what does that mean? Who is the government? The same question arises for cultural organizations. When a group of people starts a theatre company, the company is clearly theirs. They would feel so and others will recognize them as such, regardless of the formal status of the company. But to whom does the company belong after they have left? It is hard to say, especially when the company is set up as a foundation with a board of trustees. When a single individual sets up and runs a company it is clearly his, or hers. The same can be said for the family that takes it over. When the company issues shares, the owners of the shares are called the owners. But what does that mean? Most of those will never have set foot in the company, don't know anything of its daily affairs and don't really care as long as the company pays sufficient dividend. In a formal sense ownership can be merely legal; it is determined by the rules and the contracts.

In a value based approach, the emphasis is on contributions: people who contribute to an organization will experience a sense of ownership. The company becomes theirs and will continue to be so as long as they continue contributing. Such a kind of ownership could be called social or moral, in contrast to formal ownership.

Governmental organizations are collectively owned. In principle, governments belong to all citizens. Everyone contributes by paying taxes and everyone stands to benefit from the goods and services that the government provides, although some may do so more than others. When dealing with the government, you are dealing with the collective. When you receive subsidy from the government, you receive it from the collective, and when you are working for the government, you do so for the collective.

Social and cultural organizations belong to the people participating in them. Ownership here is usually not legal, but social or cultural instead (see chapter 8). You need to contribute somehow in order to benefit from their goods. You need to be a member of the church, or take part in its services in order to realize its religious and social values. The same applies to a dance company or a soccer club.

Commercial organizations belong to its shareholders. These can be families in case of family businesses, partners in case of a partnership, or anyone willing to pay the price for a share in case of joint stock companies. When dealing with such an organization, you are an instrument for the aim of the organization, which is in principle maximal financial gain for the shareholders. (I continue to stress that this is not an end in itself; for the shareholders the gain is an instrument to realize goods that are really important to them.) Even so, employees, and especially the managers among them, may say that the organization is theirs. Such a feeling is understandable since they contribute a great deal to the furthering of the organization. Formally, they are not the owners. That is why democratic procedures in business or governmental organizations may make sense.

The issue of ownership may be important to people. Some people prefer to work for the common good; they will do better working for or with governmental or political organizations. Others seek firstly financial gain (in order to realize with such the goods that are important to them); they will opt to work for commercial organizations. Then there are those people who consider social or cultural goods to be most important. They will do better working for and with social or cultural organizations.

The subsequent listing clarifies the different types of ownership.

Types of ownership

Logic

When considering the logic of organizations, we should be aware of the bounded nature of organizations. In this sense they clearly differ from social communities that usually have diffused boundaries with potential for disputes about who belongs and who does not. It is a critical characteristic of organizations that they clearly mark their boundaries so that you know when you are inside or outside of them.

Commercial organizations, for example, let you apply if you want to be inside. Some have security guards who will check your company pass before you enter and escort you out when you get fired. With money, you can buy yourself in by purchasing its shares. Buy lots of shares and you may even have a voice inside the company.

National governments guard the national boundaries. They decide which people are "legal" and which are not. Legal people are the citizens who have to pay taxes, can vote and benefit from its programs. The Dutch government will do all kinds of things for me that the Belgian government will not even consider. I am a Dutch citizen; in Belgium I would be an outsider, a **non-citizen.** If a Dutch citizen were to marry an African or Asian citizen—a social arrangement—he or she cannot be sure that the partner will become legal, that is, recognized by the Dutch government as its citizen. Furthermore, governments select their civil servants and also may have guards at their entrance.

Social organizations may require membership to determine who is in and who is out and cultural organizations are usually highly selective before they allow someone to dance, play, or perform with them.

All organizations share these formal practices; you could also say that these formal practices define the organizations. They have meetings, keep records of those (in the form of minutes), follow procedures for decision making, have protocols, standards, and account for activities and financial flows. These practices determine the logic of organizations. The logic is that of bureaucracies, as sociologist Max Weber was one of the first to observe. Anyone working in an organization has a better knowledge and understanding of that logic, lest it make their functioning impossible (Weber, 1968).

Administrative or bureaucratic logic is the logic of control, of structure, or predictability. Organizations impose structure and provide means of control by working with reports, for example, and accounting systems. It makes tasks and functions explicit and usually employs a system of hierarchy.

It is G logic that tightens rules and changes procedures in case of trouble. It is G logic that appeals to the judgment of superiors in case of doubt.

It is also logical within G to seek the expansion of its influence and scope, and to increase control of the organization. That is why organizations seek to merge with other, competing, organizations, or—as in the case of governmental organizations—aspire to centralize or cooperate, or form supranational institutions (the European Union!).

Administrative or managerial logic is objectifying since it follows clearly formulated criteria, or well-specified rules with clear terms and well-defined measures in the event of trespassing or violation. For such logic the quantification of activities works best. It helps to know what criteria an employee has to meet in order to qualify for a raise in salary. In principle, such logic rules out arbitrariness, personal preferences, prejudices, discrimination, and other such social factors. Ideally, organizational logic renders judgment unnecessary.

You learn the logic of governance at business schools and schools of public administration. They teach you the planning, strategic management, human resources, financing, accounting, procedures, protocols, mergers, and so forth.

The logic of governmental organizations is similar in principle to the logic of commercial or social organizations. They share the penchant for quantification, for objectification, and for clarity in responsibilities and hierarchies. They all need to have specified who has the position to decide what, who supervises whom.

Values
Organizations enable the valorization of values by means of the goods that they generate. These goods include jobs, work, career, status, and influence. In addition, they are vehicles for the realization of behavioral values by virtue of their logic. When people want a fast-paced life, with ample challenges, big projects, lots of travel, power, and status, they would do best to work with and for large international organizations.

But when you value working with only a few people, with lots of personal attention, relaxing lunches, and the feeling of a home, then small social or cultural organizations are the better option. As a scholar I have found the greatest satisfaction in relatively small academic institutions with lots of social interaction and little to no interference from the formal organization.

In order to be a good civil servant, you need to be able to appreciate the bureaucratic process, procedures, and due diligence and work on behalf of the politician you serve.

All organizations stand for some kind of order or structure, have procedures for the decisions to be taken, and for the valuation of the performances of its employees. (Many organizations adopt behavioral values like loyalty, team spirit, quality-driven, courageous, and creative. They come about in a social sphere and require a social logic, and are hence in principle not valorized by the logic of G. As I will elaborate below, logic spills over into other spheres. In this exercise, it is important to clearly separate the spheres and see them for what they are in their own context.)

Commercial organizations are result oriented, but so are governmental organizations, at least in some cultural contexts. They are about efficiency—an important value—and about economies of scale, influence, and power in the market place. Governmental, social, and cultural organizations may be rather about effectiveness in the sense of their power to realize their collective, social, and cultural goals.

Organizations may want to be valued as innovative, entrepreneurial, reliable, and as good employers.

Negative values of organizations become especially clear from the perspective of other spheres. From the perspective of the sphere of the market, governmental organizations seem inefficient and bureaucratic, excelling in red tape and being risk averse and overly controlling. From the viewpoint of the social sphere, governmental organizations evoke Kafkian nightmares of people caught in complex procedures, powerless in the face of inadequate rules, and unwilling civil servants.

Commercial organizations may be valued as unfair, inhuman, anti-social, ruthless, power mongering, money-driven, bureaucratic, dictatorial, exploitative, authoritarian, selfish, and so on.

Social and cultural organizations may seem naïve, inefficient, ineffective, unprofessional, and addicted to subsidies.

Virtually all organizations have the inclination to value their own continuations. That is why sustainability of their business is often an important shared value, sometimes valued even over and above profit.

The rhetoric of G

Organizations make people talk and think in certain ways. In the social sphere and at home, people will not ask to fill in forms and reject applications because of missing or wrong information. In organizations a superior can admonish, order, instruct, praise, and penalize subordinates in ways that would be illogical in any other sphere.

When people tell of a cultural organization needing to become more professional, they mean to say that it needs to strengthen its organizational logic and adopt the values that come with it. Professional logic is about "streamlining" the organization, "delegating tasks," "outsourcing tasks," "restructuring," "coordinating activities," "improving communication," "reviewing standards," "results," "efficiency," "specialization," and so on.

It is G rhetoric that evokes rules and regulations when you want to get your way, to justify your actions on the basis of the same, to call for a committee when disagreement stands in the way of a decision, or to call in the handsomely-paid consultants for their advice.

In commercial organizations an appeal to the profit motive will be persuasive in internal meetings; people working for governmental organizations may appeal to results that had been stipulated or find positive response by mentioning the common good.

Each organization tends to have its own rhetoric that you have to make your own when you want to work with or for it. It is part of their culture, the S logic at work in an organization. People cannot work with the G alone. They will be inclined to embed the formal G logic in a social logic, personalizing formal relationships, generating social talk, like gossip, to maintain their sanity. Accordingly, social logic spills over into the G sphere.

The Governmental sphere in brief

What are organizations good for?
Organizations are good for all kinds of things. We participate in and deal with organizations to earn an income, to produce goods of all kinds, varying from commodities to ideals.

Governments are good for the realization of public or societal values such as justice, security, education, health care, public infrastructure, public transport, and so on.

Relationships
The relationships in G are formal and abstract. People relate to organizations by way of contracts, rules and procedures. Within organizations social relationships rule and social logic do not apply—in principle, that is. In reality the social logic operates in organizations as well in the form of, for example, collegiality, the abuse of power, personal preferences and trust.

Logic
The logic of G is formal. It is the logic of bureaucracy, management, and law. It is the logic of procedures, protocols, meetings, hierarchies, budgets, (business) plans, strategies, accounting, results, and departments.

The logic of commercial G is that of profit generation; governmental organizations will stress the logic of the right procedure and respect for the rules.

Values

Positive values or qualities of G can be control, structure, objectivity, formality, legality, rationality, hierarchy, power, efficiency, or predictability.

Negative values or qualities of G can be bureaucracy, inhuman presence, anonymity, formality, abstraction, hierarchy, power, abuse, exploitation, or in conflict with personal values.

Rhetoric

The rhetoric of G is organizational, administrative, bureaucratic, and procedural.

"Please fill in this form, and we will get back to you."

"Why? Because I am your superior and I have made my decision."

"Since you met the additional criteria, we will place you in scale 10. Your salary from September onwards will be $8,765. If you wish to object to this decision, please do so with form …"

"So, let the minutes say that we have decided to start a new program for innovations. I'll have the human resource department draw up a text for the advertisement to recruit an innovation manager."

Note that these sentences would be illogical in the spheres of the market, society, and culture. They would not make sense in the sphere of the market either.

5) The Sphere of the Market

It seems weird to end an economics book with the sphere of the markets. However, as I pointed out above, the market is less omnipresent, less pervasive in our lives than standard economic accounts lead us to believe.

The sphere of the market is the sphere of transactions, of exchanges between suppliers and buyers of commodities. In the phrase of Adam Smith:

> "Whoever offers to another a bargain of any kind, proposes to do this. Give me that which I want, and you shall have this which you want, is the meaning of every such offer; and it is in this manner that we obtain from one another the far greater part of those good offices which we stand in need of." (Smith, 1759)

In the market we offer our wares to others, and we look for wares that others have to offer. If what we offer the other is to his or her liking we enter into an exchange: the ware in exchange for something of equal value. The trick is to determine the equivalent, which is usually an amount of money, or its price.

What is the market good for—and what not?

The market sphere has proven to be instrumental for the generation of the welfare that people have experienced in the developed world. Because of it people can specialize in one thing and become highly-productive in doing so—say in the production of computer chips. Through a series of exchanges, they procure a wide variety of other goods made by other specialized people spread all over the world.

It is also in markets that we offer our skills and efforts, that is, our labor in exchange for a wage, salary, a share in the profits, or gratitude (in case of some social and cultural organizations). That wage in turn enables us to purchase commodities, sooner or later.

As we have discussed earlier, markets cannot realize the social, societal, personal, and cultural or transcendental goods that are ultimately important to us. We do not buy friendships, trust, solidarity, faith, beauty, knowledge, skill, or wisdom on a market. But we can buy food, beer, access to education and museums, books, clothes, therapy sessions, and so many more goods and services that are instrumental to the really important goods. The market is good for instrumental acquisitions.

The market, therefore, is not only good for the procurement of a wide variety of goods, tangible and intangible, it also enables us to generate the means for buying those goods by selling our labor time, by applying our skills to serve others in exchange for a monetary amount. Yet the market is impotent in the valorization of shared goods.

Market as an answer to the how-question

When you want to valorize, say a theatre play, or an idea, an artwork, a pair of shoes you made, or a house you built, the market is an option next to the other spheres. To do it well, you may need to know certain things or certain people, such as what price to charge and how to get others willing to pay your asking price, but it is certainly worth a shot. The nice part of the valorization in the market is that you get an amount of money that directly enables you to buy the commodities you need.

Markets are intricate and complex things. Unlike organizations, you usually do not see them right away, unless you go to the local farmer's market or an old-fashioned stock market. In the latter cases you can watch a bunch of people buying and selling. It is more difficult to imagine a market when you stand by yourself at a cash register to pay the price, or when you place your order at a web shop and transfer an amount of money. No wheeling and dealing there. In most cases, the presence of a market calls for some imagination. When you are putting your house up for sale, you can imagine other people doing the same and, again, other people sitting at home wondering whether they are going to view your house and, who knows, place a bid.

As advocates of markets will tell you, markets are world wonders, miracles if you wish. It is indeed a miracle how something like a pencil—the favorite example of the late Milton Friedman—costs only a small amount of money, yet is made of materials that come from all over the world. It is a miracle, if you think about it, that if you crave a mango or a Porsche, you can get them right away, at least if you are able and willing to pay their price. It is amazing that such huge numbers of commodities, produced by so many organizations and individuals, find their way to so many customers in a more or less smooth manner. Yes, markets do crash; yes, commodities remain unsold; and yes, too many people do not have the means to buy even minimal amounts of commodities. Overall markets work, though. We travel around the world and there they are, the Starbucks, the clean water, a pretty clean bed, and food and all for a reasonable, if not dirt-cheap, price.

Since the magic of markets has done its work, say, during the last few hundred years, the number of commodities exchanged has increased dramatically and the material welfare of most people has increased tenfold, if not twentyfold. Sure, markets have a dark side, too, as I will illuminate below.

Relationships

In the formal market sphere there are no relationships. In the textbook version (just look at any economics textbook) all that is required are products, prices, individual parties offering the products, and individual parties willing to pay the price. There is no need for relationships. The price is the only information that counts, at least in principle. Once the price is paid and the product handed over, the account between both parties is settled. And that is that. There is nothing hanging in the air, no obligation, no counter gift to be considered, no unfinished business. There is simply no relationship with the other. (The standard economic approach, therefore,abstracts from relationships; in economic models there are no relationships among people.) You experience the formal market clearly when you make a purchase in a web shop. You click to put your desired item in the basket, go to the payment page, transfer the price with a few more clicks, and then wait for the delivery of the item. In all this, the other party, the supplier, remains perfectly anonymous.

In reality, market parties often develop and maintain a relationship. Financial traders exchange jokes as well as large sums of money, and go out for beer together. People about to make a deal may have lunch together and exchange niceties. I have friendly chats with the owner of the shop where I buy my groceries. Like in the governmental sphere, market logic is easily mixed with social logic.

Market logic

The logic of the market sphere is the logic of exchange. This logic consists of the following four characteristics:

1. There has to be a product. There has to be a good that can be offered for a sale. That is clear for a loaf of bread, but you have to realize that your creativity could be a product, too, that you can offer to someone else. (Question: What is the product that a museum can sell? Answer: It sells access for the price of its entrance ticket and it offers usage of its name for the price of a sponsorship.)

2. There has to be property right for the product. The selling party has to be able to claim property right for the product that is for sale. The exchange transfers the property right, as in the case of the loaf of bread, or gives the other right of usage for a certain time, as in the case of your creativity. Intellectual property rights transform intangible goods such as music, ideas, and designs into products that can be sold and bought, bestowing rights on intangible products

3. There has to be a price. In the logic of the market, the (exchange) value of the commodity is its price. Price is the value in exchange. The price indicates what the seller is asking in order to transfer the property right of a good to someone else without causing upset or disappointment. When the buyer is willing to pay the price, we can infer that he or she is valuing the good for at least that amount. (Should she have been willing to pay a higher price, then she is lucky; economists refer to this as her surplus, the consumer surplus.) The price that buyers would be willing to pay is also called their reservation price. When a visitor to the studio of an artist gets all excited about a painting and asks for the price, he or she may already have a price in mind that they are willing to pay. This is their reservation price. So when the artist names a price lower than the reservation price, they will be pleasantly surprised. Or they will be disappointed when the price is higher than the reservation price.

4. There must be a transaction. In the end the market is all about transactions, about goods changing hands, about paying and receiving the price, about turnover, and about profits and losses. Displaying your art in a gallery may give you pleasure, but the point of doing so is to sell them, to record transactions, to make a turnover. The transaction is the result of the market logic, its outcome.

Let me reiterate a point about prices that I made earlier in chapter 5. There I argued that--contrary to what most economic textbooks suggest--price is not a value. Neither is the amount of money that a price refers to. When we pay a sum of money, the price for a commodity, we forego other commodities that we could have purchased for that amount. It is not the money that counts but the commodities for which that amount stands. Likewise, when we are selling something for an amount of money, we receive the means to acquire other commodities that we want or need to realize what is important to us. It is not the monetary amount or the price that we should focus on, but the commodities that the amount represents to us. The price of a transaction is thus, strictly speaking, either an opportunity cost (that what we give up), or a suspended purchase. Accordingly, the market is good for the acquisition and appropriation of commodities, goods and services that we need as instruments

It is logical, therefore, to name something of value a product or commodity, to call its price, and to be willing to hand it over with its property right to anyone willing to pay the price. In many circumstances such a logic would fail to make sense, like when a man would walk up to me and tell me that he is willing to pay a large amount for my kid or wife. A student may consider going to the professor to offer a price for a good grade, but that usually would not be logical, at least not in a standard university. It is in the illogical propositions that you will understand best what the logic of the market amounts to.

Market rhetoric

In the market sphere people speak of "deals", of "prices", and of "sellers and buyers". In the market people become "customers", workers for a company may tell each other "the customer is king" (as long as he pays the right price, of course). In the market it makes sense to say to someone else: "Hey, you got something I want; here is something you want. Deal?" In the market you can use the rhetoric of haggling ("Oh no, that's too much. For half the price I will buy it.") In the market you can say things like "I don't care what you need or what you think, this is my price: take it or leave it." When you badly want a work of art and someone else bids more for it than you can pay, you can say that it is unfair. Well, you can say it, but it's not in accordance with the market logic.

Market rhetoric allows people to fire other people with the argument that the market conditions make this necessary. Markets are "up" or "down", markets are "stable" or "volatile". When you work in the market sphere you will quickly have to learn the appropriate rhetoric.

The market in brief

The market is good for commodities, tangible and intangible goods and services that we need in order to realize our values.

The market does not deliver shared good and ultimate goods, like a good family, knowledge, art, or enlightenment. They usually are not good for the realization of collective goods.

Relationships
Interactions in the market place are instrumental and do not require relationships, at least not in principle.

Logic
It is the logic of exchange that counts in the market sphere. It is a logic that requires the transformation of goods into commodities, the pricing of such a commodity, a willingness to sell, a willingness to pay, and an agreement between the seller and the buyer to implement the deal. Market logic stipulates that in the deal the seller transforms the ownership of the commodity to the buyer, or gives the right of usage.

Using guns or any other form of violence would be illogical, and so would the refusal of handing over the commodity after the deal is made. Giving away stuff would be illogical, too, at least in the sphere of the market. Asking to sell certain goods, like an organ, a spouse, a child, or one's life would be illogical in most contemporary cultures.

Values
Positive values or qualities come about when markets are efficient, stimulate innovativeness and entrepreneurship, and are instrumental for the realization of material welfare. Markets are a sign of civilization as they enable strangers to interact civilly with mutual benefit as the result.

Negative values or qualities that may be associated with markets are unfairness, injustice, commercialism, greed, transaction fixation, monopoly power, exploitation, anonymity, the violation of human values, being unnatural, alienation and threat to the environment.

Rhetoric

The rhetoric of markets includes expressions such as the following:
"Can I have an ounce of beef please?" "Sure." […] "Thanks." "That will be 3 dollar fifty five, please." "Here it is." "Thanks, have a good day."

"I offer you 1,000 euro for that boat of yours." "But I paid double that amount for it. For 1,700 euro you can get it." "Look at what shape it is. 1,400 is my final offer." "Okay, because you are such a nice guy."

"I am selling the firm." "But what about us? What's going to happen to us? All that we've done for you all those years, doesn't it mean anything to you?" "I am sorry. It is a bad time and I got a good bid. I also have to think about myself and my family."

"I am hungry and desperate for some food." "Can you pay for it? If not, I am sorry but I can't afford giving you any. This is not a charity."

"What is your price?"

"Let's make a deal."

Try using any of these expressions in the other spheres and you will notice that they no longer make sense—unless they are meant as a joke.

An illustration: valorizing theatre

Say you want to stage a play. To valorize your dream you first need to make it real in the social and cultural spheres. In the latter you develop your knowledge about what theatre is and particular plays and learn about their meanings and artistic values. Usually you valorize the idea in the cultural sphere along with the social sphere by attending a school for drama and socializing with like-minded people. You may decide to realize your dream with some others who share your ambition. So let's imagine you and your comrades are ready to go. What to do?

If you are in a northern-European country you are likely to automatically seek out the government. You will look up the criteria for a subsidy or grant, what forms to fill in. You will find yourself making an elaborate plan with a detailed budget because that is usually one of the conditions. You will consult an accountant to get the accounting right and seek contact with the relevant civil servants and politicians. On this path, you are being pulled into the sphere of governance.

Suppose you are denied the subsidy on the grounds of inexperience, or dubious artistic quality. You and your comrades will probably be upset and may even get angry at the procedures and at the committee that issued a negative advice. What's next?

You basically have three options left. You can exploit the sphere of the *oikos* by agreeing to forsake any income from the play, ask your spouses to finance your adventure, or get a job on the side yourself.

You can also choose to be creative in the sphere of the market. The problem here is that you need to find people willing to pay for your play. Will businesses be willing to sponsor you? It is doubtful, since you do not have much of a name or reputation yet. Another possibility would be a crowd funding campaign, but crowd funding is not an exchange really, unless you succeed in determining clear terms of a trade. An interesting option is the issuance of shares that pay out when the play is selling well. For that is what you are going to do: stage the play, find a venue, and charge a price for the tickets.

Your best options are in the social sphere. Here you appeal to the willingness to contribute, to money given with a warm hand. You can activate your social network and approach family members to get support. You may run into people who have a weakness for young talent, who would have liked to do what you are doing but did not dare to, and would like for you and your comrades to succeed. Offer them a share in your enterprise, a loan maybe, or ask them to connect you with others who may want to do such a thing. See, now you are working the social logic, building relationships, interacting with people, and figuring out what will entice them and what you will have to do in return. You are not going to pay back the same amount, mind you, for that is not part of the social logic. No, you will see how you can do the other a favor, for example by inviting your benefactor to opening night, to be interested in his or her story. Maybe the other will be sufficiently pleased that you guys end up performing your play.

I suspect that in the end the social sphere is best when the valorization concerns shared goods, like a theatre play. It is in that sphere, therefore, that churches get realized. Scientists valorize their ideas in the cultural and social sphere but depend on governmental logic for their financial income. They do pay a price for that, though.

Spillovers and crossovers

The preceding characterizations are idealizations. They highlight the characteristics that are most pronounced for each sphere. In reality, the logic of one sphere shows up in other spheres. People mix them up all the time. In many cases the mixing is problematic and impedes the valorization. A more fundamental point is that we cannot operate in one sphere alone and need to balance them somehow.

Let us consider a few important and remarkable spillovers and crossovers.

G logic in M

Actually it is difficult to observe a clean exchange. Most exchanges involve organizations—think of shops, firms, advertisement agencies, firms selling advertising space, real estate firms renting spaces for the exchange—and are embedded in governmental constructions of laws, safety and health regulations, specified rights for customers, restrictions on financing arrangements, and so on. As I noted, G logic is everywhere and does its work in the market sphere, too.

G logic in S and O

In traffic we better heed the traffic rules that governmental agencies have designed and enforce. In public spaces laws apply as well. Non-profits are organizations and so are churches and theatres. In O we are most successful in keeping G at bay. Only in case of divorce, child abuse, and the like G will make its (intrusive and inexorable) presence felt.

O logic in M

"Hey, you are my friend. You can have this stuff for a special price." The seller evokes O logic to make a deal. Good salespeople will try to do the same by speaking in familiar terms—"you have such a nice full body; this suit really looks good on you." And there are people who project *oikos* feelings on ordinary market situations. Like a friend of mine who had to buy something at a gas station in the middle of nowhere where we had stopped for gas, only to discover that the price was higher than he wanted to pay; he felt terrible for disappointing the attendant, suddenly hopeful for a rare sale that day. So he ended up paying the price anyway.

S logic in M

In some cultures people wine and dine before closing the deal to suggest some kind of relationship and create a sphere of familiarity. In Arabic markets haggling serves a social purpose: the seller feels insulted when the buyer simply pays the price. Trading parties quite often exchange niceties, social information, and the like because they want to do more business together, need to establish some credibility, or try to persuade the other to make the deal.

In art markets a lot of talking takes place. A gallery owner may not sell a work to the highest bidder because she dislikes him or does not care for his background. Traders in financial markets also talk a great deal in order to share insights, establish trust, and deal with basic uncertainties. Entrepreneurs have to be persuasive and may make use of their charisma. Operating in markets requires social skills; it is a reason to consider markets as socially-embedded, as socio-economists tend to do. When you enter a market you will notice how much socializing it requires from you. It is a reason for artists to frequent openings and for local businessmen to attend New Year receptions and other such social occasions.

Pure market exchange takes place on Internet, where one party places an order, pays by credit card, and gets the order delivered at home without any social interaction whatsoever, without knowing anything about the people on the other side.

M logic in O and S

Contrary to what economists like Gary Becker purport, the M logic does not work well in the O and S. Social goods do not lend themselves easily for an exchange and the willingness to pay tends to be inappropriate in both spheres. Even so, people may introduce the rhetoric in their social interactions like when they demand a "pay back" for social trespassing (like in the case of adultery or failing to meet a social appointment). People may want a social return for a social investment and grandmothers may give money for a birthday gift. Usually such remarks or gestures are disguised in apologies and irony.

Crowding in and crowding out

We speak of **crowding out** when the valorization in one sphere is undermined by the encroachment of another sphere. **Crowding in** occurs when the encroachment of another sphere actually adds value in the valorization process. Crowding in and crowding out are consequences of the interactions among spheres and show that spheres do not function in splendid isolation.

A strong governmental sphere tends to **crowd out** the other spheres. When the government takes care of the homeless, churches and the Salvation Army can undertake other activities. When commercial companies provide cheap clothes, housekeepers will stop sewing and mending their own clothes. When restaurants offer cheap meals, home cooking becomes too much of an effort. Likewise, strong government programs for the subsidization of the arts and the sciences crowd out the willingness to contribute or to pay.

A strong social sphere can crowd out the *oikos*. With lots of good friends the need for familial support becomes less urgent. The market, in turn, can crowd out the social sphere and the *oikos*. People will sacrifice friendships and abandon families for high-paying jobs far away. Well-paid jobs require so much time and emotional energy that not much of either is left over for family life. In such instances, M and G have crowded out O.

When artists become commercially successful, they risk their artistic reputation. When large crowds overrun a culturally well-endowed city, its cultural capital gets crowded out. When an art museum proudly announces its new commercial sponsor, the artistic world may cringe and think less of the museum as a consequence. In that case we can speak of a crowding out of the artistic reputation of the museum by the encroachment of the market sphere.

Crowding in occurs when the involvement of another sphere actually strengthens the valorization of a good. People who got rich by a clever use of the market logic may see their social status rise and their social effectiveness increase. They may even become more attractive as a partner. In that case encroachment of the M adds value to the valorization of social goods.

When an artwork is bought for a remarkably high price, interest in the artwork may increase and, with that, its artistic value. That, too, is a kind of crowding in.

Likewise, government support may give legitimacy to a project and thus enhance its social or cultural value. Companies, too, may benefit by having the government as a client.

Most significant and relevant is the crowding in as the result of encroachment of the social sphere. The application of social logic in the market sphere may generate trust and mutual sympathy and those may be good for better deals. Governments benefit from strong communities and social support for their measures and programs.

Conclusion

The five-sphere model is a critical element in the value based approach. It is for the valorization of our values and that makes the approach economical, at least if defined as the discipline that studies the realization of values. Being an economist myself, I use it all the time. It is a standard ingredient in my lectures. I have it drawn on a flip over in my government office to refer to when necessary. I use it, for example, to explain my policy towards the neighborhood. I point then to the S and warn for the crowding out of S when we from the government become too dominantly present in the neighborhood. (I usually have to explain what I mean by crowding out.)

I am writing this on the flight back from a conference on the rural economy in Korea. The question addressed was what is needed to let rural areas benefit from the creative economy. The audience consisted mostly of civil servants. I shared with them the picture of the five spheres and used it to warn against overreliance on government programs. Recalling my own experiences,

I suggested that the initiative be in the S, that the S logic is crucial for any success. They were mostly interested in tourist attractions, I had already learned. Tourism exploits the M logic and that means financial income to them. The model helped to get the thinking to move beyond M and G and to consider C and S. C makes us consider the peculiarities of Korean culture, especially in the countryside. Would the British examples that we heard in an earlier presentation be of relevance? Culture can also stand for cultural heritage that can be accentuated and exploited. How about the natural capital of the Korean countryside? Such a capital needs to be cultivated, requiring the involvement of S somehow. When local communities do not get involved, when local people do not collaborate, when there is no influx of entrepreneurial people with new ideas, governmental programs or commercial operations usually fail. Then again, a stimulating and supportive government can give private initiative a decisive push.

I emphasize the S, C, and O because they have gotten such short shrift in the instrumental age that we are on the verge of leaving them behind as far as I am concerned. We thought all the time in terms of M and G with the result that especially G, but also M seem to have become stronger than is right. When colleagues argue that we need to leave more to the market, I point at the possibilities in S. How about social enterprises? How about cooperatives? And how about focusing on qualities instead of quantities?

In the end it is not one sphere or the other. Whether we are individuals eager to valorize our values, our ideas, or our skills, whether we are part of an organization trying to make a buck or a significant contribution to a societal or transcendental goal, or whether we are politicians and civil servants serving the common good in a governmental organization, we will need to find the right balance among the five spheres.

CHAPTER 11

SO WHAT?

A few skeptical questions

Wimar Jaeger is a governor for another party than mine; he is the leader of the city council of which I am a member. We govern the city of Hilversum, right in the center of the Netherlands. When I had reached this point in the book, the concluding chapter of Volume I, he wanted to know what the book is about. The vacation had just ended, so we were quite relaxed and had the time for a probing conversation. I should add that Wimar was a businessman before he turned to politics; that makes him a pragmatic individual, eager for results. But he is also interested in ideas—he has the arts among his responsibilities—and so, every now and then, he responds to remarks I make. So I took his question seriously.

I told him that the book is about rethinking economics as a science and that it develops another perspective on the economy. I added: "It is a shift from thinking in terms of quantities to thinking in terms of qualities." Seeing his puzzled look I added: "I develop a value based approach and suggest that what you and I do in the economy is the realizing of values. We actually do that right now." I saw him making an effort to understand all this. And then he asked: "What are the practical consequences? In what ways would your perspective make a difference to me?" I had to swallow a little, since that can be the question when someone can't quite figure out what you are saying. Skip the substance and ask for the consequences. He has a point though. What is a theory worth if it has no consequences, if there is no good answer for the family man that Wimar is, and for the businessman who turned into a politician? I tried to give him the short answer—"it would motivate us to steer for qualities"—and felt dissatisfied doing so. A good answer requires more work, a concluding chapter, that is.

The what-question also inevitably pops up in interviews with journalists. They want to know "what needs to be done?" In their case the question actually is: "What should politicians do?" For most journalists an economic argument only makes sense for its policy consequences. Should the government do something? Should it intervene in educational programs, spend more money on poor neighborhoods, change the policy indicators, alter the measurements of the economy, stimulate cooperatives, withdraw from neighborhoods, or what? Only if I were to have answers to such questions, and if those answers are noteworthy somehow, would the book be worth their attention. Such a query is typical for the instrumentalist worldview: if there are no instruments for politicians, then it can't amount to much.

These journalists overlook all the other people reading and watching. Shouldn't they want to know what to do? To know what the right thing is to do?

The difficulty that an introduction of the value based approach runs up against, is precisely the prevalence of the instrumentalist way of looking at the world. People tend to think that money is the thing, and that we have to measure anything and everything with money to pinpoint their value. Accordingly, organizations presumably pursue profit, academics go after research grants, and governments cut costs and steer for economic growth, that is, for more GDP. So who cares about values? Softies, clearly. People who cannot face the harsh reality of money and whatever is measured with money. The point of the value based approach is to look beyond prices, incomes, salaries, financial wealth, income, profit, and GDP and to see how we all move around in a world of values, busy realizing the values that are important to us. The book is about doing the right thing.

An economist might want to know how the value based approach addresses questions about taxing and spending of governments, about the right interest rate for a central bank to determine, and whether protectionist measures are in order. I will grant that the value based approach as developed in this book has no answers to such questions, and that standard economics is much better equipped to deal with them. Let me reiterate here that it is not my intention to debunk standard economics. Especially the accounting that standard economics includes, with its cost-benefit kind of analysis, the accounting for stocks and flows, is most useful to deal with all kinds of instrumentalist and especially financial questions. Standard economics, therefore, covers a part of the world that the value based approach charts. It is the instrumental part, as should be clear after reading this book.

Because the value based approach is about values, or qualities, the standard remark is that it is therefore normative. My response is that stressing "efficiency" and focusing on prices, income, and other financial quantities are values, too. A standard economic account values as much as does the value based approach. We all provide a perspective on the world and make others look at it in a special and, therefore, value-laden way. Remember the blind men observing the elephant?

I can imagine that some readers are frustrated because they were looking for solutions to the problems of the world. They may have expected a devastating critique of capitalism, or of the way the health care system works. Or they may have expected a motivation for working on the sharing or circulating economy; or a substantiation of the creative economy. It's all there, I would like to respond. The value based approach enables the development of a rich and directive perspective on all kinds of issues. But that needs more work. I intend to do that work in the next volume.

Affirmative answers

Here is what I have been trying to do. My objective is to take the practice of economics beyond instrumentalist issues and to redirect it to consider issues of value. That has consequences for the type of questions that are relevant. Although the value based approach provides a context to address questions of a political nature, it encourages a change of perspective and makes us think about what is the right thing to do as members of a household, friends, members of a club, as someone working with a governmental, social, or commercial organization.

This is one ploy that I use to draw my audiences in. I ask you to imagine you are a parent who has to advise a child who is seeking a fulfilling and creative life with a warm and loving home. It is undoubtedly sound advice to tell the child to get an education in order to have a good job and it may help to give the child some money for the purchase of a house. That would be more or less the advice and type of support that follows from a standard account of the economy. Then I bring in the value based approach and point out that this approach makes clear that so much more is involved, such as the ability to initiate, develop, and sustain loving relationships, the ability to realize the qualities of a home, like the need for a creative environment, and a great deal of self-awareness or mindfulness, among other values. It makes for a more complex advice but also for a more truthful advice. You might say that such advice is obvious but if you think in instrumental terms, it is far from.

Notice that quantitative indicators don't figure into a value based advice. It is senseless to tell your child how large the income must be in order to have a fulfilling life, how many children to have, or how many contacts to maintain. A life is captured in qualities, not quantities.

Then I ask you to imagine yourself in the boardroom of a company or as a governor in a city or as the artistic leader of an artistic organization. What if you were to aim at the satisfaction of the people for whom you are responsible, for fulfilling lives and a significant contribution to society? Would your advice be all that different?

The value based approach is action oriented. If you recall the preface, it is therapeutic by raising questions like "what is important for you?" and "what is this good for?" The value based approach is also edifying in the sense that it provides a series of concepts, frames and pictures that enable a value based life, organization, politics, and economy. That is what the approach is good for.

The value based approach differs from the standard economic approach in the sense that it is less directed at feeding one's worldview. Standard accounts describe the elephant, to evoke the anecdote from the preface, whereas the value based approach tries to imagine what moves the elephant. Standard accounts may continue to be important to understand how the world or the economy works, what causes unemployment to go up or down, what explains the increase or decrease of the power of large companies, and other such issues. The value based approach will only consider such knowledge if it is relevant for knowing the right thing to do. Quite frankly, I suspect that a great deal, if not most of the insights that the standard accounts generate, fail that test. When I plan my family vacation, the sale of my house or make plans to improve the lives of the poorest in my town or to improve employment opportunities, scientific research is virtually of no use. Knowing what is going on in the world is not a must either. I do make use of the value based approach all the time, though. Values drive most decisions. Values make people do their most important things, whether they are at home, on the street or at work.

Worldview

I must acknowledge that the value based approach adds virtually no factual content to one's worldview and feeds it with few insights into how the world or the economy works. It does represent a particular way of looking at the world though, and with that, a worldview. Let me adumbrate what that worldview may look like.

The value based approach depicts a world in which people are trying to do the right thing, and are limited in their knowledge, awareness, and capability of doing so. A lot goes wrong; we make mistakes all the time. Even so, the only reasonable, mature thing to do is to strive to do the right thing. The presumption is, therefore, that people are trying to do the right thing, even if they do bad and wrong things all the time. (Ever met someone who is systematically trying to do the bad and the wrong thing?)

When we are trying to do the right thing we need to be aware of what is important to us, our values, of the goods that we are striving for, our ideals. In other words, we need to answer questions like "What is important to us?" and "What is it that we are doing good for?" That makes for a worldview that highlights values and qualities.

Remember: it is not the "house" that the economy is all about, but the "home."

We may realize that instrumentalism, or governmental logic, has become too prevalent; that market logic is needed to streamline the production and distribution of instrumental goods and values, but that the social logic needs special attention. It is by way of the social logic, by the willingness to contribute, that we generate the most important goods, and with those the good life and a good society. It is with the social logic that we realize the important qualities in our own lives, in organizations, and in societies.

In order to realize all this, transformations in governance are most likely in order. Might smaller organizations, rather than larger ones, be more amenable for the striving for good work and for quality of the goods generated? Might governments need to collaborate better with their citizens, by way of the social logic?

We may also look for changes in the social and market spheres. Think of a share economy, the circular economy, and a creative economy. It is first of all in the social sphere that initiatives will sprout to vitalize shared, circular, and creative practices.

The value based approach upstages the opposition between the market and the government. The discussion has been framed for too long as though we have a choice between a free market, and thus against big government, and a strong government that is in control of markets. The value based approach points at the *oikos* as the base of all, the dominance of the social sphere and the overarching cultural sphere. In the end the cultural is all that matters. Accordingly, the value based approach highlights the prevalence of culture (C1, C2, and C3—see chapter 2).

Those who govern may take important cues from the way we all have learned to cope with the practices of the *oikos* and the social sphere. The focus should be on well-articulated qualities. Most quantitative measurements, including the GDP and profits, have only instrumental significance and should be subordinate to the evaluation of realized qualities.

We will focus less on financial results and more on relevant qualities. We will understand that cultural organizations are about cultural qualities and social organizations about social qualities. Fighting poverty is about more than addressing financial inequality, since poverty can also be social and cultural.

The main contributions

Others will hopefully determine what the main contributions of the value based approach are and how successful its development in this book has been. Being the author I would like to point out that I really needed to write an entire book to motivate and develop this line of thought and develop the argumentation and the concepts. Even so, I too, would boil down the entire argument to a limited number of points. I anticipated them in the preface and reiterate them here shortly to refresh the reader's memory:

1.   Doing the right thing is a matter of realizing values, i.e. of becoming aware of the relevant values and making them real.

2.   The realization of value inevitably takes place in a cultural context that informs some values and renders them meaningful while rendering other values mute.

3.   The realization of values requires *phronesis*, practical wisdom (rather than rationality).

4.   The realization of values occurs by means of goods, the most important of which are shared goods. Bought goods and those goods provided by governments are instrumental and therefore subordinate to the important shared goods that tend to be social and cultural in kind.

5.   Some goods are worth striving for; so-called ultimate goods constitute the good life and good society. *Praxis* is an activity that is worth striving for, such as an artistic, scientific, or religious practice; they contain the goals as intrinsic goods.

6.   The resources, or possessions, of people consist of goods worth striving for, like the engagement in *praxes*, meaningful activities, and conversations. These resources constitute the cultural capital of people. Possession of instrumental goods, such as financial capital, social status, social capital, are potential resources. Conventional measurements of inequality focus on instrumental possessions. The most relevant inequality concerns the distribution of cultural resources. We can only guess the magnitude of that inequality.

7.   Five different spheres are available for the realization of values, or their valorization. Each sphere has a distinctive logic and rhetoric. They are the cultural, *oikos*, social, market, and governmental spheres.

The book may read as if it is philosophical and quite abstract. The reason for this is that I have yet to develop a range of new concepts and show how existing concepts can become more meaningful.

Most crucial are the following concepts:

Values: whatever people consider important, the relevant qualities of things, social entities, and practices. Values can be personal, social, societal, and transcendental.

A value based economy stresses and highlights the realization of values, and thus focuses on the qualities that constitute good practices, a good life, good work, a good organization, and a good society.

Goods: whatever people acquire in order to make their values real. Goods can be tangible and intangible, privately- and publicly-owned or shared with others. Goods can be personal, social, societal, and transcendental. Then there are all kinds of goods that are inputs in the realization of these goods.

Goods to strive for constitute the good life and the good society. They answer the question what is it that we do good for?

Praxis is a practice (or ongoing conversation) that contains the good to strive for; in that case, the good is intrinsic.

Resources constitute richness and the lack thereof, poverty. The main sources are personal, social, societal, and transcendental. In addition there are financial sources (which usually get all the attention).

Financial **inequality** in daily life is subordinate to **social, societal, personal, and transcendental** inequalities. In that way, the value based approach gives new meanings to the notion of poverty and richness.

Money or price is no value; they represent the potential for the realization of values.

Five spheres with each a distinct logic enable us to valorize our values. They include the cultural, *oikos*, social, market, and governmental spheres.

The willingness to contribute is a characteristic of the social logic and is critical for the realization of shared goods like friendship, knowledge, and art.

I was in need of these concepts to develop the value based approach. In some cases I relied on other texts and thinkers, but I must confess that I had to think them through to make sense of them and to make them meaningful. They undoubtedly will need further work and more testing to see their merit.

Some juxtapositions in brief	
Value based approach	**Standard economics**
The realization of values	The allocation of scarce resources
Value	Price
Social, societal, personal, and transcendental values	Preferences
Phronesis	Rationality
Social behavior prevails, other types are common	Self-interested common prevails
What appears altruistic is often social behavior, directed at a shared good	Altruism cannot be accounted for
Shared, private, and collective goods	Only private and collective
Social, personal, and cultural capital	Economic, Human and Financial capital
An addition to financial capital	Human capital
Five spheres: C, O, S, G, and M	Only M and G
Embedded in culture (C1 and C2)	No culture (C1 and C2)
Relationships in S and O	No relationships
Qualities	Mainly quantities
What is important to you?	What do you want?
Co-production and co-creation consumption	Production, distribution, and consumption
Substantive argument	Instrumentalist argument
Focus on doing the right thing	Focus on policy making
Substantive inequalities	Financial inequalities
Happiness as the result of doing the right thing	Happiness as the result of maximizing utility
Quality impact monitor	Quantifiable results

Practical use

I use these concepts all the time in my daily life, in my work with professionals and in my political endeavors. Quite a few of my students work with them in their research. There is actually a great deal to say with them on all kinds of topics, which I intend to do in the next volume. I intend to write on the value based approach to work, to organizations, entrepreneurship, cultural heritage, social policy, the relationship between governments and private organizations, the new economy, the creative economy, the circular economy, and other topics. Here I limit myself to a few practical consequences.

1. **The willingness to contribute in the world of the arts.** The lack of money and the cuts in government subsidies compel artists and people of cultural organizations to consider the willingness of people to pay for their offerings. I turn their attention to the importance of willingness to contribute. Make your visitors ambassadors, so I tell them, willing to contribute by talking about your work, getting others to partake in it. And sure, the willingness to contribute may also come in the form of monetary donations. But to realize that, you need to use the social logic. I actually try to get these people to visualize the social sphere with its social logic.

2. **Clarify the ideals. Be clear on the virtues and the goods to strive for. Know how to evaluate them and by whom.**
    This is the most difficult part when I work with organizations. In order to apply the value based approach, people need to articulate their ideals, their goal values and their behavioral values. When I ask them out of the blue, the answers are usually embarrassing. Even companies that have clearly defined their mission require additional work. Usually the criteria for evaluation remain unspecified, which makes the mission more or less moot. It is better to determine the mission together with the method of evaluation. In the value based approach that calls for the naming of the relevant stakeholders (see the box on the quality monitor below).
    In my experience, the exercise to clarify the relevant values and the evaluation that suits them is quite revealing and may have a lasting effect.

3. **Work with cooperatives or social enterprises.** The US and the UK now also allow for what are called public benefit corporations. All these organizational forms have in common that they have a shared good—societal, social or transcendental—as their explicit goal. I would favor a fiscal policy that treats such organizations

differently from commercial ones. As a governor I prefer working with such organizations when they serve goals that are also mine.

4. **Introduce social currencies next to official currencies (and re-introduce national currencies).** My endless battle with the euro and the thinking that underlies it finds its motivation in the value based approach. At least that is what came to my attention in the past few years. The euro is too much a product of G logic and neglects the logic of S and C altogether. The euro lacks a *demos* (a people) and, with that, political legitimacy. The response to its weaknesses and flaws has insistently been a strengthening of the G structure.

Actually, the euro has shown that a currency needs a strong S to function well. Accordingly, currencies have also a social function, by bringing about a bond in the good case, or driving people apart as in the case of the euro. I, therefore, favor local currencies to strengthen local communities and local identity. In Hilversum, I am working with a group of citizens on the introduction of such a local currency.

5. **Practices versus praxes.** Lately I had to address the problematic character of the relationship between education and research. At universities, doing research is considered to be much more satisfying than teaching. So how to improve the teaching? Research and teaching are practices, things people do by way of a series of activities. The striving should be to have people to practice either activity with commitment and dedication. The teaching and the doing of research should have intrinsic value in the sense that doing either provides sufficient satisfaction that the practitioners gain. That would make them true professionals, and that would make the practices into *praxes*. The problem occurs when the true researcher considers the teaching to be a mere chore, a practice, that is, or when the true teacher considers doing research to be an obligation of the job. In their case the practice fails to turn into a *praxis*. Deans could take this into account in the assignment of tasks or do things to develop practices into *praxes*, for example, by appreciating true teaching and true researching. (Hint: steer for qualities.)

To my students, I tell of the importance of distinguishing practices from *praxes*. They undoubtedly will engage in all kinds of activities or practices. What they want is to be able to name a practice a *praxis*, since doing the *praxis* is what gives real satisfaction in the end. I have so many stories for them of people who failed to realize *praxes* and got hopelessly stuck even when they were financially successful, or maybe especially because of such success.

6. **Altruism is the norm**. It's not only economists who consider altruism to be unintelligible. Many people do. All too often I hear people expressing their lack of faith in the good intentions of their fellow men. "People are selfish," they say, "preoccupied with what's in it for themselves." I am pleased to finally have a response to this widespread belief. First I ask them whether they are selfish themselves, as I spell out in the preface. But now I also have the notion of the shared good and the S of the social sphere. By evoking those notions I can quite convincingly state that altruistic behavior is instead the norm, at least if we consider the social behavior that is directed at the realization of shared goods. The argument is quite practical, for example for dinner conversations. It also provides me with arguments in a discussion with staunch liberals or libertarians and their radical individualism. How individualist can we be if our most important possessions are goods that derive their meanings and values from the sharing with others? When they retort that this is about enlightened self-interest I am okay, even though the remark suggests that the other has not gotten the point. ("Read my book, and we will continue the conversation," may be a sensible remark but it is still a poor argument.)

The Quality Impact monitor

When an organization, or a governmental policy is directed at the realization of qualities, it needs to be explicit on the qualities to be realized and on the evaluation of them. A theatre group has to be clear on the artistic qualities that it is striving for, and when an organization has the ambition to contribute to a better world, it needs to indicate in what ways it wants to do so and who can determine that it actually does.

The quality impact monitor is designed to monitor the realization of values or qualities. It provides leaders of organizations with clear indications of what to do, of what to change in their strategies, and it provides funders and supervisors a clear perspective on the effectiveness of the organization in realizing its goals.

We, the developers of this monitor, actually found that the process of setting up the quality impact monitor in itself is raising awareness and increasing clarity on the goals and the qualities that one seeks. Other methods usually sidestep the first stage and try to gather data from existing sources, thus forsaking the opportunities of the exploratory stage.

The first stage is dedicated to the determination of the behavioral and goal values as well as the stakeholders. Doing so requires a process, so is our experience. Leaders of organizations usually do not have those values fully articulated and if they have, they are articulated in such a way that it is not clear who will be able to evaluate them. ("We want to make the world a happier place." "We want to make the world more just.")

In the determination of the values we make use of the four dimensions: social, societal, transcendental, and personal.

Usually, leaders also want to stipulate instrumental goals such as the ideal number of visitors, amount of sponsored money, number and

relevance of external contacts, and so on. The quality impact monitor can take account of such instrumental goals but the emphasis needs to be on the substantive goals, i.e. the qualities worth striving for.

We then determine with the leaders of the organization the various stakeholders for their activities. They usually include the visitors, possibly divided into several categories (like age groups, loyal visitors and incidental visitors), the local community, businesses, local and national governments, funders, supporting organizations, experts, educational institutions, fellow artists, colleagues, the supervisory board, and—often overlooked—people within the organization.

We then ask the leaders of the organization to weigh the qualities, giving the most weight to the most important quality, and to weigh the importance of the stakeholders. We take these weights into account in the final assessment.

When we approach the stakeholders, we have two types of questions for them: what qualities do they value and how do they appreciate the qualities of the activities of the organization to be evaluated. The questions differ across the stakeholders. It is pointless, for example, to ask substantive questions on, say the artistic qualities to incidental visitors. The latter may be able to say how moved they were, inspired or bored but they usually lack the experience and knowledge to be able to appreciate the craftsmanship involved or the societal relevance.

There are several methods to get the evaluations of the various stakeholders, such as surveys, interviews, panels, and visitation committees. The latter consist of knowledgeable people with a variety of backgrounds who will spend a day or two talking with a select number of stakeholders, reviewing data and reports, and, following a certain procedure, conclude with a qualitative assessment of the qualities realized.

The evaluation of the instrumental goals usually requires the collection of quantitative data. The leaders, the supervisors and the funders can draw two types of conclusions from the gap observed between the stated qualities and the appreciation of stakeholders. For example, when the quality impact monitor concludes that visitors find the plays of the theatre company too experimental and too difficult, the leaders can decide to change their strategy in two different ways. Either they can plan plays that are less difficult or they can start a campaign educating people to appreciate complexity, innovation, and being challenged. In the latter case, they aim at changing the values of visitors.

In conclusion of this book, I encourage others to make, and continue making, contributions in the same spirit:

- I expect and hope that students will continue working with the value based approach.

- I expect and hope that organizations will start with monitoring the qualities that they strive to realize.

- I expect and hope that we will leave the dominance of instrumentalist thinking behind us, and that it becomes normal to think of substantive qualities first before we consider quantities.

This book intends to be a contribution to all of that. There is much work still to be done. The conversation is far from over.

BIBLIOGRAPHY

Adams, R. M. (2006). A Theory of Virtue: Excellence in Being for the Good. Oxford: Clarendon Press.

Anderson, E. (1993). Value in Ethics and Economics. Cambridge: Harvard University Press.

Aristotle, Ross, W., & Brown, L. (2009). The Nicomachean ethics. (W. Ross, Trans.) Oxford: Oxford University Press.

Arnold, M. (1869). Culture and Anarchy: An Essay in Political and Social Criticism. New York: MacMillan.

Augustine, & Blaiklock, E. (2009). The Confessions of Saint Augustine. London: Hodder & Stoughton.

Aurelius, M., & Gill, C. (2013). Meditations. Books 1-6. Oxford: Oxford University press.

Barnes, J. (1989). A History of the World in 10 1/2 Chapters. New York: Knopf.

Becker, G. (1976). The Economic Approach to Human Behavior. Chicago: University of Chicago Press.

Beugelsdijk, S., & Maseland, R. (2014). Culture in Economics: History, Methodological Reflections and Contemporary Applications. Cambridge: Cambridge University Press.

Bourdieu, P. (1986). Forms of Capital. In J. R. (ed), Handbook for Theory and Research for the Sociology of Educatoion (pp. 241-258). New York: Greenwood.

Buchanan, J. (1965). An Economic Theory of Clubs. Economica, 1-14.

Bustamente Kuschel, P. G. (2012). Rationality and Phronesis in Economics: A Rhetorical Moment. Retrieved from Erasmus University Rotterdam: http://hdl.handle.net/1765/38053

Cameron, K., & Quinn, R. (1999). Diagnosing and Changing Organizational Culture: Based on the Competing Values Framework. New York: Addison-Wesley.

Chandler, A. D. (1977). The visible hand: The managerial revolution in American business. Cambridge: MA: Belknap Press.

Cicero, M. T., & Gardner, R. (1958). Speeches. London: Harvard University

Press.

Debreu, G. (1959). The Theory of Value: An axiomatic analysis of economic equilibrium. New York: Wiley.

Dewey, J. (1915). The school and society. Chicago: The University of Chicago Press.

Drucker, P. (1992). Managing the Non-Profit Organization — Principles and Practices. New York: HarperBusiness.

Elias, N. (2000). The Civilizing Process . Oxford: Wiley-Blackwell.

Florida, R. (2002). The Rise of the Creative Class . New York: Basic Books.

Folbre, N. (2008). Valuing children: Rethinking the economics of the family. Cambridge: Mass: Harvard University Press.

Foot, P., & Adams, R. M. (2006). A Theory of Virtue: Excellence in Being for the Good. Oxford: Clarendon Press.

Foucault, M. (1969). The Archeology of Knowledge. (S. Smith, Trans.) London: Routledge.

Foucault, M. (1970). The Order of Things . London: Pantheon Books.

Foucault, M., & Senellart, M. (2008). The birth of biopolitics: Lectures at the Collège de France, 1978-79. Basingstoke: Palgrave Macmillan.

Frey, B. (1997). Not just for the money: An economic theory of personal motivation. Cheltenham: Edward Elgar Pub.

Geertz, C. (1972). Deep Play: Notes on the Balinese Cockfight. Indianapolis: Bobbs-Merrill.

Goede de, M. (2005). Virtue, Fortune, and Faith: A Genealogy of Finance. Minneapolis: University Of Minnesota Press.

Graeber, D. (2001). Towards an Anthropological Theory of Value: The False Coin of Ou Dreams. New York: Palgrave MacMillan.

Granovetter, M. (1985). Economic Action and Social Structure: The Problem of Embeddedness. American Journal of Sociology, 481-510.

Grube, L. E., & Storr, V. H. (2015). Culture and economic action. Cheltenham: Edward Elgar Publishing.

Gudeman, S. (2008). Economy's Tension The Dialectics of Community and Market. Oxford: Berghahn Books.

Habermas, J. (1984). The Theory of Communicative Action. Boston: Beacon Press.

Hardin, G. (1968, December 13). The Tragedy of the Commons. American Association for the Advancement of Science, 1243-1248.

Hicks, J. R. (1939). Value and Capital: An Inquiry into Some Fundamental Principles of Economic Theory. Oxford: Clarendon Press.

Hillesum, E. P. (1983). An interrupted life: The diaries of Etty Hillesum, 1941-1943. New York: Pantheon Books.

Hoffman, D. D., & Richards, W. A. (1985). Parts of Recognition. Cognition, 65-96.

Hofstede, G. (2003). Culture's consequences: Comparing values, behaviors, institutions and organizations across nations. Thousands Oaks: SAGE.

Inglehart, R., & Welzel, C. (2005). Modernization, Cultural Change, and Democracy: The Human Development Sequence. Cambridge: Cambridge University Press.

Jacobs, J. (1993). The Death and Life of Great American Cities. New York: Random House.

Johnson, J. (2006). Russell and Strawson on Significant Sentences. Aporia, 16(1), 1-10.

Keynes, J. M. (1963). Essays in Persuasion. New York: W. W. Norton & Company.

Klamer, A. (1996). The Value of Culture. In A. Klamer, The Value of Culture: On the Relationship Between Economics and Arts. Amsterdam: Amsterdam University Press.

Klamer, A. (2003). The Gift Economy. In R. Towse, A Handbook of Cultural Economics (pp. 243-247). Cheltenham: Edward Elgar Publishing.

Klamer, A. (2007). Speaking of Economics: How to Get in the Conversation. New York: Routledge.

Kopytoff, I. (1988). The cultural biography of things: commoditization of process. In A. Appadurai, The Social Life of Things: Commodities in Cultural Perspective (pp. 65-91). Cambridge: Cambridge University Press.

Lane, R. (1991). The Market Experience. Cambridge: Cambridge University Press.

Lasch, C. (2013). The True and Only Heaven. New York: W.W. Norton & Company.

Leemans, I., & Johannes, G. (2013). Worm en Donder. Utrecht: Prometheus.

Lohman, R. (1992). The commons: New perspectives on nonprofit organizations and voluntary action. New York: Jossey-Bass Inc Pub.

Luhmann, N. (1997). Die Gesellschaft der Gesellschaft. Frankfurt am Main: Suhrkamp.

MacIntyre, A. (1981). After Virtue. Parijs: Notre Dame University Press.

Mandela, N. (1964). Nelson Mandela's statement from the dock at the opening of the defence case in the Rivonia Trial [Recorded by N. Mandela]. Pretoria, South Africa.

Marx, K., Engels, F., Moore, S., & McLellan, D. (1992). The Communist Manifesto. Oxford : Oxford University Press.

Maslow, A. H. (1943). A Theory of Human Motivation. Psychological Review, 370-396.

Maslow, A. H. (1954). Motivation and Personality. New York: Harper.

Mauss, M. (1967). The gift: Forms and functions of exchange in archaic societies. New York: Norton.

McCarthy, T. (1984). Theory of Communicative Action. Boston: Beacon Press.

McCloskey, D. N. (1982). The applied theory of price. New York: Macmillan Pub. Co.

McCloskey, D. N. (2007). The Bourgeois Virtues: Ethics for an Age of Commerce. Chicago: University of Chicago Press.

McCloskey, D. N. (2011). Bourgeois Dignity: Why Economics Can't Explain the Modern World. Chicago: University of Chicago Press.

McCloskey, D. N. (2016). Bourgeois Equality: How Ideas, Not Capital or Institutions, Enriched the World. Chicago: University of Chicago Press.

Meinong. (1904). Untersuchung zur Gegenstandstheorie und Psychologie.

Menger, C. (1871). Principles of Economics. Auburn: Ludwig von Mises institute.

Merton, R. (1968). The Matthew Effect in Science. Science, 56-63.

Mirowski, P., & Sent, E.-M. (2008). The Commercialization of Science and the response of STS. In E. J. Hackett, O. Amsterdamska, M. Lynch, & J. Wajcman, Handbook of Science and Technological Studies (pp. 635-689). Cambridge, MA: MIT Press.

Moody-Adams, M. (2006). Reflections on Appiah's The Ethics of Identity. Journal of Social Philosophy, 292-300.

Nelson, M., & Singh, R. (1998). Democracy, Economic Freedom, Fiscal Policy, and Growth in LDCs: A Fresh Look. Economic Development and Cultural Change, 677-696.

Netzer, D. (2011). Non-profit organizations. In R. Towse, A Handbook of Cultural Economics (pp. 304-312). Cheltenham: Edward Elgar Publishing Limited.

Nussbaum, M. (1986). The Fragility of Goodness: Luck and Ethics in Greek Tragedy and Philosophy. Cambridge: Cambridge University Press.

Oslington, P. (2014). The Oxford handbook of Christianity and economics. Oxford: Oxford University Press.

Ostrom, E. (1990). Governing the commons : the evolution of institutions for collective action. Cambridge: Cambridge University Press.

Piketty, T. (2014). Capital in the twenty-first century. Cambridge: The Belknap Press of Harvard University Press.

Plato, & Jowett, B. (1941). Plato's the Republic. (B. Jowett, Trans.) New York: The Modern Libary.

Polanyi, K. (1944). The great transformation: The political and economic origins of our time. Boston: Beacon Press.

Ray, L., & Sayer, A. (1999). Culture and Economy After the Cultural Turn. Thousand Oaks: SAGE.

Robbins, L. R. (1932). An essay on the nature & significance of economic science. London: Macmillan.

Rorty, R. (1979). Philosophy and the mirror of nature. Princeton: Princeton University Press.

Sahlins, M. (1972). Stone Age Economics. Chicago: Aldine-Atherton.

Samuelson, P. (1947). Foundations of economic analysis. Cambridge, MA: Harvard University Press.

Sandel, M. J. (2012). What money can't buy: the moral limits of markets. New York: Farrar, Straus and Giroux.

Schön, D. (1984). The Reflective Practitioner, How Professionals Think in Action. New York: Basic Books.

Scitovsky, T. (1976). The Joyless Economy: The Psychology of Human Satisfaction. Oxford: Oxford University Press.

Sen, A. (1985). Commodities and capabilities. Amsterdam: North-Holland.

Sennett, R. (2008). The Craftsman. New Haven: Yale University Press.

Severin, T. (2003). In Search of Robinson Crusoe. New York: Basic Books.

Smith, A. (1759). The Theory of Moral Sentiments. London: A. Millar.

Smith, A. (1776). An Inquiry into the Nature and Causes of the Wealth of Nations. London: Methuen & Co.

Taylor, C. (1991). The Malaise of Modernity. Toronto: House of Anansi.

Taylor, C. (1992). Sources of the Self. Cambridge, MA: Harvard University Press.

Thatcher, M. (1987, October 31). Woman's Own. (D. Keay, Interviewer)

Thompson, E. P. (1971). The Moral Economy of the English Crowd in the Eighteenth Century. Past & Present, 76-136.

Throsby, D. (2001). Economics and Culture. Cambridge: Cambridge University Press.

Tilly, C. (2008). Credit and blame. Princeton: Princeton University Press.

Van Staveren, I. (2013). The values of economics: An Aristotelian perspective. Routledge.

Walzer, M. (1983). Spheres of Justice: A Defense of Pluralism and Equality. Oxford: Basil Blackwell.

Waterman, R., & Peters, T. (1982). In Search of Excellence. New York: Harper and Row.

Weber, M. (1968). Economy and Society . California: University Of California.

Weber, M. (2001). The Protestant Ethic and the Spirit of Capitalism. (T. Parsons, Trans.) New York: Routledge.

Zelizer, V. A. (1985). Pricing the priceless child: The changing social value of children. New York: Basic Books.

Zelizer, V. A. (2005). The Social Meaning of Money: Pin Money, Paychecks, Poor Relief, and Other Currencies. Princeton: Princeton University Press.

INDEX

A

Adams, R. M. 60
Amariglio, J. xxi
Appadurai, A. 96
Aquinas, T. 24, 28, 58
Aristotle 24, 58, 78, 88, 102, 104,
    135, 157, 194
Arnold, M. 9
Art is a conversation 93
arts ix, 12, 23, 25, 30, 51, 61, 86,
    122, 134, 225
Augustus 119
Aurelius 74
Austin 57
authentic 62, 112
autonomy xi, 51, 62, 116, 167

B

Barnes, J. 122
base 7
Baumol, W. 15
Becker, G. 15, 156
Benhamou, F. 15
Beugelsdijk, S. 17
Beus de, J. xxi
Boulding, K. xiii
Bourdieu, P. 17, 130
Bruni, L. xiii
Buchanan, J. 91
Bustamente Kuschel, G. 27

C

Cameron, K. 17
Capital
    cultural 130
    economic 130
    financial 130
    human 130
    social 130
capitalism 16
cardinal virtue 27
Chandler, A. D. 161, 198
characterization xviii
Cicero, M. T. 112
civilization x, 6, 16, 61, 63, 107,
    118, 134, 136, 142, 154, 165,
    191
co-creation 41, 89, 184
Coleridge, S. xvii
Collins R. 13
commodities xiv, 91, 96
commons 12, 83, 91, 182
communists introduced 169
communitarians 169
conversation introduced 12
co-production 89
corporatism 169
courage 28, 54
craftmanschip introduced 115
crowding in 96, 154, 214
crowding out 214
Crusoe, R. 76

cultural heritage 136
culturalists 11, 48
culture
  culture 1 (C1) introduced 12
  culture 2 (C2) introduced 12
  culture 3 (C3) introduced 12
  culture introduced 11
currency introduced 176

D

Debreu, G. 56
Dekker, E. xxi
design defined 32
Dewey, J. 73
Dickens, C. 14
DiMaggio, P. 164
domain
  personal 116
  social 115
  societal 118
  transcendental 119
Drucker, P. 107

E

Eckhart, M. 110
edifying xvii, 121
Egmond van, K. 105
elephant allegory xviii
Elias, N. 9
Engels, F. 36
evaluation 33, 37, 72, 144, 225
external economy 52

F

faith 58, 76, 138
Fisher, I. xxi
Florida, R. 16
Foot, P. 28
Foucault, M. 167
Frey, B. xxi, 15

Friedman, M. xii, 166, 194, 207

G

Gadamer, H. 13
Geertz, C. 18
gift introduced 184
Goede de, M. 17
good life x, 10, 131, 223
goods introduced 75
  club 92
  collective 91
  common 91
  cultural 119
  hyper 118
  personal 116
  private 91
  shared 92
  social 115
  societal 118
  transcendental 119
  ultimate 118
good society x, 108, 221
goods to strive for 106, 115, 223, 225
Goto, K. xxi
governance introduced 147
Granovetter, M. 19
greed 42
Grube, L. E. 17
Gudeman, S. 19, 154, 164
Guggenheim museum, Bilbao 16

H

Habermas, J. 13, 164
Hardin, G. 86
Harrison, L. 17
Hayek, F. 166, 194
Hegel, G. W. F. 164
Heusden van, B. xxi, 18
Hicks, J. R. 56

Hillesum, E. P. 119
Hofstede, G. 17, 63
hope 58, 138
humanomics xiii
Huntington, S. 17
Hutter, M. xxi, 154

I

ideals 32, 101, 108, 110
impartial spectator 28
individualism xi, 111, 116, 227
inequality introduced 142
Inglehart 61
Inglehart, R. 61
instrumental xi, 41, 66, 80, 99, 102,
       110, 121, 218, 221, 224, 229

J

Jacobs, J. 10
Jaeger, W. 217
Johannes, G. 17
joke of the drunkard 8
justice 58

K

keynesians introduced 169
Keynes, J. M. xiii, 101, 112, 160
Kierkegaard, S. A. 110
Knight, F. xiii
Komter, A. 184

L

Landy, M. 140
Lane, R. 17
Lasch, G. 9
Lavoie, D. xiii
Leemans, I. 17
liberals 167, 169
logic

bureaucratic 201
cultural 189
governmental 153, 221
market 210
social 153, 184
Lohman, R. 87
love 58
Lucebert 23
Luhmann, N. 154

M

MacIntyre, A. xxi, 24
Magala, S. xxi
Mandela, N. 74, 108
Marx, K. 36, 56
Maseland, R. 17
Maslow, A. H. 24, 53, 102
Mauss, M. 157, 184
McCloskey, D. N. xiii, 17, 24, 28,
       57, 58, 138
McLellan, D. 36
memories introduced 125, 137
Menger, C. xiii, 78
Merton, R. 23
Mirowski, P. 15
Mises von, L. xiii, 194
mission 24, 32
Moore, G. E. 112
Moore, S. 36
Moore, T. 122

N

neo-liberal xii, 167, 169
Netzer, D. 107
New Public Management xii
Nobel Prize xii
normative economics xx
norms 69
Nussbaum, M. 24

O

Oakeshott, M. 13
Oberholzer-Gee, F. 96
oikos 12, 132, 150, 171
Oslington, P. 15
Ostrom, E. xiii, 86
ownership 201

P

Peters, T. 17
phronesis xv, 27, 31, 38, 52, 69, 71,
    144, 168, 224
Piketty, T. 142
Plato 5, 111, 135
Ploeg van der, R. 29
Polanyi, K. 19, 158, 164
positive economics xx
Potok, C. 119, 136
poverty introduced 141
power 130
praxis defined 114
price or value 51
Prins, A. xxi
prudence 58

Q

quality impact monitor
  explained 227
Quinn, R. 17

R

Rand, A. 122
rational choice xi, 15, 28, 72
Ray, L. 12
realizing values introduced 21
richness introduced 141
Robbins, L. xiv
Rorty, R. xvii, 13

S

Sahlins, M. 156
Samuelson, P. xiv, 56
Sandel, M. J. 164
Sayer, A. 12
Schön, D. 33
Schumacher, E. F. xiii
Schumpeter, J. xiii
Scitovsky, T. 57
Seiz, J. xxi
selfishness 42
Selkirk, A. 81
Sen, A. 130
Sennett, R. 115
Sent, E. M. 15
seven classical virtues 28, 59
Shakespeare 62, 69, 70, 72, 86, 103
sharing economy xiii
Skidelsky, R. 24
Smith, A. xiii, 19, 24, 28, 49, 140,
    158, 193, 205
social democrats introduced 160
socialists introduced 160
sources defined
  financial 138
  intellectual 134
  material 138
  social 133
  societal 137
spheres
  cultural 150
  governance 152
  logic 175
  market 151
  oikos 150
  regulation 161
  relationship 175
  rhetoric 176
  social 149
  value 176
spillovers 212

standard economics defined xiv
standard logics 147
Steinbeck, J. 14
Storr, V. H. 17
substantive reasoning xii

T

Taylor, C. xi, 24, 110
temperance 58
Thatcher, M. 164
therapeutic xvii, 6, 25, 41, 121
Thompson, E. P. 159
Throsby, D. xxi, 15, 61
Tinbergen, J. xii, 160
Towse, R. 15
tree of life 131, 138
Tzu, L. 110

U

utopia exercise 122

V

valorization introduced 22
value based approach introduced xv
values 47
  cultural 63
  extrinsic 64
  financial 64
  intrinsic 64
  moral 64
  personal 62
  scientific 63
  social 62
  societal 63
  transcendental 63
  use 64
van Staveren 24
Veblen, T. xiii
Velthuis, O. xxi
Verbruggen, H. xxi

virtue 19, 27, 49, 57, 71, 176, 225
vision 32

W

Walzer, M. 96
Waterman, R. 17
Weber, M. xiii, 16, 17, 31, 201
Welzel, C. 61
Wilde, O. 48
willingness to contribute 88, 212, 223, 225
willingness to pay 52, 88
Wolfe, T. 14
worldview defined 32

Z

Zelizer, V. 19, 164
Zhuangzi 110, 135
Zuidhof, P. W. xxi, 154, 167

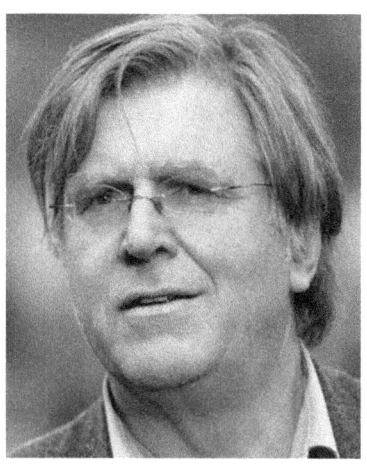

Arjo Klamer is professor of cultural economics at the Erasmus University, lector in social innovation at Fontys university, and governor of the Dutch town of Hilversum. Earlier he taught at several American universities. His most famous book is Conversations with Economists (1984), a source of inspiration for budding economists. Other books of his are Speaking of Economics: how to be in the conversation (2008) and the edited volume Value of Culture: the relationship between economics and the arts (1996).

He actively participates in discussions about alternative economic approaches and solutions, such as the share, creative and circular economy. He presents seminars on the value based approach around the world.

He is married and has 5 children.

www.klamer.nl
www.doingtherightthing.nl